MEDICARE
FOR ALL,
REALLY?!

www.amplifypublishing.com

Medicare for All, Really?!: Why A Single Payer Healthcare Plan Would Be Disastrous for America

For more information, please contact:
Amplify Publishing, an imprint of Amplify Publishing Group
620 Herndon Parkway #320
Herndon, VA 20170
info@amplifypublishing.com

Library of Congress Control Number: 2021911872

CPSIA Code: PRV0422A
ISBN-13: 978-1-64543-678-2

Printed in the United States

For those who believe Medicare For All is wrong,
this book is a must-read.

For those who believe Medicare For All is right,
you'll want to read this book to understand why it's wrong.

To Ann, Mitchell, Spencer, and Rob

MEDICARE
FOR ALL,
REALLY?!

WHY A SINGLE PAYER HEALTHCARE PLAN
WOULD BE DISASTROUS FOR AMERICA

RICH YURKOWITZ

HEALTHCARE ACTUARY

OPEN LETTER TO THE MEMBERS OF CONGRESS

Please read this book, and consider its solutions to US healthcare problems. You'll see that healthcare costs are not as high as commonly believed (proper context is required), that the laws of supply and demand work, that everyone points to everyone else as the cause of the problem (and ignore that they themselves contribute to the problem), and that the federal government is less efficient than the private marketplace.

Your decisions should create an alternative healthcare system that will help the US flourish. It will require adjustments as you develop the plan, flesh out details and the markets (insurance, healthcare providers, even state regulations), pass legislation, promote the viability of the new program (assuring support to those with preexisting condition and bankruptcy concerns), and then monitor its successes and failures. I propose a Catastrophic Plan for All (CAT4ALL), a program with easy-to-modify features to fit cost and other parameters, a program which the federal government would run in collaboration with the private market providing underlying insurance.

I urge you not to oscillate back and forth. Repealing Obamacare only to someday institute another plan like Medicare For All (M4A) will not work. Programs need twenty-five to fifty years to achieve viability. An adoption of CAT4ALL makes sense for the long-term.

CONTENTS

PROLOGUE

"You can't measure what didn't happen."
–Rich Yurkowitz, 2020

People die. As the WHO (the World Health Organization) reported, all the amazing cures and healthcare over thousands of years have not impacted humans dying. Headline: "World Death Rate Holding Steady at 100 Percent." "World Health Organization officials expressed disappointment Monday at the group's finding that, despite the enormous efforts of doctors, rescue workers and other medical professionals worldwide, the global death rate remains constant at 100 percent. Death, a metabolic affliction causing total shutdown of all life functions, has long been considered humanity's number one health concern. Responsible for 100 percent of all recorded fatalities worldwide, the condition has no cure. Many are suggesting that the high mortality rate represents a massive failure on the part of the planet's healthcare workers."

"I was really hoping, what with all those new radiology treatments, rescue helicopters, aerobics TV shows and what have you, that we might at least make a dent in it this year," WHO Director General Dr. Gernst Bladt said. "Unfortunately, it would appear that the death rate remains constant and total, as it has inviolably since the dawn of time." Okay, *The Onion*, a well-known satirical online newspaper that puts issues into perspective, created this tongue-in-cheek article.

Beyond this fantabulous finding that we all die anyway, what is life? We try to live to the fullest, even though the end is the same for everyone. In a perfect world, we would all have a great education, a home and a car, a meaningful job, people to love, and a healthy life with purpose. That healthy life would extend to the average age of eighty, and then I guess we would die because we all must at some point.

Why care? Because for eighty years on average, we want everything. We want the best education we can get, a home and a car, a meaningful job, people to love, and a healthy life with purpose.

But what is health and why care about it? To a significant portion of the already healthy population, they want to remain that way. To a disabled person, they may want to walk. To a chronically ill person, they may want more time—at least if it's pain-free. We want a perfect life so we don't suffer and have to spend resources to extend an unhealthy life.

Some of these desires are merely to be made whole—defined as what someone else has. In other words, if all humans couldn't walk, the desire to walk would not be a high priority. It may sound silly, but humans can't fly, so we don't desire that personal ability (ignoring airplanes and other artificial abilities). The goal with healthcare must ultimately be defined as what's "medically necessary," or else it goes too far.

Does everyone have the right to a heart transplant because heart transplants are now viable? What about in 1967 when heart transplants were "experimental"? Of course not.

But why do we always want to know how someone died, especially in the tragic loss of a young person? Why do we prefer someone be elderly or suffering to deem the death acceptable? Because in our equation, that person wasn't young or healthy before they died, so death "makes sense."

We are living longer than ever, so one might think we're doing rather well. A person born in 2014 can expect to live seventy-one years (seventy-one is the world average; the US average is seventy-nine years; Hong Kong and Japan are the highest at eighty-four years). Fifty years ago, the world average life expectancy was fifty-six years (seventy years in the US). This increase is remarkable.

We know that income is key when considering life expectancy, as data from across the world shows:

- High Income: 81 years
- Upper Middle Income: 74
- Lower Middle Income: 68
- Low Income: 63

This data sometimes gets misread to say that the rich get something the poor do not. Regardless, there is an advantage to moving up the income ladder to improve longevity.

If we compare the US healthcare system based on longevity of life, the US is above average but below average for similar-income countries (I won't bother showing you the details, trust me). This is a major complaint against the US healthcare system.

Back to our perceptions about life since longevity isn't the only consideration.

What do we want while living? Abraham Maslow (of Maslow's Hierarchy of Needs fame) wrote in 1943 that we strive toward higher-order needs after we accomplish lower needs:

MASLOW'S HIERARCHY OF NEEDS

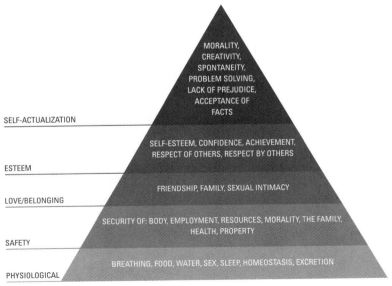

Individuals prioritize needs. Society can create an environment supporting the achievement of needs, but it is up to individuals to achieve their specific needs. People don't want more stuff; they want more life.

Some claim healthcare is a human right. However, it wasn't societal perception that birthed healthcare plans after WWII, but instead, US employers who recognized the need and offered coverage to employees as a fringe benefit. Employers provided coverage during a time when it was not available. Some now chastise employers for not providing portable coverage, thereby demanding government control of the industry.

Healthcare is a system that the government cannot and should not control. In his book, *Genome: The Autobiography of a Species in 23 Chapters*, British author Matt Ridley wrote about centralized systems: "The truth is that nobody is in charge. It is the hardest thing for human beings to get used to, but the world is full of intricate, cleverly designed and interconnected systems that do not have control centres. The economy is such a system. The illusion that economics run better if somebody is put in charge of them—and decides what gets manufactured where and by whom—has done devastating harm to the wealth and health of peoples all over the world, not just in the former Soviet Union, but in the west as well. Economies are not centralized systems; they are markets with decentralized, diffuse controls."

Humans desire control but need to recognize that controlling everything is not possible. From poverty and the weather, to finances and healthcare, many elements are not controllable. Attempts to control the uncontrollable can make things worse, such as with poverty (which is worse today than five other times in the last fifty years as illustrated in Chapter 2).

Government planners cannot determine the needs of 325 million people. Instead, individuals should control what they each want and need, with markets providing. "Why are there twenty-three brands of underarm sprays?" quips Senator Bernie Sanders. He argues that there are too many choices in deodorant.

While talking about a comedian's funny question is interesting for a time, no one should latch on to rhetoric just because it's ironic. We laugh, think about it for a moment, then move on. That's what Matt Ridley warns about—that no one individual can dictate what people want, nor should anyone who represents government.

That the people demand twenty-three brands, and there are twenty-three suppliers/brands that meet the need, means the market works and our economy is successful enough to have generated such products. Multiple companies and brand availability reflect a healthy mix of competition, not a conglomeration of corporate greed.

That someone lives in poverty somewhere does not mean that the economy should shift from twenty-three "needless" brands to solve every heart-wrenching situation. If it did, we'd fail miserably as a country because then we'd solve each individual case of poverty at the cost of not having markets. Ultimately, we'd have no wealth in which to "solve poverty" in the first place, sacrificing the long-term for the short-term.

If we take this kind of thinking to its logical end, humans should not spend any resources on the arts, NASA, investigation for the sake of learning, etc. Further, spending should be on poor children and not wasted on entertainment from movies, TV, games, or books.

There has always been and always will be poverty about which we claim we need to do something. There will be poverty in the year 2100, this we know. The claim to affordable care for all requires free coverage so that no one ever has a concern. "*Anything short of that is unacceptable.*"

I use a lot of sarcasm in the book, so I put sarcastic commentary in quotes with *italics* because of their double entendre meanings. For example, I say, "*squeeze the balloon*" to represent the solving of one problem while ignoring others (a sarcastic comment about how attempting to solve one problem may cause other problems). The quotes signify that it's my statement and the italics signify sarcasm, rather than to declare "sarcasm on/sarcasm off."

These healthcare ideals involve tradeoffs, as unaffordable, high-cost premiums lead to lack of care for all. Obamacare premiums have more than doubled since 2014. Allowing the government to take over the system may provide care for all, but at a significant price. Free care adds the incomprehensible element of increasing demand without changing supply; higher demand with stagnant supply is a recipe for disaster.

Americans tend not to be very accepting of shortages in anything. For example, during rush hour, there is a shortage of roads in which to get somewhere. Shortages lead to a flurry of bad behavior, and shortages in healthcare would be no exception. Imagine rush hour attitudes in the ER. Sadly, we're near that.

It's great to espouse the virtues of "Maslow's hierarchy" and to say that Mother Teresa was a great human being because she gave to others before herself. Human nature doesn't work that way since humans lean toward selfishness (part of our evolution that has kept us alive). We can't force all 325 million Americans to act like Mother Teresa. Once we realize that, we will stop trying to implement programs that depend on the success of everyone changing to something they're not. Considering all these aspects, should we overhaul the healthcare system or let it develop into the best it can be?

Here are some food-for-thought quotes on healthcare and related topics from notable sources:

"I don't think healthcare's a right. The only right you have is the ability to go out on an even playing field and work, and then purchase health insurance, or whatever it is." — Adam Carolla

"The essence of a government health care system—for people who have never lived under it and don't know—is waiting, waiting, waiting. You wait for everything. You wait for years for operations that are routine in America." — Mark Steyn

"Access to a waiting list is not access to health care." — Canadian Supreme Court (Chief Justice Beverley McLachlin)

"Costs for liability insurance are higher than costs for many procedures. There is a need to reform liability laws to stop out-of-control health care costs." — Temple Grandin, 2011

"One rough test of the various explanations that have been proposed is to see if they help us understand why the U.S. is the last major developed country without national health insurance. Several reasons for the lag can be suggested. First, there is a long tradition in the U.S. of distrust of government." — Victor Fuchs, 1976

"That is their [Monarch's] argument, and this argument of the Judge [democratic Senator Stephen Douglas] is the same old serpent that says you work and I eat, you toil and I will enjoy the fruits of it." — Abraham Lincoln, 1858

"To act on the belief that we possess the knowledge and the power which enable us to shape the processes of society entirely to our liking, knowledge which in fact we do not possess, is likely to make us do much harm." — Friedrich Hayek, 1974

"No one should die because they cannot afford health care, and no one should go broke because they get sick." — Barack Obama, 2009, to Facebook users to post as their status

"Science is not just about seeing, it's about measuring, preferably with something that's not your own eyes, which are inextricably conjoined with the baggage of your brain. That baggage is more often than not a satchel of preconceived ideas, post-conceived notions, and outright bias." — Neil deGrasse Tyson, 2017

"The curse of me and my nation is that we always think things can be bettered by immediate action of some sort, any sort rather than no sort." — Plato, 400 BC

"The worst form of inequality is to try to make unequal things equal."
— Aristotle, 350BC

"The measures we are applying, and all of the changes that are necessary for the modernization of the economic model, are aimed at preserving socialism, strengthening it and making it truly irreversible." — Raúl Castro, 2010

"The whole gospel of Karl Marx can be summed up in a single sentence: Hate the man who is better off than you are. The envious are more likely to be mollified by seeing others deprived of some advantage than by gaining it for themselves. It is not what they lack that chiefly troubles them, but what others have." — Henry Hazlitt, 1966

"A government that robs Peter to pay Paul can always depend on the support of Paul." — George Bernard Shaw, 1944

"Democracy and socialism cannot go together. You can't have it both ways." — Alexis de Tocqueville, 1848

"Democracy is nothing more than mob rule, where fifty-one percent of the people take away the rights of the other forty-nine." — Unknown

"Anyone who after the 20th century still thinks that socialism, nationalism, imperialism, mobilization, central planning, regulation, zoning, price controls, tax policy, labor unions, business cartels, government spending, intrusive policing, adventurism in foreign policy, faith in entangling religion and politics, or most of the other 19th-century proposals for governmental action are still neat, harmless ideas for improving our lives is not paying attention." — Dierdre McCloskey, 2012

"The lessons of history, confirmed by the evidence immediately before me, show conclusively that continued dependence upon relief induces a spiritual and moral disintegration fundamentally destructive to the national fiber. To dole out relief in this way is to administer a narcotic, a subtle destroyer of the human spirit. It is inimical to the dictates of sound policy. It is in violation of the traditions of America." — Franklin Delano Roosevelt, 1935

"Socialist governments traditionally do make a financial mess. They always run out of other people's money. It's quite characteristic of them. Then they start to [nationalize] everything, and people just do not like more and more [nationalization], and they're now trying to control everything by other means. They're progressively reducing the choice available to ordinary people." — Margaret Thatcher, 1984

"The 'free market' ideology was developed mainly by a handful of sociopathic assholes, like Milton Friedman and Ayn Rand—pushed by academics, some of their acolytes, like within the Chicago School of Economics—and fleshed out into something 'smart' and appealing. And then, this ideology was sold to the public at large, by puppet politicians such as Reagan and Thatcher." — Sammy Kayes, educator and activist in Chicago, 2017

As an actuary, I am uniquely qualified to analyze healthcare because I can look at aggregate data to discern trends. One classic joke tells that actuaries help to drive a car by looking out the back window. The best an actuary can do is to tell the driver where to turn by saying, "You missed the turn!" Some help that is. A book like this allows me to step back and look at the big picture and then extrapolate to predict the future, which is not simple, but possible.

Like with any prediction, one must look to the past to have a chance at getting close to forecasting accurately. But the past is littered with mistakes and poor decisions. For example, the Food and Drug

Administration (FDA) suggested we eat six to eleven bread portions per day twenty-five years ago. The latest food pyramid doesn't suggest anywhere near that amount. Should we trust current thinking? What if it's wrong? The 1992 food pyramid came from Sweden, so it must be right. We hear the same line of thinking with healthcare—that countries like Sweden have figured it out. But following someone else's lead, only to make the same mistake they made, is disastrous.

Many people think healthcare costs are a real problem and that the US spends too much and gets too little in return. I'm not so sure. Cost comparisons across countries have flaws, and we know our system is excellent. Our healthcare providers are the premier providers in the world. Data that shows otherwise doesn't capture reality.

Unquestioningly, healthcare costs are too high. But what is the point of watching TV ads that incessantly mention four-hour side effects, whether someone has been injured in an accident, whether someone may have mesothelioma (why do I even know what that word means?), or that death is a potential outcome of some obscure drug that applies to only a hundred of us? The answers lie in the waste within the US system of high drug utilization, higher legal costs, frivolous lawsuits, and punitive damages. Only the US and New Zealand allow direct-to-consumer prescription drug advertising. We should not make individual and aggregate choices like this only to complain about the resultant costs. We are our own enemy.

Be careful what you wish for. Before you support the government banning drug advertising, then what about alcohol advertising? What's next, soda? Snack foods? Fast foods? You really don't want to live in a society where someone from the government decides what can be advertised and consumed. I'm not proposing eliminating drug advertising, but we should realize why costs are so high. And if you like seeing someone get one million dollars from an insurance company, instead of thinking that's good because companies are bad, realize that we all pay for large awards through higher prices.

There are also claims from people watching drug advertising who can't buy the drug without a prescription anyway: "*The pharmaceutical industry spends twice as much advertising drugs as they do developing drugs*" (untrue, if you lazily compare sales and marketing costs to Research & Development (R&D) without considering total investment), or "*that's why drugs are so expensive—advertising costs money and then people take these drugs that cost more money.*" These simple arguments ignore economics to help draw simple conclusions. For example, the reason a drug costs ten times what it does in Canada is that the price in the US bears the full cost of development of the drug, whereas the price in Canada covers just the marginal cost of producing pills. We either need to demand the same price be charged in the US (and suffer the consequence of drug makers scaling back R&D because there's no profit incentive), or we find a way to force manufacturers to charge the same price in Canada.

The reason the healthcare system has a problem is there's money to be made by companies and lawyers, adding to our healthcare costs. In each case, the US government may deem these actions as appropriate (for example, freedom of speech), but the public must understand the added cost. We need to ask the tough questions as to why we've let this happen. Instead, we ask the lazy question as to why our healthcare costs are so high. The answer leads to knee-jerk reactions, ignoring root causes.

No industry has been assailed like healthcare. Our healthcare system gets rampaged as if it's the poorest in the world. How can one draw such a conclusion? US healthcare is rated #37 in a 2000 World Health Organization study, which hasn't been updated since. Other studies show equally poor outcomes of US healthcare. Did I miss this degradation, or are they false as well?

Similarly, banks are often chastised because what they produce is nebulous; there is a perception that what they produce is unnecessary, that they are a middleman. However, banks have prospered all over the world by providing vital services. Banks are a conduit for moving resources to where they're needed, besides the mundane tracking of account transactions. How can one possibly complain about big banks and bankers getting rich? Does that thinking also apply to you, the reader, in your personal situation, that you desire to make a lot of money? I thought that's perceived to be greedy.

Another industry that gets beat upon is oil production, where ExxonMobil is the largest and sometimes chastised company because they produce "*dirty oil*." But what they produce is vital to the economy and to each of us. Humans cannot live without the energy they provide, including the powering of vital-to-life computers and mobile phones. One cannot chastise an industry for what it produces, for which people pay for at will, while idolizing the not-for-profit industry that produces, say, water for underprivileged communities abroad. Each has its own place, and using a valuation system other than economic benefit is ruinous.

The last two questions pose an error, which I call Looking at the Forest. Aggregate data can be misleading. The opposite but classic error is Looking at the Trees. Both are employed in analyzing the healthcare system, to the detriment of the perception of the system.

Some people like to find unusual things to justify and popularize their studies, making them famous for being ironic. Some don't try very hard to explain their research, leaving results in studies to shock the reader and validate a purpose. But healthcare analysis influences public policy, so the data needs to be put in perspective to be better understood.

The topic of nationalized healthcare has been debated for the past hundred years. I remember quoting Victor Fuchs in a high school debate in 1978. The topic that year was, "Resolved: That the federal government should establish a comprehensive program to regulate the healthcare system in the United States." Fuchs, who is now eighty, said recently to the *Journal of the American Medical Association*, "[T]he way to make universal health insurance affordable is to curtail use of mammograms, costly new drugs and diagnostic technologies."

So that in mind, it's time to debate the future of healthcare in the US. To begin the discussion, I've simulated a theoretical debate with my rebuttal right-justified.

We should try Single Payer.

Why should we? It will fail, and it will be thirty years until we have proof of failure. Our healthcare system might never recover.

But it works in many other countries.

Name one.

Sweden.

They have as many people as North Carolina. Swedes are essentially one relatively healthy nationality. Plus, they're heading toward less government involvement in healthcare, not more.

But their healthcare system costs just 11 percent of GDP (Gross Domestic Product) versus 17 percent in the US.

It's silly to think that changing the US healthcare system will cut costs by a third. If a change to the US healthcare system could save 10 percent, then it's worth 10 percent. You can't change an apple into an orange.

Why not? It works for Sweden.

You can't compare the costs for different populations. For example, the US car accident rate is four times higher than Sweden's, and the obesity rate is 50 percent higher. Those rates aren't going to change under a new healthcare system.

Why are you opposed to trying what the rest of the world uses, and that's Single Payer?

Since when does the United States follow other countries? Ours is a system that is unique, built on Capitalism.

But this isn't about Capitalism versus Socialism. The USSR is gone, and we should try what Scandinavian countries found works.

Yes, the USSR (Union of Socialist Soviet Republics) dissolved. There's no proof the Scandinavian system will work here. The only reason we're even talking about Socialism is because Capitalism has given you security in which to consider options for improvement.

Then what's your idea?

Evolution, not revolution.

Can't we just try it? How about offering it as an option?

Then why is Social Security mandatory and not offered as an option? You don't want to offer Social Security as an option, and I don't want to offer Single Payer as an option. With healthcare, the federal government can just demand the lowest prices and eliminate all competitors. There would be no choice. So that ends that discussion.

Why are you against trying? Are you against lower-cost healthcare for all?

Stop with the all-or-nothing arguments. No one is against a lower-cost system that provides care to all. What I'm against are subsidies to get there, subsidies that are unfair and incite bad behavior (that's what Obamacare is). We could have just spent more money on the problem.

Then why not just spend more?

You mean like making Medicaid available to anyone without coverage? That could have been done at an incredible cost.

But costs are lower in every other country than in the US. It must be the result of Single Payer.

That's like following a recipe but using different ingredients and expecting the same cake.

But we'd be more efficient if the government paid claims because the government cost is just 3 percent of premium instead of insurers that charge 20 percent.

The government costs more than 3 percent of premium. That figure represents Medicare overhead which doesn't account for rent, tasks performed by other agencies, and tax-favored status, among other elements. Second, insurers don't charge 20 percent of premium as that figure represents small-group companies. The average of all companies is 12 percent, not 20 percent. An apples-to-apples study shows that government costs are actually 12 percent higher than the market (see Chapter 9).

I've never heard that comparison.

And why do you suppose that is? Perhaps because that study was underreported?

But Sweden ranks twenty-third in the same study that the US ranks thirty-seventh.

I'll address that in my book. Suffice it to say that comparison is from 2000 and reflects weights that skew results toward Single Payer systems. Further, that study has been debunked repeatedly.

But every other country with Single Payer has lower costs. There must be something to it.

For the second time, you can't perform an experiment with different chemicals and get the same product. You get a by-product of the chemicals used in the experiment. And we can't afford another experiment like Obamacare (the Affordable Care Act, or ACA).

I'm glad you mentioned it. Obamacare worked for most people.

Really? Just because some people were better off? According to that measurement, the government should just give everyone $10,000.

But too many people were previously excluded from coverage.

Excluded how? Some of those people chose not to be covered (to spend money on something else).

But all people don't have to worry about preexisting conditions anymore. That's a good thing.

If you wanted to eliminate preexisting limitation exclusions, just do that. The ACA was a monstrosity for such an "easy to fix" problem.

But there were 42 million people without healthcare coverage before the ACA took effect. And all other countries cover more of their people.

Again, if you just wanted to cover more people, we could have increased Medicaid availability to more people. The complexity was unnecessary unless the real purpose was to hide the goals.

That's untrue. The ACA needed to be complex because healthcare is complex.

Really? A 2,700-page bill with twenty thousand pages of regulation, none of which could be read and understood because it read like, "Strike the word 'create' and add the word 'amend.' "

But regulations need to be complex. For instance, there were 80,000 pages of regulations of all types issued in general last year.

Thanks for reminding me about something else that needs to be fixed.

But cost control is what's needed. Who better to do that than the government?

Cost control is what brought HMOs to the forefront in the '90s. People rejected that because they didn't like "cost control." The only alternative is to sacrifice quality, access, or innovation.

What hasn't been tried is having one buyer—a monopsony—where the government controls the price of goods.

Every apparent issue with the cost of healthcare derives from a cause that's further upstream, such as the high cost of an ER visit due to cost shifting from the government underpayments from Medicare and Medicaid.

You've gotta be kidding me. The high cost of the ER is due to Medicare and Medicaid?

Don't take my statements out of context as if that's the only cause. But it's an important one—the new school thinking is that there hasn't been a true free market in healthcare since 1965 when Medicare and Medicaid were passed. This distorted the market for healthcare.

But isn't cost-shifting from government just one of the components of healthcare cost inflation?

Yes, however, 1 percent per year cost shifting over fifty years compounds to 65 percent.

But shifting costs between the public and private sectors does not influence the overall cost of healthcare, which is 17 percent of GDP in the US.

Yes, that's the classic line. And we're back to your original argument. Here, read this:

"If we expanded Medicaid [to] everybody—we would be spending such an astronomical sum of money that, you know, we would bankrupt the nation." -Bernie Sanders, 1987

MEDICARE

FOR ALL—OMG!

"It is amazing that people who think we cannot afford to pay for doctors, hospitals, and medication somehow think that we can afford to pay for doctors, hospitals, medication, and a government bureaucracy to administer it."

-Thomas Sowell, 2004

HEALTHCARE COSTS IN THE US ARE TOO HIGH

We all agree on that. But it's important to define the word "high" and put costs into context.

Why is this important? Because Single Payer—or Medicare For All (M4A)—is being pushed as a solution looking for a problem (that we shouldn't spend more than other countries on healthcare). As I discussed in the prologue, all statistics need context. GDP does not correlate very well with an individual's decision to purchase health-care. Disposable income does. But percentage of GDP is how healthcare spending is always put into context. Case in point:

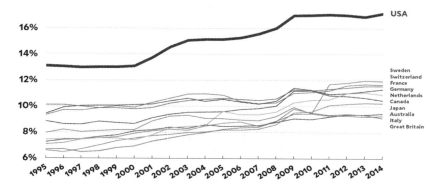

Health Care Spending as % of GDP
1995-2014

Source: World Bank

We have been told for generations we spend too much on healthcare and get too little in return. I have followed this line of thinking for years. It bothered me, but I just couldn't move on as expected. Then I found the following graph comparing spending to income.

HOUSEHOLD DISPOSABLE INCOME

A measure for context better than GDP is Household Disposable Income:

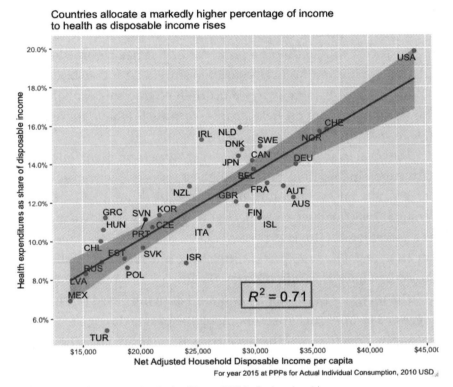

Countries allocate a markedly higher percentage of income to health as disposable income rises

$R^2 = 0.71$

Source: Random Critical Analysis. (Note: CHE is Switzerland.)

The graph, developed by blogger *Random Critical Analysis*, explains US healthcare spending better than any other. It shows spending *is appropriate* when compared to Household Disposable Income (HDI). Indeed, US disposable income far exceeds that for every country shown in the GDP graph. Healthcare spending as a percentage of HDI is reasonable, as the shaded area shows.

Household Disposable Income is the bottom line that affects decisions made by consumers, not the country's GDP. Never have I said, "We're all doing well collectively, so I can afford to spend more on my family's consumption of healthcare." For decades, we've been told that the US should not spend such a high percentage of GDP. But this graph says, "Yes, it should!" Data should be correlated, not just related.

The difference is that GDP relates but indirectly correlates with healthcare spending, while HDI directly correlates. GDP is what the economy produces while HDI is the result of that production, and that's specific to me: GDP is a proxy for HDI. It has become less correlated with income due to globalization since 2000. Incredibly, Household Disposable Income is so well correlated that this explains why the US spends more on healthcare—because we have more available to spend.

The graph shows the US spends nearly 20 percent of HDI on healthcare, much higher than the next highest country (Switzerland) at 16 percent. But our Average HDI per person is 20 percent higher ($44,000 versus $37,000 for Switzerland). That means our healthcare spending as a percentage of HDI is 25 percent higher than in Switzerland, while our HDI per capita is 20 percent higher, so our spending is above the projection line but within the gray range.

The US has a much higher standard of living based on HDI than suggested by GDP! That's because more GDP passes through to individuals as income than in other countries. HDI doesn't have the imprecision of GDP due to trade deficits, individual savings, cross-country GDP generation, etc. And the more a person has available to spend, the more willing they are to spend on health.

My argument is that we're much richer than other countries, much more than comparisons of GDP would imply. Here are the thirteen countries with higher GDP per capita than the US (2019), in order:

- Monaco
- Liechtenstein
- Luxembourg
- Bermuda
- Cayman Islands

- Macao
- Switzerland
- The Isle of Man
- Ireland
- Norway
- Channel Islands
- Iceland
- Singapore

Many of these countries have wealthy residents and are the size of US cities. We knew we had a higher standard of living; we just didn't have the right data to show it. HDI proves the US has a higher average standard of living than *every* major country in the world, and it is higher than *every* country in Europe—countries which are often promoted as having lower cost healthcare. A main reason for higher HDI than GDP is due to taxes and investment, which favor the US.

The US is unique in the HDI graph—an outlier versus other countries that clump together in the middle. Who should the US be compared to? The common approach has been to compare the US to developed countries, those that are part of the OECD (Organization for Economic Co-operation and Development). But the graph shows that OECD countries are nowhere near the US in HDI.

As other countries continue to increase in HDI, their healthcare spending as a percentage of HDI will undoubtedly increase toward the US level. At that point, we may know how to compare the current US healthcare spending. Maybe a comparison would be appropriate in 2030. Until then, it's premature to argue we're spending too much. As a population achieves lower-order Maslow needs, the desire for higher-order needs increases. Other countries will someday desire what Americans have collectively desired in the past decade or two.

That means the US healthcare system has and will continue to forge a new path. There is no other system in the world like it, so the US healthcare system is the only system that it could be compared to (compared to itself). This is disconcerting to all who wish to make sense out of the data, that there must be some pattern. I'll discuss that desire in the next section. Suffice it to say, it's not sufficient to find correlation, it must be causation.

Let's compare the US to Sweden (SWE) on the HDI graph since Scandinavian countries are often held up as models for US healthcare. Sweden's healthcare expenditure is well above the line of best fit, like in the US. Using this comparison, Sweden spends too much relative to the comparable acceptable range in gray, while the US is within the gray range. That means something is wrong in Sweden (and right in Finland, which is well below the gray range).

A significant reason for this overexpenditure is Sweden's lower HDI relative to the US (28 percent less), such that Sweden's allowable healthcare expenditure is much lower than it might otherwise be if they had higher HDI.

The US compares well to all the Scandinavian countries: Norway's expenditure is in the acceptable range; Denmark and Sweden, above acceptable; and Finland, well below acceptable. One could conclude that a country's spending could be increased or decreased based on this relative comparison—that if a country is above the line that less spending is warranted, and vice versa. And the degree of concern is greater where a country's spending is outside of the gray range.

How can such disparate pictures of healthcare spending result? And which one is more accurate? Undoubtedly, GDP is widely chosen because it's easy and shows what some want it to show—that the US has a healthcare spending problem.

But healthcare spending as a percentage of GDP is just a two-dimensional calculation, while the HDI chart shows a third dimension. Put differently, the GDP graph shows healthcare GDP divided by total GDP (two dimensions). The HDI graph incorporates a third dimension, that of Disposable Income Per Capita (the graph plots healthcare spending as a percentage of HDI versus Disposable Income Per Capita).

The two-dimensional chart only highlights the problem so that proponents can declare an emergency exists. The HDI graph shows the HDI percentage relative to HDI per capita, establishing a correlation with a third dimension that explains why the percentage is high.

It's amazing that the US political infrastructure didn't overreact to the Single Payer phenomena. Had it, we would never know this truth about the affordability of the current system (based on HDI). We would only know what we'd been told, that the US healthcare system is unaffordable. Any decision to change the system is vital to the healthcare industry and its sixteen million employees (about 11 percent of all workers).

There should be options, affording people who want to save by spending less. Alternatively, some people want more healthcare and value it above buying, for instance, another TV. Market options allow them to do that, instead of one-size-fits-all government programs.

WHAT DOES THIS MEAN?

This is incredible! How could this chart have never been noticed? Because the media doesn't want any other picture to be considered, other than that healthcare costs are one dollar out of every six dollars of the economy. At a minimum, this chart casts doubt.

But it's heretical to even mention there isn't a cost problem. *"People can't afford healthcare in America, don't you know?"* But what about those who can't afford food? Or shelter? Or higher education? Or transportation? Or clean water? Or a smart phone? Or Wi-Fi? Or insurance? The list goes on and on.

Do we spend more as a percentage of GDP than other countries? Yes. And do we spend more per capita (adjusted for purchasing power parity) than other countries? Yes. And do we spend more per HDI than other countries? Yes.

But the percentage we spend is appropriate relative to other countries because our HDI per person far exceeds HDI per capita in other countries. What I'm asking is that the standard analysis of measurement—that of GDP—needs to be HDI instead, and that the comparisons to other countries need to stop, as I show later in Chapter 6. I show that comparison to other smaller, dissimilar countries is inappropriate.

The bottom line is we spend a lot for our healthcare. Some of the extra cost is due to innovation. What if no other country would pay for innovations in medicine going forward? Does that mean we shouldn't? Healthcare R&D is expensive, but it's worth it. It would be great if we continue to prosper from innovation and other countries pay their share of it. Until that happens, we can't just give up on the current system.

Understandably, we're ready for major change in our healthcare system. I'll propose an alternative change in Chapter 3 that makes more sense than M4A. In the interim, let's continue analyzing healthcare from all angles.

CONTEXT FOR MEASUREMENT

Two data elements can be related, but that can be coincidence. A website and book have evolved from this concept, called *Spurious Correlations* by Tyler Vigen. Here is one of the graphs:

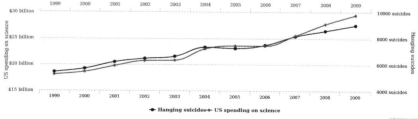

This chart illustrates how comparing data just because there may be correlation can be meaningless. There is a continuum of relationships in any two sets of data: no relationship; related; correlated; partial causation; full causation.

Data can be related by:

A classic method of putting a number in context is to divide it by a contextual number (putting a numerator in context by dividing it by a denominator). This helps to understand what "100 percent" means. But dividing any two numbers should be done carefully. For example, a false comparison is to divide a person's rent by their income (versus dividing by their take-home pay). Both income and take-home pay are useful, but take-home pay is clearly more appropriate in this context. Does dividing healthcare spending by total GDP suffer from this issue of context? And why is such a calculation performed only for the healthcare industry?

So one must be careful when analyzing data. The human mind wants to see patterns even where none exist (there are myriad examples at tylervigen.com). It's still important to lower total spending, but it's not necessarily important to lower spending per capita, unless total spending also decreases. If we knowingly lowered the per capita figure but raised total spending, that would be an abomination. And that's what some changes in Obamacare did. An example is the requirement to purchase coverage or face a tax penalty. Average per capita costs decreased because Obamacare now covered people with little in claims, which didn't lower total spending and may have increased it (when something is free, utilization increases).

Bad data and bad analysis haunt the discussion of healthcare in many ways:

- Some claim that the US spends too much on healthcare using GDP as context—again, a poor proxy versus HDI, as shown above.
- Some claim that the government adjudicates claims at a much lower cost than the private sector should be laughed at rather than taken seriously (I'll discuss in Chapter 9).
- Some claim that it must be someone else's fault that healthcare is so expensive. People rarely look at themselves. For example, thinking of using medical benefits at the end of the year because it's free once one meets the out-of-pocket maximum. Or timing an expensive healthcare service to optimize coverage. Or filling a prescription not based on need but because "*I deserve it*" even though the need for more pills has subsided.
- Some claim that life expectancy is shorter in the US because of the healthcare system when we know that there are numerous other factors being ignored, like lifestyle and demographics.
- Some claim that life expectancy is longer in other countries (like Japan, Scandinavia), when this was true fifty years ago well before implementing any healthcare policies.
- Some claim that waiting for services (like in Canada or the UK) will be acceptable in the US.
- Some claim that eliminating profit under Single Payer will generate continued innovation as if there is no cost to eliminating incentives.
- Some claim that free healthcare will not increase care and cost.
- Some claim that Single Payer systems work in every other developed country for half the price. If you think about it, researchers' analyses has been appalling to reach such conclusions.

The harm of false statistics has already occurred: The urgent passage of the ACA took place because something needed to change. This is akin to pulling a fire alarm and then claiming the action warranted because it started a conversation.

SCANDINAVIA

The perception of socialism begins with Capitalism. Scandinavian countries know this, and they are becoming more capitalistic every day. In 2015, Denmark's prime minister said, "I know that some people in the US associate the Nordic model with some sort of socialism, therefore I would like to make one thing clear. Denmark is far from a socialist-planned economy. Denmark is a market economy."

And as reported by CNBC on March 8, 2019, "Finland's government resigned on Friday after ditching plans to reform the healthcare system, a key policy, the Finnish president's office said, throwing the country into political limbo. Financial constraints are colliding with the healthcare costs imposed by Finland's fast-ageing population. But cutting those costs is a major political obstacle in a Nordic country that historically has provided an extensive and expensive healthcare system."

And in Sweden, just 9 percent of Swedes call themselves Socialists.

Put differently, Scandinavian countries are not Socialist; they're Capitalist with more government oversight. So, let's see: "*We should be more like Scandinavia*," and they're capitalists with higher taxes. The bottom line is we could increase our tax rates to be more like Scandinavia. Since 1913 (when the income tax was first created), it has been the goal of Democrats to call for increasing taxes. So how is this different?

Further, Scandinavia is becoming more capitalist to counter the Socialist policies from the 1970s and 1980s. Capitalism can survive without socialism, but not the other way around. The amount of Economic Freedom (a term coined by the Heritage Foundation) is markedly higher under Capitalism and lower under socialism, all other things being equal. But trying to match what Scandinavia is doing is like trying to hit a moving target.

Let's compare the US population to that of Scandinavia to see how dissimilar they are:

2015	US	DENMARK	FINLAND	NORWAY	SWEDEN
POPULATION	321 MILLION	6 MILLION	5 MILLION	5 MILLION	10 MILLION
RATIO	64	1	1	1	2
GEOGRAPHIC SIZE (MILLION KM²)	9.1	0.04	0.3	0.4	0.4
RATIO	228	1	8	10	10
HEALTHCARE SPEND % OF GDP	16.8%	10.2%	9.7%	10.1%	11.0%
HEALTHCARE GDP	$3.1 T	$31 B	$23 B	$39 B	$55 B
RATIO	135	1	1	2	2
LARGEST ETHNIC GROUP PERCENT OF THE POPULATION (2017)	72%	92%	98%	96%	91%
ADULT OBESITY RATE (2016)	36%	20%	22%	23%	21%
CAR ACCIDENT RATE PER 100,000	10.9	3.1	4.9	2.3	2.6
HOMICIDE RATE PER 100,000	5.0	1.0	1.5	0.5	1.2
DENSITY (PEOPLE PER KM²)	36	134	18	14	25
MIGRANTS (NET)	+992,000	+21,000	+16,000	+44,000	+51,000

Sources: Various (see Endnotes), Author's Calculations

I chose to compare 2015 numbers because in Chapter 2, I update the 1990 charts that presidential candidate Ross Perot showed, and I wanted to compare numbers twenty-five years earlier and later rather than thirty years. Little has changed from 2015 to today in the relationships. And data from 2015 is consistently available for the US and other countries.

Apples and oranges make for poor comparisons. Yes, both have outer peels. But cherry-picking features that one likes is disingenuous.

Scandinavian countries have strong work ethics and strict citizenship requirements to become part of their homogeneous nations. Suggesting we repeat their experiment is like saying that all we need to do is to stay as a small group of people in the Northeast, avoid wars along the way (remaining neutral to World Wars and other atrocities), attain higher morals with less corruption (Scandinavian countries are the least corrupt countries in the world, per Transparency International), and work hard under a system of high taxes. We, too, could have a successful, homogeneous healthcare system. *"That's all it would take."*

One could say that the US works hard and plays hard. Regardless of the reasons that US obesity is high at all ages, that driving is reckless, and that homicide rates are four times as high, there is little similarity between the US and Scandinavian countries. The cultures are very different, exemplified through a survey of trust of others, where Scandinavian countries are at the top in the world, while trust amongst the US population measures about half that in Scandinavia (per the World Value survey).

One final comparison: The Index of Economic Freedom by the Heritage Foundation. While the US often is deemed to be capitalist, and Scandinavian countries deemed to be socialist (by US Democratic Socialists), their rankings are essentially the same with regards to Economic Freedom. In 2020, the US had a score of 77 on a 100-point scale, while Scandinavian countries averaged 76. For context, Cuba, Venezuela, and North Korea were at the bottom with scores of 27, 25, and 4, respectively.

So how can a Socialist country rank high in Economic Freedom? Obviously, they're not socialist. Scandinavian countries score well compared to the US in the following areas:

- Scandinavian countries score high in Open Markets, reflecting high scores for Trade, Investment, and Financial Freedom.
- Scandinavian countries score high for Fiscal Health, reflecting Public Debt of just 50 percent of GDP on average (versus the US where Public Debt is 106 percent of GDP).
- The US scores lower for Government Spending and Fiscal Health.

A Swedish economist once said to US economist Milton Friedman, "In Scandinavia, we have no poverty." Milton Friedman replied, "That's interesting, because in America among Scandinavians, we have no poverty either."

OBAMACARE

We tried a Socialist solution in Obamacare, and it didn't work. In place since 2014, a rational analysis of the ACA is needed. Here are average Obamacare increases by year:

OBAMACARE		
	AVERAGE INCREASE	CUMULATIVE
2014	25%	25%
2015	14%	43%
2016	8%	54%
2017	25%	92%
2018	37%	164%
2019	5%	177%

Source: Health and Human Services (HHS). Note that the first-year increase is described as the Obamacare plan average increase versus individual market plans available in 2013.

Astoundingly, the average increase from 2013 to 2019 is 177 percent, meaning if a plan cost $10,000 in 2013, it would cost $27,700 in 2019! Why is this not widely known? It would cost a family over $100,000 in premium every four years, likely increasing at double-digit rates over the next decade.

I recognize there is a potential disconnect of the 177 percent Obamacare increase while overall spending in healthcare didn't increase nearly this much; if it had, we would have noticed. The reason is that Obamacare represents such a small percentage of the healthcare system since the increase in number of insured people of thirteen million is just 3 percent of 325 million people in the country.

Some have been trying to figure out what's wrong with Obamacare and have concluded that:

- premiums are very high,
- insurers lost money,
- insurers left the market, and
- there are still twenty-nine million uninsured.

All legitimate issues, but they counter with:

- premiums have always been high,
- insurers make too much money,
- insurers left the market, so the government should step in, and
- there are still twenty-nine million uninsured, so we need to go further.

Some people talk about needing a revolution. The push now is for M4A to replace private insurance with government control of the health-care system. Obamacare already failed, so why should we try one more complex solution? When in history have we allowed a CEO to fail and then let them try again?

What causes healthcare costs to be so high? There is an old saying in business: "Cheap, fast, and accurate: Pick two." While trite, this saying implies that we can accomplish two out of three objectives, but that in attempting to accomplish the third, we will unknowingly sacrifice one of the two we already have. If healthcare today (or at least the market we had before the ACA) is fast and accurate, we must live with expensive. Alternatively, we can regulate price through Single Payer and force healthcare to not be as fast (or accurate).

We collectively choose what we want through the free market system, and to the extent we would like to have our cake and eat it too (i.e., coverage for low cost), we would collectively need to choose which sacrifice we are willing to make. Choice of quality is not an option, so our decision comes down to cost versus speed. And the fact is that no one in Single Payer countries likes the waiting for services (for non-emergency care, such as waiting to get screened for cancer). How would it be possible that people in the US would be willing to sacrifice speed for cost with one's life? The answer is we wouldn't (and shouldn't).

Politicians are so frustrating in that they talk about one side of the equation without mentioning the other side. They promote free things that everyone will ultimately have to pay for but rarely mention the taxes. When they do, they wave their hands at the question as if high costs today allow for high taxes tomorrow. They claim families will save thousands of dollars in outlays for healthcare, with no mention that the cost side will offset most of the savings.

In addition, I want to tackle some of the dumb things I've heard and read about the US healthcare system:

- **We're being gouged by rich healthcare companies.** Really? That happens in healthcare more than in other industries? For-profit companies run just 20 percent of hospitals, and only about half of insurance companies are for-profit (because many insurance companies are not-for-profit, like many Blue Cross Blue Shield plans, Kaiser Permanente, many HMOs, and ACA Co-operatives—the four that are still in business). Not-for-profit companies are a large part of healthcare costs. And the "*bad-and-evil*" health insurance industry profits average just 3 percent of revenue.

- **It's the middlemen**. Really? They skim off the top and aren't necessary to the healthcare system? Insurance is important to a fair allocation of resources (their customers all agree to the rules of paying average premiums to get coverage for small and large claims). Purchasing healthcare directly works for a few risk-taking individuals, but that's a recipe for disaster for most of the population. And if there was a better, cheaper alternative, a new insurance company would provide just that (that's what competition does). Like often said, nobody wants to be a middleman for an expensive product, because then you get blamed for the cost. Bottom line: it's not the middlemen.

- **It's the lobbyists.** Really? Yes, millions spent on lobbying focus on a special interest, but lobbying extends to many interests (be it doctors, hospitals, insurance companies, etc.). In some cases, the lobbyists are employees; in others, they are contractors who act like employees. How much of what they do is educational, and how much of what they do is what opponents view as counter to the public interest? "*They should all go away.*" Really? So the AARP shouldn't have a voice in elderly issues? "*Okay, then the insurance lobby and the NRA should go away.*" I see. It's the voices you don't like. Believing in free speech means accepting all voices and all lobbyists. And lobbyists are there to represent the hospitals, doctors, nurses, insurance, etc.

- **The pharmaceutical industry makes too much.** Really? Prescription drugs represent about 20 percent of all healthcare spending, and while the pharma industry's profits are above average versus other industries (profits averaged about 17 percent of revenues from 2006 to 2015, lower than many industries and lower than some would have you believe), shouldn't their profits be above average for providing something that not just anyone can create, something that's vital to life? And many drugs never get approved, so the risk is very high (high risk, high reward). Bottom line: 17 percent profit times 20 percent of healthcare costs equals just 3 percent of overall costs; again, not the amount some would claim.

- **It's those CEOs and their pay.** Really? Take the largest insurer, UnitedHealthcare, which had revenues of $242 billion in 2019. CEO pay and pay for the top five executives in any company varies widely from year to year and is often indeterminable until the executive purchases and sells company stock. For simplicity, let's assume the top five executives averaged $20 million. That would be $100 million total, or 0.04 percent of the premium for United-Healthcare, just 0.003 percent of total US healthcare spending. Even if there were one hundred such companies, their top five executives would be paid just 0.3 percent of healthcare spending. So let's put an end to this concern that someone is making too much money at the expense of someone else.

- **It's the shareholders.** Really? If that's the case, pension invest-ments would boom because all they would need to do is invest in healthcare companies. And then I would be rich (I'd invest my 401k in these companies, and I would even borrow to make money investing in these lucrative companies because it's guaranteed). As Ben Stein says, companies are owned by widows and orphans (through pensions and 401k plans). *"Yes, the shareholders are the evil ones."* Okay, so that's not it.

- **Healthcare is one of the few industries where competition increases the cost of care.** Really? The argument goes something like, "If a community adds a hospital, the number of procedures must increase in that community for the hospital to survive." But that's not the case in any other industry, such as with banks. If a new bank enters a community, we can make the same argument that there are more mouths to feed. But through competition, existing banks either get better (better quality, cheaper prices) or they go out of business. Overall, that's good for the consumer, and the same is true with healthcare. Further, competition has worked with dental coverage, vision coverage, and LASIK surgery to bring down prices. Market forces through competition led to lower prices, so that should be the approach for healthcare.

- **Purchasing healthcare is so complex that the average person cannot contemplate all the information.** Really? That's not the case in other industries, such as investing in complex financial instruments? There is a ton of information to consider, yet the average person can handle decisions about what's important to them. A counter argument is often, "But healthcare is a more important purchase than a financial instrument"—all the more reason to not have the government involved in decisions, but to let the individual decide with the counsel of healthcare professionals.

- **It's all that administration; I don't want to pay any more than necessary.** Really? Then why did you buy that beer at a bar, over six times the cost in a store? Plus, much of healthcare administration is due to government paperwork. Don't get mad at the office person who asks you to fill out a form that requires more details than needed to solve your healthcare problem or the doctor who doesn't spend much time in the exam room because they have paperwork to fill out or have to dictate or type details about your health in case they get sued.

- **Healthcare purchasing is inelastic (unlimited demand, so the price can be unlimited).** Really? Many purchases are relatively inelastic, such as food, water, and energy (electricity and gas), having few sources of substitution. True, healthcare is inelastic when an inca- pacitated person cannot take part in the decision-making process, so that's why buying insurance beforehand when coherent can over- come this issue. A counter argument is often, "But the insurance company has different goals than just my health." That's where government regulation is vital to making sure the insurer honors commitments to provide or arrange for proper care. Before you sal- ivate over government decision-making versus for-profit insurer decision-making, remember that both insurers and the govern- ment have a reason to deny claims to save money. The government would answer your phone call about payment of claims instead of an insurance company, and that government decision is final with no appeal. The government never goes out of business.

- **It's them!** Really? Doctors say it's the hospitals. Hospitals say it's the doctors. It's always somebody else. There are a lot of fingers pointing at lobbyists and the PBMs (Pharmaceutical Benefit Manag- ers), partly because they're nameless and faceless. It's easy to claim lobbyists and PBMs are there to make money for themselves at the public's expense. But what lobbyists and the PBMs do is important to the provision of healthcare. Try the system without PBMs and see what the price of undiscounted drugs amounts to.

- **It's all the above!** Really? If you throw every idea up against the wall to see what sticks because the amount of "gouging" isn't very high for any specific cause, maybe it will be high enough to con- sider in total. *"Yes, at least the total amount is worthy to consider, but that means incredible complications in any solution to fix all the issues at the same time."* That's why proponents want Single Payer, to claim that although each argument is poor by itself (arguments like, "competition doesn't work in healthcare"), somehow life will be better with the government in charge of every aspect. Even though that has never been the case in any industry at any time.

- There's a case to be made that we should solve smaller problems that represent, say, 1 percent of total spend since 1 percent of $3 trillion in spending is $30 billion per year (worthy of the effort). The problem is, how far upstream is the actual problem? For example, if we don't go far enough upstream, we might attempt to solve a problem with drug prices where the federal government demands the negotiation of prices. That solution may cause more problems than this Band-Aid approach can solve, like the lack of innovation. Alternatively, we might go too far upstream by changing drug patent law to be twelve years instead of twenty. This upstream solution would again lead to long-term unintended consequences. So, obviously any solution will need to be well-thought-out, not knee-jerk.

- Speaking of how far upstream, it's important to place blame appropriately. For example, we commonly blame CEOs as the cause of high healthcare costs (among other ills). Blame is typically two-fold: CEO pay is X times the lowest-paid worker (or the median wage), implying that the CEO takes from someone else or that CEO pays their employees as little as possible so that the CEO makes more. Some claim that it's not fair that someone makes so much and that it's not fair that they control what other people make. Instead, one should accept that CEOs make a lot more than the average worker, and as President John F. Kennedy famously stated in a speech in 1963, "a rising tide lifts all boats."

- One more, I couldn't resist: **People under Single Payer in other countries have lower rates of diabetes due to management.** Really? It's not because certain nations with homogeneous populations have lower rates of diabetes in the first place? Sheesh.

Everyone blames everyone else for the problem. There's a desire to claim to be a victim, as if that avoids any blame. This is true in all aspects of society, not just healthcare.

It goes something like this: *"I'm just trying to be a good doctor to my patients. If it wasn't for all this paperwork, I'd spend more than five minutes talking to you. But don't alleviate the problem by allowing nurse practitioners, physician assistants, or C students do what I do, because no one can provide care as perfectly as I do. I'm constantly nagged by insurance companies to prove my planned course of treatment. Don't they know it's the right plan?"*

There is an incongruous comparison that the US spends more on its healthcare system compared to other countries. The error is assuming that healthcare is the same in each country, as if the products are the same. For instance, an office visit is not the same in the US and Canada. While both doctors are well-educated, and quality is comparable, the US doctor has more alternatives to consider, albeit at higher cost:

- The US develops more drugs because US patients use more drugs. Regardless of the reason, they do. And note that studies often categorize drugs as being developed in the manufacturer's country, but the US market drives much of the R&D. I question origination because it makes little sense to give credit, say, to a French company which domiciles in Canada for tax reasons while their motivation for innovation emanates from the US drug market. Simply put, the manufacturing and sale of drugs is global, while the purchasing and use is local. The US market receives over a third of the world's developing new drug patents. The bottom line is that US physicians must keep up on all the various drug studies if they prescribe more medicine for patients than in Canada.

- Four of the world's top ten hospitals for treating cancer are in the US, according to *Newsweek*, and no other country placed over one hospital in the top ten.

- Hospitals in the US typically have private rooms. Other countries typically have both private and semiprivate rooms, including

Canada. Private rooms have shown in various studies to have infection rates that are 20-50 percent lower than in two-or-more rooms. There is sparse data on this element (private rooms by country), but from reviewing multiple sources, US hospitals commonly offer private rooms, while Canada has few private rooms even available.

- Advancement in medical devices is like prescription drug R&D since companies innovate because of profit incentives. For example, we have seen progress in bioabsorbable stents and needle-free injections. Like with prescription drugs, US doctors prescribe more medical devices than in Canada.

- We can scan the entire body without having to address symptoms. Some feel scanning the body without symptoms is a waste, but the fact is we have access and the means to conduct such care. There are three times as many CT scanners per person than in Canada and six times the number of MRI machines. Whether Canada has too few or the US too much is a separate question, but that there are more devices allows for the possibility of scanning, even if unnecessary in the medical sense. Like with Socialist thinking that would eliminate Capitalism because there are twenty-three brands of deodorant on the market, Socialist thought would eliminate scanning the body to detect maladies before they become symptomatic. Cheaper in the short term, costlier in the long term.

- We have the highest percentage of specialists per physician than any other country. While perceived as a negative because we'd like to have more primary care physicians, the US system has evolved beyond primary care. A hundred years ago, it made sense that one primary care physician treated a wide variety of health problems. Today, we benefit from the variety of training, and that training needs specialization because healthcare is so complex. This means specialists focus on their training and that benefits consumers. It's like thinking a primary care physician can also operate on internal organs or perform transplant surgery.

- US patients trade cost for inconvenience. One reason there are so many MRI machines in the US is that patients want their MRIs performed at the hospital where they're admitted. They expect to get a prescription at every appointment or think the doctor didn't do his job, that "I need something for the pain." We are our own worst enemy regarding healthcare costs.

- US patients willingly abuse the system. For example, who hasn't said, *"I might as well use my healthcare because I've hit my out-of-pocket maximum for the year, and it'll be free until year-end," "So, let's go ahead with that cortisone shot even though its effects are temporary,"* or *"I'm planning on having the surgery in December, so I won't have to pay for it"*?

GDP

My original goal was to figure out how much we spend on food, clothing, and shelter (to compare to Maslow's hierarchy). I could not find an all-encompassing source for what we spend. We're told that we spend 10 percent of GDP more on healthcare and another 10 percent more on the military, so I couldn't wait to find out what we spend 20 percent less on (it must be a great deal!) So, what do we forgo? According to the Centers for Medicare and Medicaid (CMS), US healthcare spending was 16.8 percent of GDP in 2015. However, I couldn't find any pie charts that show this figure, only ones that show healthcare GDP at 7.1 percent (in 2015):

2015 GDP

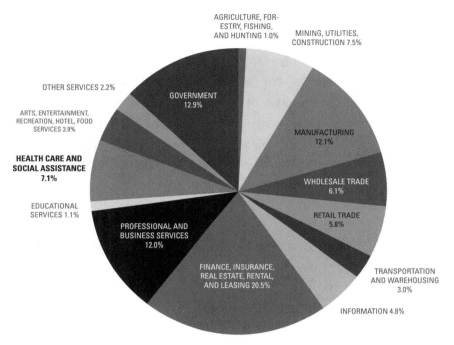

Source: Bureau of Economic Analysis (BEA)

I was shocked to find Health Care and Social Assistance at just 7.1 percent of GDP instead of 16.8 percent! These are not new pie charts, as they have been available on the internet for years. Anyone can readily see similar charts by Googling "US Industry GDP Pie Charts." I call this a dangling data point.

I contemplated these findings for a long time. What was I missing? Could both be right, that these charts are correct as well as claims that healthcare represents one-sixth of the economy? I reviewed the underlying data, hoping to reconcile the two sources. But reconciliation never happened. That's because the sources of data are separate and inconsistent.

Robert Kornfeld of BEA reconciled the BEA versus CMS figures in 2010, but the starting point was 15 percent, rather than 7.1 percent. The analysis never tied back to the 7.1 percent pie charts available on the internet because that wasn't the focus. I wanted to see how 7.1 percent translates into 16.8 percent as there are numerous pie categories that would have to give up their share of GDP to the healthcare category.

After a lot of review, I'm convinced the CMS figures are accurate, that the US spends 17 percent of GDP on healthcare. However, I decided that GDP provides such poor context that I tossed out these figures in favor of the HDI chart from earlier in this chapter. That means we should not argue over whether healthcare spending is 17 percent of GDP; it doesn't matter. What matters is that healthcare spending is 20 percent of HDI, and that's reasonable, compared to other countries.

Since the industry pie chart reflects the only available information for US GDP categories, I compared spending across countries with data that's already available (comparing spending to GDP is acceptable since those are the only figures available across countries; HDI is preferable to GDP, of course). Only Canada and the UK provide GDP data by industry. (Many other countries do not even have healthcare-specific data because their healthcare numbers blend in with other government spending.) Here is a comparison of figures for those countries:

2015	HEALTHCARE GDP / TOTAL GDP* PIE CHARTS	REPORTED HC SPEND / TOTAL GDP**
US	7.1%	16.8%
ENGLAND (UK)	7.4%	9.1%
CANADA	6.6%	10.4%

*Per BEA, the Office for National Statistics UK, and Statistics Canada

**Per World Health Organization

In the immortal words of Doc Brown from *Back to the Future*, "Do you know what this means?" It means Canada's and England's costs are too high! But seriously, are their costs too high, or are US costs too low (because we have it in our heads that the US healthcare system costs too much)?

Here is a comparison of all the GDP percentages with Canada and the UK:

2015 % OF GDP	US	UK	CANADA
HEALTH CARE AND SOCIAL ASSISTANCE	7.1%	7.4%	6.6%
FINANCE, INSURANCE, REAL ESTATE, RENTAL, AND LEASING	20.5%	20.7%	19.7%
GOVERNMENT	12.9%	4.7%	6.3%
MANUFACTURING	12.1%	10.1%	10.4%
PROFESSIONAL AND BUSINESS SERVICES	12.0%	12.2%	5.5%
MINING, UTILITIES, CONSTRUCTION	7.5%	10.0%	17.9%
WHOLESALE TRADE	6.1%	10.8%	5.7%
RETAIL TRADE	5.8%		5.3%
INFORMATION	4.8%	6.0%	3.1%
ARTS, ENTERTAINMENT, RECREATION, HOTEL, FOOD SERVICE	3.9%	4.5%	2.9%
TRANSPORTATION AND WAREHOUSING	3.0%	4.5%	4.4%
OTHER SERVICES	2.2%	2.5%	5.3%

EDUCATION SERVICES	1.1%	6.1%	5.3%
AGRICULTURE, FORESTRY, FISHING, AND HUNTING	1.0%	0.7%	1.6%
TOTAL	100.0%	100.0%	100.0%

Sources: US—BEA, UK—Office for National Statistics, CAN—Statistics Canada.

This chart provides an amazing array of statistics never compared before. Government looks unusually high in the US, but that's a reflection of military spending and Social Security (and apparently, healthcare). In the end, all countries spend 100 percent.

Also, other than for education, we don't spend a lot less in any category (ignoring mining, utilities, construction, which is very high in Canada). If the data were available that reallocates percentages to healthcare spending, then certain categories in the US would be lower. For now, this table allows us to highlight categories that stand out, and education is the only one.

Where is the 10 percent excess being spent on the military and the 10 percent excess on healthcare? It must be under government. As I've mentioned, one would need to transfer 9.7 percent from government and other categories to get from 7.1 percent to 16.8 percent for healthcare GDP. But then there would be no excess left in government. The bottom line is there are obvious flaws in the apparent understating of healthcare spending. I sidestep this problem by saying that HDI is better than GDP anyway, so let's quit worrying about GDP because it just leads to false conclusions.

HEALTHCARE SPENDING COMPARISONS

Admittedly, the amount the US spends on healthcare is difficult to estimate. Any accounting of a $3 trillion figure has details behind it that would befuddle any economist. For example:

- The BEA states: "The emergency housing or healthcare services provided by nonprofit institutions serving households (such as the Red Cross)" are included. While it makes sense to include Red Cross costs in the healthcare bucket, these costs may not be comparable to other countries' spending.

- VA costs are included, which means the US must include additional costs that no other country must include (since US military healthcare spending far exceeds that for any other country). No study ever accounts for this.

- Costs of people from Canada and Mexico (and other tourism) are included. That means the inclusion of costs for people incurred without corresponding counts.

- Costs of care provided overseas, where US healthcare entities provide medicines and other services to poor countries. For example, cost is included for Doctors Without Borders and for the US Navy ship that parked off the coast of South America in 2018 to provide free medical and dental treatment to Venezuelans.

- Other potential plusses and minuses versus other countries. One consideration is the high cost of innovation (especially with prescription drugs), which is disproportionally higher in the US than in other countries.

CONTINUING THE LEFT-RIGHT THEORETICAL DEBATE

There are thirteen million fewer uninsured because of the ACA.

So the ACA's level of complexity covered just one-third of the uninsured. It should have had one-tenth of the level of complexity to fix 75 percent of the problem.

What would you have done to give health insurance to thirteen million people?

> I'd have figured out who were the forty-two million people not covered and why they weren't covered. For instance, many of the twenty-nine million people still uncovered have subsidies available to them and choose not to pay premiums.

So if the ACA was successful in lowering the number of uninsured people, shouldn't we increase the incentives to further reduce the number of uninsured?

> Let me get this right: Obamacare spent up to $10,000 per person in subsidies and solved one-third of the problem, and you want to increase the amount spent in hopes of chipping away at this issue?

But the current system is so complicated. What are you saying, keep the current system?

> I would keep what makes sense. Just because you've declared there's an emergency doesn't mean we need a grand plan to control every transaction. I get that repeal without a replacement would lead to an unknown outcome, and that's concerning. So, replace is also necessary.

What would you replace it with?

> I would give catastrophic coverage (over $100,000) to all through the government, so that those who choose to buy other things instead of healthcare are covered for anything catastrophic, but not for the underlying coverage that they won't purchase (I outline my idea in Chapter 3).

How many people would still be uninsured?

None.

But no one would be provided coverage under $100,000. You can't expect people to be able to afford supplemental coverage.

Why not?

Because only the rich can afford it.

But if healthcare is of such importance, it should be the first thing anyone would consider purchasing before cable TV, phone, internet, etc.

So if forty-two million people choose not to buy coverage, then there would still be forty-two million people uncovered for their first dollar of coverage.

You could say that. However, that would be their choice.

But Canada has done it successfully for years. Let's try that.

Why? Because everyone is covered?

Yes. And Single Payer works for them.

Canada has significant supplemental coverage that Canadians purchase (about two-thirds purchase supplemental coverage).

So likely one-third of Americans would not purchase your plan's market coverage if given the choice.

Yes.

The Canadian healthcare system costs just 11 percent of GDP, just like in Sweden, versus 17 percent in the US.

And our cost would start at 17 percent, with changes that add/subtract from that.

So we could save under Single Payer.

If the net of all the changes saves money, yes there would be savings. But adding coverage for preexisting conditions adds on the order of one-third to double the total cost, offsetting any potential savings.

Why?

Because the cost of covering those who chose to go without coverage is so high, compared to the average premiums they pay. It's one of the costs the ACA had to overcome and is one reason Obamacare premiums are so high.

So we've already overcome that cost under the ACA. That's why it's been so expensive.

To some extent, yes. But insurers had to guess at their initial premiums in 2014 (Obamacare's first year), and to the extent they were wrong they had to catch up, for example, with an average 25 percent premium increase like in 2017.

Will there be more recovery?

We don't know. Covering more of the uninsured, where their decisions to purchase coverage apply each year, costs everyone else more. Those individual decisions continue under Obamacare.

But under the ACA, doesn't the system either collect the premium from everyone, or the tax penalty?

Yes. But the penalty was $700 per person in 2017, versus premiums that are about $10,000. Many people submitted silent tax returns, which means that they didn't answer the question about whether they had coverage. Plus, the penalty has been eliminated going forward.

So all the Obamacare problems can be avoided with Single Payer. Let's start with a clean sheet.

We don't have a clean sheet. What you're saying is that Obamacare has problems that are known, but rather than fix them or fixing the current system, Single Payer is the answer?

Yes. Sounds better than trying to fix something we both don't want to fix.

But Obamacare wasn't a good answer in 2010 when it was passed. Nor was Single Payer as that wasn't passed either.

What's better?

Competition. It works for all other industries.

But competition doesn't work when you're in an ambulance and need care immediately.

There you go again with the "all-or-nothing" argument. Much of healthcare is not life-threatening. The ACA only covers 6 percent of the population, yet it affected everyone.

GUIDELINES FOR REVIEWING THE CHARTS IN CHAPTER 2

Before you review the charts in Chapter 2, here are some thoughts to help you analyze them (and for reviewing any material created by the media):

- **Think about context.** I try to put the charts in context, but it's important not just to look at what the creator points the reader to look at. For example, the creator of "Healthcare Expenditures per Capita as a Percent of US Expenditures: 1997" wants the reader to think poorly of US healthcare, but I turn the findings on their head and conclude something the creator didn't think of.

- **Think again about context.** I show historical charts as a percentage of GDP to show how healthcare has historically been shown to cost too much. Think about the HDI chart at the beginning of Chapter 1—a chart you've probably never seen before. If healthcare spending as a percentage of HDI makes sense to you from what you observe in daily life, change your perspective.

- **Think again about unintended consequences.** Too often people think only about what they hear. For example, we think about a government policy to raise the minimum wage. Analysis typically focuses on the impact of getting a raise from, say, $7.25 an hour to $15 an hour. The unintended consequences (aka, the unseen) are the lost jobs and the jobs that never materialize. Sometimes, an increase in the minimum wage costs more than the value of the job, such that it's cheaper to have another employee do the work or mechanical alternatives that are now viable because they cost less relative to the minimum wage.

- **Be open-minded.** For example, while "The Most Important Graph in the World" is surprising, realize that it points out something we don't understand from our position in the world: the world is remarkably better off today than in history. We may know this, but sometimes it takes a chart to remind us. Otherwise, it's like thinking the world is flat because that's what we see from where we're standing.

- **Remember facts you used to know and build on that knowledge to think about healthcare beyond what's in the media.** For example, you know that China and India dwarf the US in size. But the US dwarfs other countries in commerce such that none of the countries being compared to the US for their healthcare systems are similar. "Population Statistics" reminds you which countries have the top ten populations in the world, none of which are ever compared to the US for their healthcare systems. You should ask yourself why that is.

- **Understand the numbers.** Focus on millions compared to millions, billions compared to billions, trillions compared to trillions. The chart, "A Collection of Various Measurements," shows numbers with units (millions, billions, trillions) such that comparisons can be made. Also, notice figures which are annual, ten-year accumulations, and sometimes, "as of" (like a balance sheet, the measurement is "at the moment" and not over time).

- **Don't let credentials fool you.** Yes, a doctorate (Doctor of Philosophy or PhD) requires years of education, but only 2 percent of the US population achieve a PhD, and that credential is used to imply logical thinking. I do not have a PhD, and most writers don't, but arguments need to be logical.

- **Think about what you hear and read and then think again.** For example, you've never heard of Dr. Jha, but his analysis in "Dr. Jha Healthcare System Ranking" is unique in that, despite various studies showing that the US healthcare system is poor, the US system ranks well once logic influences the analysis. His analysis portends the US system ranks third out of eight countries.

- **Know that the news media promotes only liberal causes, and that the media has created an emergency in healthcare with the goal of enacting Single Payer.** The media is the reason that democrats fight like hell because they are always supported by the media and why Republicans "fold like lawn chairs," because their proposals are not supported by the media. An example of a question that never gets asked is why, as shown on the chart, "Price Changes January 1998 to June 2020," the highest increases have occurred for Hospital Services and College Tuition, Fees, and Textbooks. Healthcare and Education have had the least amount of competition of all the items compared in the chart, so Single Payer goes in the wrong direction.

- **We've heard from the media incessantly about wait times, that waiting for services is just the price we have to pay so everyone can get healthcare insurance.** But look at the waits in Canada in the chart "Canadian Wait Times." How would we accept waiting over seventeen weeks on average when six weeks is the weighted median clinically acceptable wait? Seventeen weeks is over four months! There is no way that's acceptable in the US.

- **If a writer or speaker has to say, "This is a nonpartisan take on an issue," it probably isn't nonpartisan.** You can think, *"Thanks for telling me, I wouldn't have even thought about your bias and would have listened to what you had to say as potentially unbiased, but now that you mention it, I will listen from a position of doubt."* Once a source is known to be partisan, can anything they ever say be considered nonpartisan? So the charts in Chapter 2 are not nonpartisan, and they've been created by a myriad of sources (at least twenty-seven) who have all sorts of partisan reasons for what they created. So be it.

"Healthcare should be between the doctor and the patient. And if the doctor says something needs to be done, the government should guarantee it gets paid for."

-Michael Moore, 2007

DAMNED STATISTICS

I devoted this chapter to charts I found on the internet, and rather than showing them as an afterthought in an appendix, Chapter 2 allows the reader to draw their own conclusions about the state of healthcare today and in the recent past. A picture says a thousand words, and graphs and charts are their equal. The reader can see charts, pulled together by others, and decide for themselves.

Historically, the media created data and charts that collectively form what I call dangling data points, which rarely get analyzed and put into context. It's as if academic researchers like to imply conclusions with their research, allowing politicians to make statements like, "Single Payer is the answer."

Not only were these charts relatively unnoticed, the creators used them to lead the reader to their point of view. I turn that view on its head.

ROSS PEROT CHARTS

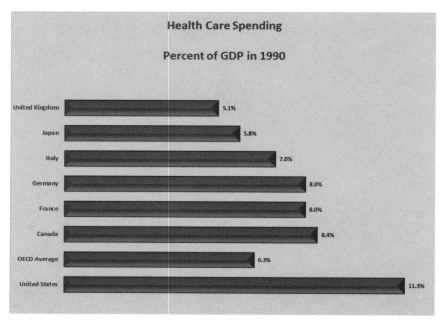

This chart and the following two use the same data that Ross Perot (Independent) produced in his run for president in 1991 (he garnered 19 percent of the national popular vote, losing to Bill Clinton with 43 percent and George H. W. Bush with 37 percent. The Electoral College vote was Clinton—370, H. W. Bush—168, Perot—0). He spoke through campaign infomercials, half-hour presentations called electronic town halls shown on most networks during prime time.

The charts shown here use GDP instead of the original GNP (Gross National Product) because GDP doesn't have the additional noise of productivity of US nationals working or investing abroad. The change to GDP does not significantly alter the relationships between countries. Also, I've added a bar for the OECD (The Organization for Economic Co-operation and Development) thirty-five country average.

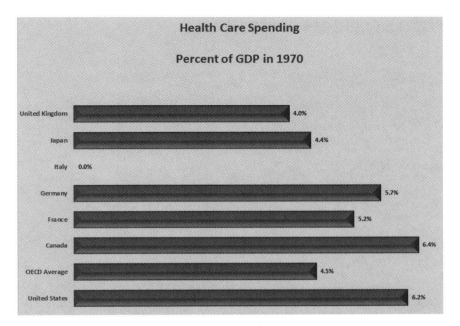

This chart shows that healthcare spending in the US didn't stand out as an issue in 1970. I agree this means healthcare spending now stands out as a problem needing a solution (despite the HDI chart I show in Chapter 1). However, my conclusion is not one of emergency but that of alarm. We shouldn't spend as much as we do on healthcare, but Medicare For All is a bad solution.

PEROT HEALTHCARE SPENDING

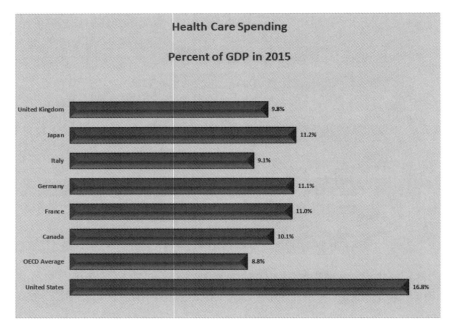

This chart shows that healthcare spending in the US has gotten worse since Ross Perot sounded the alarm. However, this antiquated context (GDP) should be replaced with HDI. We then have less of an emergency and can develop an appropriate response rather than overreacting and declaring a revolution.

These three charts, the "Ross Perot" charts, show that healthcare as a percentage of GDP has been an issue for many years, and that's why Ross Perot and most everyone else complains about the high cost of healthcare. HDI shows that complaint should stop.

DR. JHA HEALTHCARE SYSTEM RANKING

According to Dr. Ashish Jha, Dean for Global Health Strategy, Harvard School of Public Health, the US ranks higher than he and others expected when he ranked eight countries' healthcare systems as follows (in August 2017):

1. Switzerland
2. Germany
3. US
4. UK
5. France
6. Australia
7. Canada
8. Singapore

While surprising, Dr. Jha said access to healthcare in Single Payer systems is offset by wait times that keep patients from receiving the vital care they need. The individual patient looks at access versus wait times in a combined manner, so analysts should as well.

Dr. Jha continues his analysis: "If you take a big step back and look at the data, Americans do better than average in timely access, especially to specialty services and 'elective' surgery (which is often not that elective). They tend to be among the leaders in acute care quality, when health care means the difference between life and death, although the quality of primary care could surely be better. And America is the innovation engine of the world, pumping out new drugs and treatments that benefit the whole world. All of that earns America a high rank in my book—behind Switzerland and Germany but ahead of others."

Table 2. Country Performance on Selected Indicators

			Australia	Canada	France	Germany	Singapore	Switzerland	UK	USA
Access	**Wait Times** [a]	Able to Get Same-Day/Next-Day Appointment When Sick	67%	43%	56%	53%	N/A	57%	57%	51%
		Waited Two Months or More for Specialist Appointment	13%	30%	4%	3%	N/A	9%	19%	6%
		Waited Four Months or More for Elective Surgery	8%	18%	2%	0%	N/A	7%	12%	4%
	Cost Related Access [b]	Medical Test, Treatment or Follow-Up Skipped Due to Costs	3.2%	5.6%	9.5%	5.6%	N/A	7.4%	2.5%	21.3%
Quality	**Mortality Rates**	Breast Cancer Five Year Survival Rate [a]	88%	88%	N/A	86%	N/A	N/A	81%	89%
		Ischemic Stroke 30 Day Mortality (per 100 patients) [b]	9.3	10	7.9	6.4	5.9	6.9	9.2	3.6
		Mortality After Hospital Admission for Acute Myocardial Infarction (per 100 admissions) [b]	4.1	6.7	7.2	8.7	12.4	7.7	7.6	5.5
	Preventable Hospitalizations [b] (per 100,000 population)	Diabetes Hospital Admission (per 100,000 population)	141.3	95.3	180.6	216.3	403	43.9	64.3	198
		Congestive Heart Failure Hospital Admission (per 100,000 population)	240	178.8	238	382.4	277	174.4	99.4	366
	Safety [a]	Health Professional Did Not Review Their Prescription in Past Year	16%	16%	47%	19%	N/A	27%	21%	14%
	Care Coordination [a]	Experienced Gaps in Hospital Discharge Planning in Past Two Years	29%	40%	60%	28%	N/A	45%	28%	22%
	Preventive Health Care [a]	Percentage of Children with Measles Immunization	93%	95%	90%	97%	94%	93%	93%	91%
		Percentage of Population Age 65 and Older with Flu Immunization	N/A	63.1%	48.5%	58.6%	N/A	N/A	74.5%	67.9%
Innovation	**Pharmaceutical** [c]	Percent of New Chemical Entity Output [d]	N/A	N/A	6%	6%	N/A	13%	8%	57%
Cost	**Overall Healthcare Spending** [c]	Percentage of GPD Spent on Health Care	9.0%	10.5%	11.8%	11.0%	4.9%	11.4%	10.2%	17.2%
		Out of Pocket Health Care Spending	$532	$644	$305	$664	N/A	$1,815	$586	$1,034

[a] Data from the 2016 International Profiles of Health Care Systems from the Commonwealth Fund. [b] Data from OECD Health Care Quality Indicators. [c] Data from OECD Main Science and Technology Indicators. [d] Data from 2001-2010 from "The Global Biomedical Industry: Preserving U.S. Leadership," Milken Institute 2011.

THE CHART OF THE CENTURY

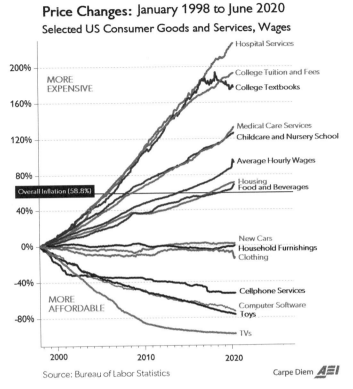

Price Changes: January 1998 to June 2020
Selected US Consumer Goods and Services, Wages

Source: Bureau of Labor Statistics   Carpe Diem *AEI*

The chart above, created by economist Mark Perry, shows price changes for the last twenty years in which various commodities and services for more competitive markets have had lower cost increases, while less competitive markets have had higher cost increases. Healthcare and education have had the highest increases. Both are the opposite of free market and are government run, more so than for the other categories.

In education, government-run education is a monopoly for K-12. For colleges, subsidized loans and four-year undergraduate programs (versus three years) adds to costs. In healthcare, less competition under Obamacare leads to higher prices. Further, supply has not kept up, as the number of hospitals and the number of physicians graduating from medical school have not kept pace with demand.

THE MOST IMPORTANT GRAPH IN THE WORLD

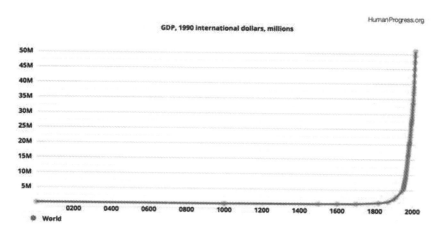

GDP, 1990 international dollars, millions

HumanProgress.org

Source: Angus Maddison

In a 2016 article, *Reason Magazine* said the world benefited immeasurably from capitalism starting in the 1950s when the average wealth in the world skyrocketed. Jonathan Haidt, an NYU psychologist, created it with the title "The Most Important Graph in the World."

If this chart shocks you, it should. There's never been a better time to be alive. How in the world is it possible that there are complaints about poverty and how some groups aren't doing very well? Makes you think of the word "ingrateful"—not an actual word, but one I made up, on purpose. If the chart above showed a bell-shaped curve of how everyone faired, every group would be better off than in the past. And many in the poorest classes today would be better off than the richest classes in history.

So what happened in the world? Capitalism brought about an incredible number of conveniences not available to those in the past that we often take for granted. For example, we have electricity which extends our day, instead of going to bed because it's dark outside. We have indoor plumbing. We have hot and cold water. We have TV that comes to our house via electricity (cable) or airwaves (dish). Not to mention the internet.

LIFE EXPECTANCY

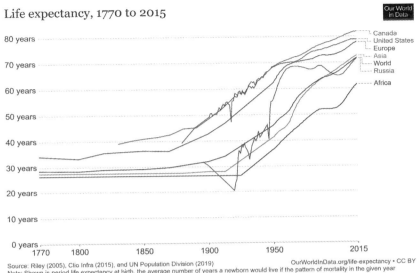

Life expectancy, 1770 to 2015

Source: Riley (2005), Clio Infra (2015), and UN Population Division (2019)
Note: Shown is period life expectancy at birth, the average number of years a newborn would live if the pattern of mortality in the given year were to stay the same throughout its life.

OurWorldInData.org/life-expectancy • CC BY

The above chart shows life expectancy of populations over time and across the world. One can glean from the data the general trend of increasing life expectancies, that Africa lags (and the toll that AIDs took in the 1980s), that Russia languished from 1960 until recently, and that Canada life expectancy has outpaced that in the US.

LIFE EXPECTANCY AT POINTS IN TIME

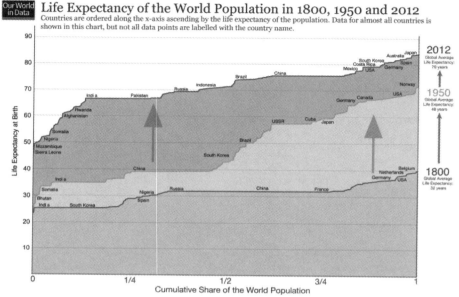

Life Expectancy of the World Population in 1800, 1950 and 2012

Countries are ordered along the x-axis ascending by the life expectancy of the population. Data for almost all countries is shown in this chart, but not all data points are labelled with the country name.

Data source: The data on life expectancy by country and population by country are taken from Gapminder.org
The interactive data visualisation is available at OurWorldinData.org. There you find the raw data and more visualisations on this topic.

Licensed under CC-BY-SA by the author Max Roser.

The chart above is a fascinating look at life expectancy at three points in history. Of particular interest is where the US was relative to other countries, and in 2012, the US had fallen relative to 1950, as well as in 1800. In 2012, several countries passed the US—many countries I named earlier. What strikes me is the relative advancement of life expectancy for all countries (the arrows that show increases around the world).

One could question the improvement in the US but not as much as some of the other countries. That is alarming, but not if you think it reflects poorly on the US healthcare system. Deaths caused by accidents, obesity, violence, et cetera, are more prevalent in the US and, undoubtedly, are a key part of the relative life expectancy picture.

HEALTHCARE EXPENDITURES PER CAPITA AS A PERCENT OF US EXPENDITURES: 1997

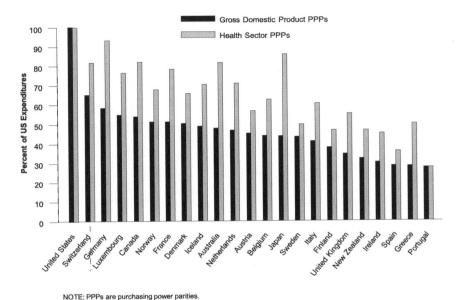

NOTE: PPPs are purchasing power parities.
SOURCE: (Organization for Economic Cooperation and Development, 1999a.)
Source: *Health Expenditure Trends in OECD Countries, 1970-1997,* Manfred Huber, Ph.D.

One can conclude from this 1997 chart that the US spent more on healthcare per capita than every other country (as shown by the gray bars). We also know that US total GDP per capita is more than for the other countries (as shown by the black bars). That leads one to conclude, "The US spends too much on healthcare, and if we didn't, we would have more money to spend on other things."

Conversely, the higher the spending on healthcare, the higher a country's GDP. The more we spend on healthcare, of course, the higher the GDP since healthcare spending counts toward overall GDP. But only Portugal comes close to the US in spending an equal percentage on healthcare and the benefits of GDP (Portugal's black and gray bars are close to each other). All other countries spend more on healthcare than their resultant GDP (relative to US spend and GDP). We can draw an alternative conclusion, that "The US may spend more on healthcare, but healthcare spending has a positive effect on our success as shown by high GDP." That means we should not view healthcare in isolation, but in context to the entire GDP picture.

This classic analysis is what I refer to as looking at one tree (US healthcare spending). But that analysis misses the bigger picture of the forest (total US GDP). Is US healthcare spending inefficient, or is it an important productive part of the overall US economy? If other countries spent more on healthcare, would they be more productive?

Note the US GDP is $57,000 per person while the world average is $15,800.

The chart on the next page shows the relative population of the US. While not even close to China and India in population, the US is much larger than all European and other healthcare (OECD) comparator countries (none of those countries are even in the top ten). Note the lack of discussion on the success stories of these other top ten countries' healthcare systems. Claiming the US should follow what a Scandinavian country the size of North Carolina does is like saying the US should follow the healthcare program of Massachusetts.

Remarkably, the median age varies appreciably amongst countries, and the US population is relatively old. The US median age is thirty-eight while the weighted average of the median age of the world is thirty-one. We know that, on average, a year of age leads to higher healthcare costs of about 4 percent per year, which multiplicatively (1.04 raised to the seventh power) would be 32 percent higher in expected healthcare costs, all other things being equal.

Also, immigration is significant: people are leaving most other countries in the top ten versus the net migration to the US, which also impacts healthcare costs. The top three countries with positive migration are the US (+900,000), Germany (+370,000), and Turkey (+305,000).

POPULATION STATISTICS

#	COUNTRY	POPULATION (2019)	YEARLY CHANGE	NET CHANGE	DENSITY (P/KM²)	LAND AREA (KM²)	MIGRANTS (NET)	FERT. RATE	MED. AGE	URBAN POP	WORLD SHARE
1	CHINA	1,420,062,022	0.35 %	5,016,094	151	9,388,211	-324,919	1.6	39	60 %	18.41 %
2	INDIA	1,368,737,513	1.08 %	14,685,659	460	2,973,190	-490,000	2.3	28	34 %	17.74 %
3	U.S.	329,093,110	0.71 %	2,326,362	36	9,147,420	900,000	1.9	38	84 %	4.27 %
4	INDONESIA	269,536,482	1.03 %	2,741,502	149	1,811,570	-165,000	2.3	29	56 %	3.49 %
5	BRAZIL	212,392,717	0.72 %	1,524,763	25	8,358,140	6,000	1.7	33	86 %	2.75 %
6	PAKISTAN	204,596,442	1.88 %	3,782,624	265	770,880	-214,356	3.4	23	40 %	2.65 %
7	NIGERIA	200,962,417	2.60 %	5,087,180	221	910,770	-60,000	5.4	18	52 %	2.60 %
8	BANGLADESH	168,065,920	1.02 %	1,697,771	1,291	130,170	-470,000	2.1	27	37 %	2.18 %
9	RUSSIA	143,895,551	-0.05 %	-69,158	9	16,376,870	160,000	1.8	40	73 %	1.87 %
10	MEXICO	132,328,035	1.20 %	1,568,961	68	1,943,950	-60,000	2.1	29	79 %	1.72 %
	WORLD TOTALS / AVE.	7,714,574,904	1.08%	81,757,598	234	3,669,685	0	2.5	31	55%	100%

Source: Worldometers.info http://www.worldometers.info/world-population/population-by-country/

CANADIAN WAIT TIMES KEEP GETTING WORSE

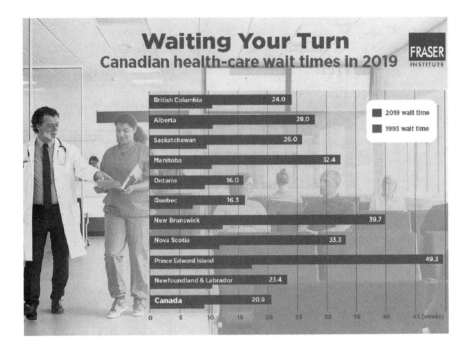

Waiting Your Turn
Canadian health-care wait times in 2019

FRASER INSTITUTE

Province	2019 wait time
British Columbia	24.0
Alberta	28.0
Saskatchewan	26.0
Manitoba	32.4
Ontario	16.0
Quebec	16.3
New Brunswick	39.7
Nova Scotia	33.3
Prince Edward Island	49.3
Newfoundland & Labrador	23.4
Canada	20.9

Legend: 2019 wait time, 1993 wait time

The chart above shows how the Canadian healthcare system wait time seems to be getting worse. One might quibble with wait times in Canada in 1993 since waiting for proper healthcare is natural. But when wait times are double in 2019 versus 1993 and are more than double in many provinces, it's time to wake up and realize how dire the situation really is.

The US is much more rural than most countries, so there are many more hospitals needed, which leads to higher costs per person. Interestingly, the US is one-sixth as populated as the world average (thirty-six people per square km versus the world average of 234). I showed in Chapter 1 that the US is similar in density to Scandinavia, and I'll show in Chapter 10 that Europe is much denser.

CANADIAN HEALTHCARE SYSTEM WAIT TIMES

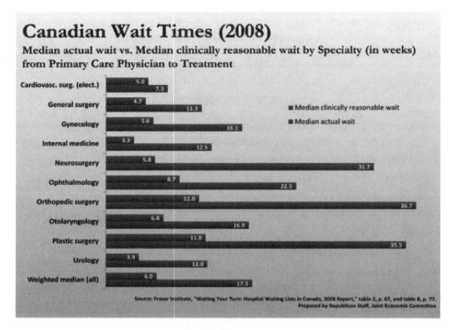

Canadian healthcare costs are lower than in the US, and the Canadian healthcare system is often heralded as a potential solution for the US. However, based on the chart above, there is no way that US citizens would find wait times acceptable.

Another way to put this is that if the Canadian healthcare spent more to improve their wait times, that system might be more palatable. But that would erode any perceived advantage. And 90 percent of Canadians live within one hundred miles of the US, so the US healthcare system often becomes the fallback system when Canadians can't wait—evidenced by the anecdotally high percentage of Canadians using US facilities near the border. That means the US healthcare system builds up spare capacity in which to handle peak demand, including additional Canadian healthcare.

THE GOLDEN HOUR OF MEDICINE

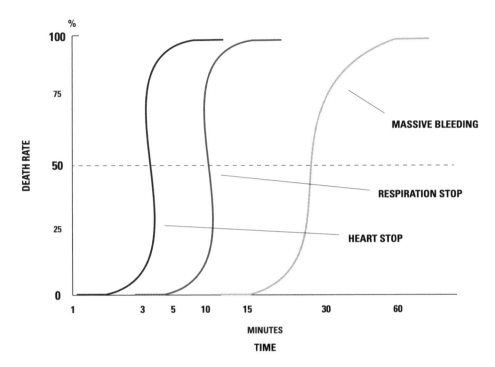

The chart above describes the "Golden Hour of Medicine", a phrase that illustrates the need for immediate care for certain conditions. The US must spend more than some other countries to meet healthcare needs in its more rural areas, since emergency care and access is vital to all people.

Sources of waste in American health care

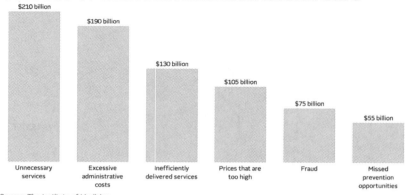

Source: The Institute of Medicine

The above chart from 2013 shows an estimate of waste in US healthcare. Some contend that Single Payer could alleviate some waste (such as #2, excessive administrative costs, and #4, prices that are too high).

But offsetting those savings may mean increased costs for #1, unnecessary services (since services would be free, the demand would increase significantly), and #5, fraud (Medicare and Medicaid are already fraught with fraud). Touting savings in one category but ignoring higher costs in another category is disingenuous.

Note that a separate estimate of fraud under the current Medicaid and Medicare programs alone may be $70 billion to $110 billion, implying that this chart may understate fraud waste at $75 billion.

GROWTH OF ADMINISTRATION

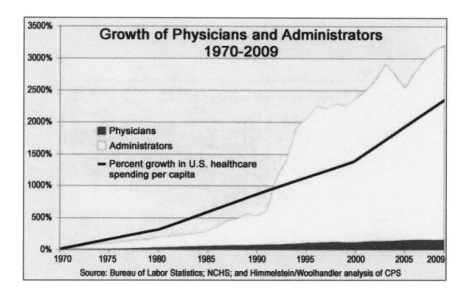

The chart above shows the incredible rise of administrators relative to the slight increase in the number of physicians. The dramatic increase began in the 1990s and reflects insurance requirements, legislation, lawsuits, and attempts at managing care.

PREVALENCE OF SELF-REPORTED OBESITY AMONG US ADULTS BY STATE AND TERRITORY, 2017

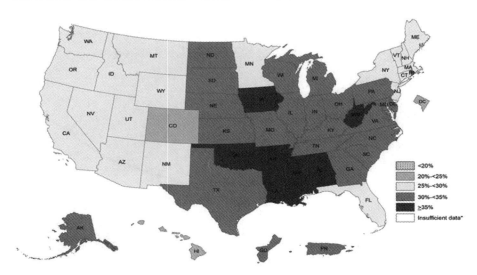

Source: Behavioral Risk Factor Surveillance System

The chart above shows how rampant obesity is in the US. Healthcare costs are higher than average to treat obesity (on the order of double the average).

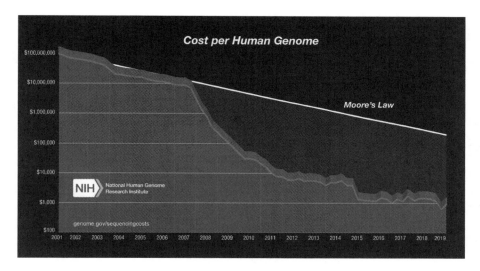

The chart above shows how the cost to sequence an individual's genome has dropped, and it's now less than $1,000. A prediction for future cost is less than $100, so everyone in the US likely will benefit soon. Moore's Law predicted that the processing power of semiconductors would double every two years, and the cost for sequencing the human genome has beaten that general measure significantly.

In the future, sequencing an individual's genome will be vital to treatment. Today, dementia is a disease that befuddles doctors, but there are signs that genome sequencing may provide answers as to what works for certain patients. With costs for dementia care projected to amount to $1 trillion per year by 2050, genome sequencing is vital to finding solutions.

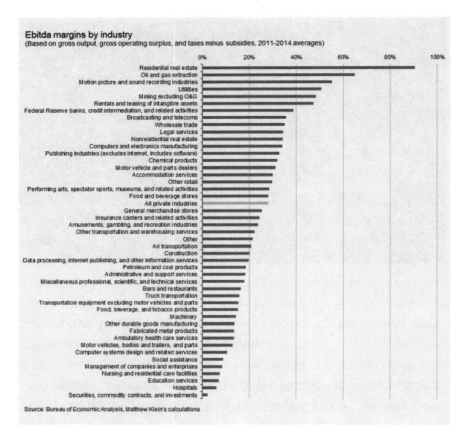

Ebitda margins by industry
(Based on gross output, gross operating surplus, and taxes minus subsidies, 2011-2014 averages)

Source: Bureau of Economic Analysis, Matthew Klein's calculations

Supply and demand drives profits for all industries. Insurance profits are below average (in the chart, insurance is the second bar below "All private industries" [the light gray bar] and historically, health-care insurance profits [not shown] are even lower than the insurance average).

Note that EBITDA stands for Earnings Before Interest, Taxes, Depreciation, and Amortization (essentially, EBITDA is the same as earnings or profits).

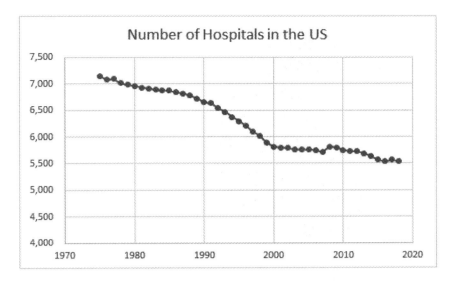

Source: American Hospital Association

The chart above shows the number of hospitals in the US since 1975, and due to closings and consolidation, the number of hospitals overall has declined in number. The 1990s decline resulted from consolidation and closings, many in urban areas.

Now, at approximately 5,500 and likely to remain above 5,000 for the foreseeable future, hospitals lack competition in many markets and, sometimes, have no competition (often in smaller communities). Larger hospitals (due to mergers and acquisitions) may lead to lower costs in the short-term, but often less competition in the long-term. Care in more rural communities will need competition that's allowed to evolve beyond full hospitals, such as minihospitals, urgent care, and surgery centers.

It is impossible to dictate every situation in every city, such that some inner-city neighborhoods and rural locations are underserved. There is also the challenge of meeting individuals' needs that are different than the community's.

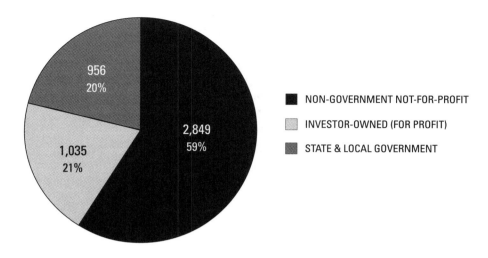

Source: Based on AHA Hospital Statistics, 2018 ed., Health Forum, an American Hospital Association affiliate, 2018

The chart above shows the breakdown of community hospitals to show that for-profit hospitals represent just 21 percent of hospitals in the US. Note that, not included, are non-community hospitals, such as prison hospitals and college infirmaries, of approximately seven hundred in number.

More than 9 in 10 primary care physicians accept Medicare—similar to private insurance—but acceptance of *new* Medicare patients is comparably lower

Percent of non-pediatric primary care physicians accepting new/current patients, by insurance type, 2015

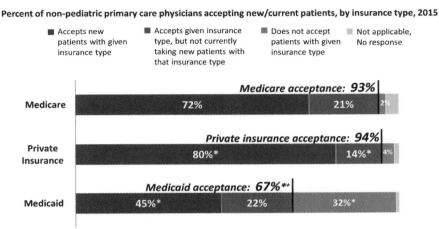

NOTE: Analysis excludes pediatricians. (+) The overall percent of primary care physicians accepting Medicaid increases to 71% when pediatricians are included in analysis. (*) indicates statistically significant difference at the 95% confidence level from Medicare. Percentages may not sum to 100 due to rounding.
SOURCE: The Kaiser Family Foundation/ Commonwealth Fund 2015 National Survey of Primary Care Providers

The chart above shows Medicare, Medicaid, and private insurance acceptance by primary care physicians (PCPs). While overall acceptance is reasonable for Medicare and private insurance (over 90 percent), acceptance is poor for Medicaid (67 percent). Worse is the much lower acceptance for new patients (72 percent, 80 percent, and 45 percent, respectively). The latter levels of acceptance will occur incrementally as newer patients become an increasing percentage of those covered by each program. These lower acceptance levels reflect current reimbursement levels and administrative complexities inherent in each program.

How many PCPs accept direct pay? The answer is, of course, 100 percent. So, for new patients, the survey would show 100 percent self-pay acceptance, 80 percent private, 72 percent Medicare, and 45 percent Medicaid.

The bottom line is that physicians are averse to new patients covered by the government programs. Direct pay is gaining ground as the preferred payment approach for physicians, often offered as a choice by doctors, with large discounts.

2015 CONSUMER EXPENDITURES ($56,000 TOTAL)

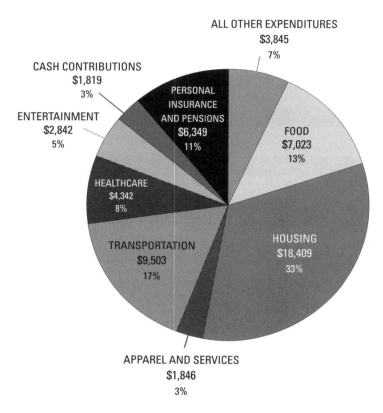

ALL OTHER EXPENDITURES
$3,845
7%

CASH CONTRIBUTIONS
$1,819
3%

ENTERTAINMENT
$2,842
5%

PERSONAL
INSURANCE
AND PENSIONS
$6,349
11%

FOOD
$7,023
13%

HEALTHCARE
$4,342
8%

TRANSPORTATION
$9,503
17%

HOUSING
$18,409
33%

APPAREL AND SERVICES
$1,846
3%

Source: Bureau of Labor Statistics

The chart above shows consumer expenditures per person, representing a perspective on spending different from the prior charts that focused on GDP. Healthcare (8 percent) is a relatively small piece of total consumer expenditures, in which some claim that this leads to higher utilization of services.

MEDICAL CPI VERSUS GENERAL CPI

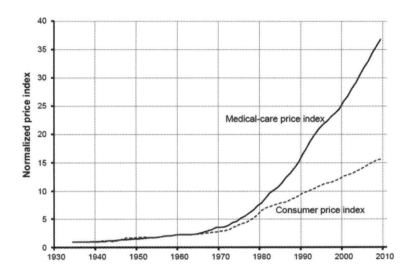

Figure 1: An Indexed Comparison of Health Care Inflation and Consumer Price Index in the US from 1935 to 2009 (Source: US Census 2013) https://mises.org/wire/how-government-regulations-made-healthcare-so-expensive

The chart above shows how medical care CPI (aka, CPI-M) closely matched overall CPI until about 1965, then escalated exponentially. Economist Milton Friedman wrote, "Enactment of Medicare and Medicaid provided a direct subsidy for medical care. The cost grew much more rapidly than originally estimated—as the cost of any handout invariably does. Legislation cannot repeal the non-legislated law of demand and supply: the lower the price, the greater the quantity demanded; at a zero price, the quantity demanded becomes infinite. Substituting some method of rationing for price has to be in order, which invariably means administrative rationing."

POVERTY RATE THROUGHOUT HISTORY

Number in Poverty and Poverty Rate: 1959 to 2020
(Population as of March of the following year)

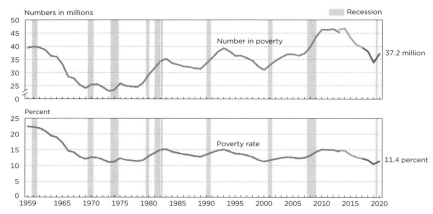

Notes: The data for 2017 and beyond reflect the implementation of an updated processing system. The data for 2013 and beyond reflect the implementation of the redesigned income questions. Refer to Table B-4 for historical footnotes. The data points are placed at the midpoints of the respective years. Information on recessions is available in Appendix A. Information on confidentiality protection, sampling error, nonsampling error, and definitions is available at <https://www2.census.gov/programs-surveys/cps/techdocs/cpsmar21.pdf>.

Source: U.S. Census Bureau, Current Population Survey, 1960 to 2021 Annual Social and Economic Supplements (CPS ASEC).

Why is poverty so difficult to defeat? The war on poverty began in 1964, just after a precipitous decline in the early 1960s (some would argue this is like wearing a belt and suspenders—the belt would have been sufficient, but President Lyndon Baines Johnson ushered in the war on poverty anyway). LBJ declared a "war on poverty" in January 1964, and $22 trillion later (per Robert Rector, The Heritage Foundation, September 23, 2014) we have poverty today at the same level as when we started. The poverty rate has oscillated between 10 percent and 15 percent since 1965. How could that be, especially since the goal was to eliminate poverty in one generation? Either we should not attempt to manage a system that works best on its own, or our definition of poverty is too antiquated and always shows a problem in need of fixing.

Amazingly, other than for CPI, the definition of poverty has remained static since 1969. Updating the definition may be good news, that the war on poverty was more successful than thought, or vice versa. That begs for an updated definition.

Do we really want to conduct a war on healthcare like the war on poverty? What if twenty trillion dollars later we still have the same healthcare problems in fifty years? We would look back and say we shouldn't have spent the money.

With healthcare, barriers likely will forever impede the ability to enable all individuals to have coverage. Cost versus wait time will be the tradeoff. *"Wouldn't it be ideal if everyone had coverage?"* At what cost? With wait times like in Canada and the UK?

WHO PAYS TAXES?
U.S. income tax is progressive, but enough to be 'fair'?

2015 individual income tax statistics, by adjusted gross income

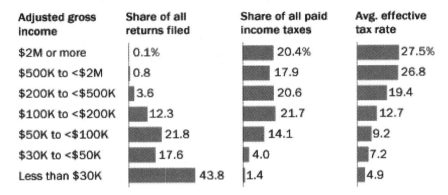

Adjusted gross income	Share of all returns filed	Share of all paid income taxes	Avg. effective tax rate
$2M or more	0.1%	20.4%	27.5%
$500K to <$2M	0.8	17.9	26.8
$200K to <$500K	3.6	20.6	19.4
$100K to <$200K	12.3	21.7	12.7
$50K to <$100K	21.8	14.1	9.2
$30K to <$50K	17.6	4.0	7.2
Less than $30K	43.8	1.4	4.9

Note: For each income group, "effective tax rate" is defined as the total income tax due as a percentage of total adjusted gross income, on returns with tax liability. Share totals may not equal 100% due to rounding.
Source: Pew Research Center analysis of Internal Revenue Service data.

PEW RESEARCH CENTER

There is a lot of misinformation about income taxes, much of it due to the private nature of personal income. But just because personal information is scant doesn't mean that it's right to ignore aggregate information. I'll discuss the chart above in Chapter 7 in talking about the rich and how we should be careful in vilifying this group as not paying their fair share.

An example of misinformation is that the rich avoid paying taxes through tax-avoidance schemes. There are methods to sidestep certain income taxes, but the bottom line is that the rich still pay over 25 percent of their income to the federal government. And with state income tax averaging about 7 percent, the "rich" are paying over one-third of income in taxes, plus other consumption and local (property) taxes which typically bring the overall tax percentage to about half of income.

TAXES ON THE RICH

Taxes on the Rich Were Not Much Higher in the 1950s
Average Effective Tax Rate on the Top 1 Percent of U.S. Households

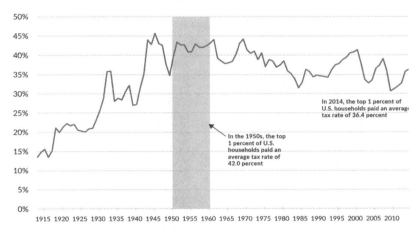

In 2014, the top 1 percent of U.S. households paid an average tax rate of 36.4 percent

In the 1950s, the top 1 percent of U.S. households paid an average tax rate of 42.0 percent

This chart is useful to consider bygone eras of taxes and proposals that the rich should pay 70 percent to 90 percent of their income in taxes. The top tax rate was 91 percent in the '50s, but that didn't translate into taxes nearly that high. Deductions and other adjustments brought the top 91 percent bracket down to average just 42 percent overall and just 5.6 percent higher than in 2014.

Today's proposals to tax the rich at 70 percent typically ignore unintended consequences (such as the rich leaving the US, making profits overseas, and making less than they otherwise would have). The bottom line is that raising the marginal tax rate to 70 percent will not increase taxes as much as surmised and could even lead to less tax revenues (if a person stays in the US if taxes are 40 percent of income but leaves the country when above 50 percent, the effective tax rate under the two scenarios are 40 percent and 0 percent, respectively).

The reason actual taxes in the 1950s reached nothing close to 91 percent was due to tax loopholes and other nontaxed related income. The federal income tax paid by that group amounted to just 17 percent, nowhere near 91 percent. Corporate income, estate income, and investment earnings were taxed at lower rates, and the total amounted to just 42 percent.

COMPANY SIZE

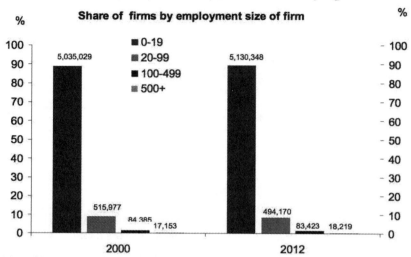

There are 5.7mn companies in the US. 90% of these have less than 20 employees

Share of firms by employment size of firm

Note: Total number of Firms in 2000 and 2012 were 5,734,538 and 5,726,160 respectively
Source: Census, DB Global Markets Research

What many people don't realize is that most companies are small businesses with under five hundred employees. Nearly half of all employees work for employers with fewer than five hundred employees. Some say there are too many to fail.

Some believe companies will only get bigger over time, that large companies grow and buy up smaller companies such that the average size will expand and no small businesses will exist. That's not true, as the graph shows that, over time, the number of small businesses grows through "creative destruction," a term coined by the Austrian economist Joseph Schumpeter. The concept suggests that while many companies go out of business, new (and usually smaller) companies form to meet the needs of consumers.

What's larger than the largest company, which produces just one product and demands a monopoly for that product? The government.

INFLATION BY COUNTRY

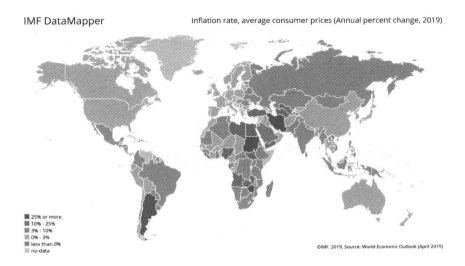

IMF DataMapper   Inflation rate, average consumer prices (Annual percent change, 2019)

- 25% or more
- 10% - 25%
- 3% - 10%
- 0% - 3%
- less than 0%
- no data

©IMF, 2019, Source: World Economic Outlook (April 2019)

Inflation in the US is 1.9 percent. The world average is 3.6 percent. Today, Venezuelan inflation (known as hyperinflation) is 10,000,000 percent. (Venezuela is gray in the graph, because of no available data from this source; however, it was 1,000,000 percent last year and 500 percent the year before, from other sources.) Examples of hyperinflation in history: the German Weimar Republic in the 1920s; Zimbabwe from 2004 to 2009; and Confederate currency in the US during the Civil War (1861-1865).

Inflation below 2 percent, often represented by developed countries with competition, implies stability. Hyperinflation cases like in Venezuela have historically represented a point of no return.

A COLLECTION OF VARIOUS MEASUREMENTS

MEASUREMENT (2015, UNLESS NOTED)	TIME PERIOD	AMOUNT
WORLD DEBT		$199 T
US DEBT	AGGREGATE (NO TIME PERIOD— AKIN TO A "BALANCE SHEET")	$18 T
MEDICARE UNFUNDED LIABILITIES		$28 T
SOCIAL SECURITY UNFUNDED LIABILITIES		$13 T
WORLD GDP	1 YEAR	$74 T
US GDP	1	$18 T
MERCATUS PROJECTIONS:		
TOTAL NATIONAL HEALTHCARE EXPENDITURE UNDER M4A (MIDPOINT)	10 YEARS	$58 T
FEDERAL BUDGET COST INCREASE UNDER M4A (LOW END OF RANGE)	10	$32 T
PROJECTIONS OF THE CBO:		
MARCH 2009 ACA EFFECT ON THE FEDERAL DEFICIT	10 YEARS	<$143> B
MAY 2010 ACA EFFECT ON THE FEDERAL DEFICIT	10	<$28> B
APRIL 2014 ACA EFFECT ON THE FEDERAL DEFICIT	10	UNSURE
MEDICARE 2017-2026 MANDATORY OUTLAY PROJECTION	10	$9 T
ACTUAL MEDICARE PAYMENTS:		
1967	1 YEAR	$3 B
1990	1	$110 B
2010	1	$526 B
2017	1	$708 B

ACTUAL MEDICAID PAYMENTS:		
1966	1 YEAR	$1 B
1990	1	$72 B
2010	1	$402 B
2016	1	$577 B

ACTUAL SOCIAL SECURITY PAYMENTS:		
1938	1 YEAR	$5 M
1950	1	$784 M
1970	1	$30 B
1990	1	$250 B
2010	1	$706 B
2017	1	$945 B

Sources:

Total World Debt estimated by The Institute of International Finance.

Ten-Year M4A estimated by the Mercatus Center at George Mason University for 2022-2031.

Congressional Budget Office (CBO) projected Medicare spending annual report for 2017 to 2026 (Medicare becomes insolvent in 2026).

Congressional Budget Office (CBO) estimated the net effect of the ACA on the federal deficit before and after passage of the law. In April 2014, the CBO declared in a footnote that it could no longer determine the effects of the ACA, due to changes in the law after its passage.

Office of Management and Budget (OMB) OASDI and Medicare Trust Fund payments 1937 to 2017.

2017 Actuarial Report on the Financial Outlook for Medicaid, Office of the Actuary.

The Annual Report of the Board of Trustees of the Federal Old-Age and Survivors Insurance and Federal Disability Insurance Trust Funds, seventy-five-year estimates, 2015.

The Annual Report of the Boards of Trustees of the Federal Hospital Insurance and Federal Supplementary Medical Insurance Trust Funds, seventy-five-year estimates, 2015.

I created this chart to consider large numbers in a way that no other source compares: Trillions compared to trillions, billions to billions, millions to millions. While we often hear that some program or change will cost X billion, what is the context for that change? We sometimes are told what a comparison point is, such as X is Y percent of Z, but is this a lot? We don't know because we don't know what other things cost. So, this chart allows the reader to understand the context.

Also, there is a difference between something that costs just one time, versus another that's an annual cost. Then there are figures over ten years, and in the case of Obamacare, figures that were quoted representing ten years but four years from now (in 2010, when the law was passed, Obamacare didn't go into place until 2014). Add to that costs for Social Security and Medicare for the next seventy years. Then there are projected numbers versus actual costs. How should all these numbers be compared?

3

SO THEN WHAT?

"Healthcare is the most deeply dependent on science and technology of any field of human endeavor. No one is smart enough to fix a system that big and that complex in one giant reform."

-Newt Gingrich, 2018

Some people think Single Payer is a good idea. But what if they're wrong, and we move to it only to find out that the healthcare system is worse ten years from now? Twenty-five years from now? Then what, we move back? We keep oscillating until the grass is greener?

Let's see, if I don't like those running M4A, it may take a lifetime to vote politicians out of office. But if I don't like an insurance company, I can change tomorrow.

Instead of the overhaul with M4A, consider this: Peter Fisher, former treasury official, once said, "Think of the federal government as a gigantic insurance company (with a sideline business in national defense and homeland security)." The government can assure payment much like insurance companies do.

The best way to optimize that ability is government-provided catastrophic coverage along with an underlying insurance market. A catastrophic approach to healthcare insurance fits with the concept of insurance, not first-dollar coverage.

CAT4ALL

We should change the current system to be market-provided below $100,000 and government-provided above $100,000 (what I call CAT4ALL). The dividing line, which I've chosen to be $100,000, is per-individual per-year, such that a person has an incentive to buy market healthcare coverage every year, with the government covering an individual's costs over $100,000.

Why? A famous finding in healthcare is that "20 percent of the people have 80 percent of the claims." Also, "5 percent of the people have 50 percent of the claims." This means costs are skewed, sometimes exceeding $1 million, and large claims represent the bulk of healthcare costs. Insurance makes sense for large claims, not small costs.

There is no way to separate the 20/80 percentage groups before the fact. If known ahead of time, the premiums for 80 percent of the group would be small and the premiums for 20 percent of the group would be astronomical. Instead, this CAT4ALL plan separates the groups *after* their claims occur. The federal government would be like a large insurance company, its main strength.

Insurance should provide catastrophic coverage, not coverage for the budget-able stuff (like oil changes, gas, dings with auto insurance). The value insures against bad accidents where loss of life is the main concern. CAT4ALL provides everyone with catastrophic coverage like with other insurance.

This high-level concept requires the development of many details, such as what's the right dividing line, and how to index the amount. Also, should all other plans be kept (Medicare, Medicaid, employer-provided, etc.) and CAT4ALL apply only to the individual market? I think so, but I'll leave those details to Congress. Another vital decision is whether healthcare provided through an employer should continue to be tax deductible. And if so, what will tax on premiums look like for other groups (such as individuals)?

In the meantime, I'll describe some details below.

The new market will have much lower premiums than under Obamacare, since the government will pay the bulk of the costs for large claims. I assume premiums will be about one-third of what they are now (that may be a goal for the choice of the dividing line). So, instead of average premiums of $10,000 per year, premiums would be $3,000 per year. This math isn't exact, and the cutoff for where the government begins payment is to be determined, but $3,000 should be in the ballpark.

Importantly, taxes would need to increase significantly so that the government can pay claims over $100,000. All of this would lead to winners and losers compared to the current system, much of which may not be fair or palatable. Government costs would be $7,000 per person, and the tax increase needed to pay for this would be formidable.

There will be questions about how the government will pay claims and at what discount level. If they pay claims at the current Medicare level, they might reimburse providers at just 70 percent of cost. The government reimburses Medicare physician services today using RBRVS (Resource-Based Relative Value Schedule). That would create a sudden jolt to the market, leading providers to leave the market and there being less competition (remember, I'm trying to encourage more). So the government would need to reimburse closer to cost, a level not well known today, and it varies by service, provider, and geography.

CAT4ALL PLAN

Coverage for the CAT4ALL plan could be 100 percent. Alternatively, there could be copays or some other feature to continue to engage utilizers of coverage so that continued use of services is not free. A simple way to accomplish that is to apply coinsurance (such as 10 percent up to an out-of-pocket maximum), requiring patients to pay a portion of every bill. This adds billing complexity, of course, which adds complexity.

The government needs to figure out how the design will apply to families. The last time the government designed family deductibles and out-of-pocket maximums, they screwed it up. In 2003, the Medicare Modernization Act (MMA) was created to provide prescription drug coverage for seniors. But the government defined family coverage in a way never used before by any government program or insurer.

Typically, insurance companies limit the number of individual deductibles and out-of-pockets maximums to double or triple the amounts for individuals. Put differently, if an individual had a $1,000 deductible, two family members reaching $1,000 each, or $2,000 in total, could meet the family maximum deductible.

But the MMA definition created a new concept, the aggregate deductible, meaning that one individual could only contribute up to their individual deductible toward the family deductible, with the rest coming from another family member. Insurers had to re-program for this while consumers had to learn how it worked. The bottom line is the designers didn't understand how insurance works and created a new plan design that added little to the value of the benefit. The private market would have designed this simpler.

Other questions to be discussed: When should the government pay? When does an individual reach $100,000? The answer could be:

- when the gross claim amounts exceed $100,000
- when the net claim amounts exceed $100,000 (net of discounts)
- some measure other than gross or net

It makes sense to use the second approach—to wait until the net claim exceeds $100,000. The reason is that the gross amount never gets reimbursed and is arbitrary (if a provider initially asks for $1,000 for a service, but ultimately gets paid $700, the $1,000 amount doesn't really matter). This approach leads to lower costs for CAT4ALL and higher premiums for the Market Plan.

Also, there is significant leveraging that will occur with a fixed threshold of $100,000. This means, assuming claim trends are 3 percent per year, claims would increase by 3 percent for every claim, but the government cost would increase by, say, 4 percent due to leveraging (because claims that were previously below $100,000 are now over $100,000). The solution to this issue is to index the $100,000 amount, another important decision.

IDENTIFYING A SPECIFIC PROBLEM-SOLUTION APPROACH

One of the glaring weaknesses with passing Obamacare was that proponents never identified what problems needed to be fixed. I prefer solutions to specific problems because of the explicit measurement of success.

For example, fixing the cost problem by making prices transparent does little because the consumer needs to have skin in the game. That's similar to expanding your TV to 4320p (4K) capability when TV is still broadcast at 1080p.

Some proposed solutions to these problems have proven to be red herrings, and I'll discuss those below. Specific problems should have solutions.

I'll address each of the following:

- Preexisting condition limitations—change the market rules
- Bankruptcy—create CAT4ALL
- Provider administrative costs—let the market work
- Claims adjudication—the market is more efficient
- Technology—let the market work
- Regulations—guardrails, not control

- Malpractice—tort reform
- Fairness—premiums and copays should be appropriate
- Insurer profit—it's not that much
- For-profit—eliminating for-profit slows motivation

PREEXISTING CONDITION LIMITATIONS

There are heartbreaking stories where preexisting limitations affect out-of-pocket costs and care. But there are also stories of cases where a healthy individual skipped coverage and saved the premium, then signed up after the fact. No one chastised these people, as they were often lauded as smart. Why not sign up for coverage once pregnancy begins? Why not sign up for coverage once a cancer is revealed? I personally would do the same if the rules allowed that I could sign up for something after-the-fact and get more in return than the premiums I pay.

The problem: the natural tendency to optimize one's financial equation versus those truly in need. And when people take advantage of those truly in need by waiting, why do we blame the insurance company? Do we blame the government for those who take advantage of a government program? We never seem to blame the individual. So, how can we appropriately create the right rules to handle both the optimizer and the needy?

And why is health insurance different from other insurances? There is an attitude with health insurance to win, meaning to get more money back in claims than premiums. This same attitude doesn't exist with life, auto, or homeowners' insurance. We don't think, "If only my auto insurance claim would pay back more than the premium." I'm convinced that the attitude arises because life, auto, and homeowners' insurances provide catastrophic coverage, such that the value of paying premiums buys protection from catastrophic events. Healthcare coverage is more than for catastrophic coverage, and the more part leads to the attitude of "*trying to get what I have coming to me.*"

This isn't that hard. I'll propose an obvious solution at the end of this section.

Let's look at some numbers. Just 115,000 people enrolled in the new Obamacare risk pools through the first three years of the law (after the law passed but before 2014). This number, 115,000, is likely low because of lack of information about the risk pools. But another study, prior to Obamacare adoption, showed just 257,000 individuals were denied coverage in 2009 due to preexisting conditions by the four largest for-profit health insurers (Aetna, Humana, UnitedHealth Group, and WellPoint). Yet another analysis that looked at both figures estimated that Obamacare covers just 500,000 individuals with preexisting conditions, a far cry from the millions of people claimed by the media.

Just 5 percent of the population faced limitations. Here's a chart that shows prevalence when Obamacare was enacted:

PLAN (2010)	PREEXISTING LIMITATIONS	ENROLLMENT	PERCENTAGE
MEDICARE	N	44,000,000	14%
MEDICAID	N	49,000,000	16%
MILITARY	N	13,000,000	4%
EMPLOYER	N	169,000,000	55%
INDIVIDUAL MARKET	Y	16,000,000	5%
UNINSURED	N/A	50,000,000	16%
TOTAL		306,000,000	

Sources: US Census Bureau, Kaiser Family Foundation. Numbers shown exceed 100 percent because the Census Bureau counts all coverages an individual may have during the year (coverage is not mutually exclusive). The total of individuals above is correct, but the categories are over-represented. This could have been avoided by counting only the *main* coverage an individual enrolls in, but that wasn't the case. So, the percentages require mental adjustment.

What are preexisting condition limitations? Prior to the ACA, insurance companies required that, if an illness existed before the patient purchased insurance, they would not pay the claim on that illness, since an insurable event had not taken place. Rejecting preexisting claims avoided adverse selection and kept premiums lower for illnesses that were not preexisting.

Insurers continued to notice large claims for certain individuals who waited to purchase coverage until needed (and in some instances, after initial treatments). Since underwriting often did not identify individuals with preexisting conditions, insurers began limiting the coverage for illnesses after the claim occurred, because only then would the preexisting claim become known.

There were two types of conditions considered preexisting: known and unknown. State regulations often limited the definition of preexisting conditions to the first category, while forty states limited how long individuals have had the preexisting condition, often to one year or less (addressing both types of preexisting conditions).

A 2017 McKinsey study estimated that elimination of preexisting condition limits may have added up to 76 percent to premiums. The exact percentage is unknown and varies by group. The variation depends on the number of preexisting condition cases that occur, as every preexisting case increases the number of higher-cost claimants versus lower-cost claimants. And since the higher-cost claimants with preexisting conditions can cost ten times the average of the low-cost claimants, the cost increase is significant.

If the public prefers that no limitation exists, the change is relatively simple. However, instead of charging more to those who do not maintain continuous coverage (like Medicare does), Obamacare passed the cost to everyone, building the extra cost into the system in such a way that no one knows the true cost. Obamacare architects misled the public about protections that already existed. Concerns became overstated with 95 percent of those covered through government and group coverage not having the issue and HIPAA protecting many cases in the individual market.

An appropriate solution would be to require those who do not maintain continuous coverage for sixty days to pay 1 percent per month (for each month without coverage) more than someone who maintained coverage (similar to what Medicare charges if someone chooses to not sign up when first eligible). This approach is a better alternative than charging everyone.

Another solution is to increase the stability of the Obamacare exchanges. One way would be to add the approximately eight million people covered separately in the Federal Employees Health Benefit program (FEHB) into the exchanges, as the higher numbers of people in the exchanges will increase stability and help with preexisting condition charges.

BANKRUPTCY

Bankrupting healthcare costs are an important concern in the US. Some proponents of Obamacare claimed medical claims in over 60 percent of all bankruptcy cases cause bankruptcies.

Their studies muddled correlation versus causation (tainted by the selection of data). Other studies showed hospitalizations caused just 4 percent of individual bankruptcies among nonelderly US adults (two papers published in the *American Economic Review* and the *New England Journal of Medicine*).

Some would say the percentage doesn't matter, and I agree. When I am bankrupt, probabilities don't matter anymore. But the real question is, how often do healthcare costs cause bankruptcy? More than they should, but less than some have claimed.

So the catastrophic plan for everyone is the protection that's needed. Arguably, there would be no more catastrophic claim bankruptcies. We need no further discussion with CAT4ALL.

PROVIDER ADMINISTRATIVE COSTS

Why is healthcare so complicated? For example, doctors must spend enormous amounts of time to justify their billings and patient care. They hire administrative staff, many of whom coordinate payment for care in lieu of providing care. Hospitals loaded with administration beyond just the purchasing of supplies spend much of their time getting paid and even coordinating on behalf of patients.

Other countries don't have this complexity. Studies that compare administrative costs in the US versus elsewhere always show more complexity here. These studies verify what we thought: that doctors' offices, hospitals, and patients spend more time on the dizzying array of rules. Plus, healthcare in the US has more administrative costs than with other US industries.

There are two sides to the administrative cost issue: the measured one, administering claims payments, and the unmeasured one, which is the cost to providers for administrative claim services.

M4A proponents suggest having government oversight to streamline payments so there would be just one set of rules to follow, rather than multiple approaches. Let's look at an analogy to Social Security. In 1935, the government decided there should only be one base retirement-savings plan.

"Yes, and Social Security is much more streamlined than those unwieldy investment companies with their complicated rules. It's much better to take retirement savings and invest it collectively through the government, only to find out it's not being invested since it's become a 'pay-as-you-go' system that generates low rates of return. We could save on the administrative costs of marketing, customer service, billing, claims review,

quality assurance, and information technology. All of that is waste."

"Who would possibly commit fraud in this idyllic world?" Not the doctor, who just wants to care for people, and not the patient who just wants to recover. But it would occur—and that's exactly why insurance companies must create complicated rules—because many gamed the system in the past and that led to rules like preexisting condition limitations.

Let me reiterate: the development of preexisting condition limitations occurred because people gamed the system.

As always, there is a reason the rule exists, and it's not because insurance companies were greedy. It's because customers (individuals) were greedy.

Haven't we learned that when we squeeze the balloon, something else sticks out, like fraud? *"But all those rules won't be needed under a streamlined government system."* Really? And people won't feel the need to optimize their situation by gaming the faceless bureaucrats working for the government? *"No one tries to game Social Security, Medicare, Medicaid, Food Stamps, the IRS, Unemployment Insurance, Disability, or Obamacare."*

We don't know about fraud that goes undetected. Further, the General Accounting Office (GAO) determined that just 15 percent of known individuals who commit fraud are ever prosecuted, which is just one out of seven!

Why is healthcare so darn complicated? Here are a few examples:

- There are 10,000 procedure codes for doctors in which to bill.
- There are 70,000 diagnosis codes required for doctors to choose from, some added to designate left or right side of the body.
- There are 20,000 drugs available.
- Medicare reimburses through RBRVS, a coding system with nearly 10,000 procedure codes, and DRGs (Diagnosis Related Groups) with 1,000 categories.
- Fifty insurance commissioners regulate healthcare in the states, with myriad state-mandated benefits. (The number of state-

mandated benefits has increased from 252 in 1979 to 2,133 in 2009, an average of forty-two per state!)

- Myriad legislation impacts healthcare through Medicare and Medicaid, ERISA, the HMO Act of 1973, COBRA, EMTALA, HIPAA, SCHIP, and ACA.

Government regulations and agencies created many of these examples of complexity. Some people like Single Payer for no other reason than the apparent simplicity, that since the current array of programs is difficult to understand, simplicity would be good for that reason alone. But is complexity a reason to consolidate? Why not make things less complex, rather than overhaul the system, hoping to create a simpler program? Obamacare was meant to simplify things. Did it, with its 2,800 pages of law and 20,000 pages of regulations? *"Maybe the next major overhaul will do it."*

Over time, insurance companies created many ideas worth implementing. But they are also willing to pare back programs that they deem otherwise. For example, UnitedHealthcare discontinued the requirement to coordinate care through PCPs. While debates continue over each decision, successful programs win out, while government programs rarely stop once they start.

For example, libraries still exist across the nation. Had libraries been privately held, and the internet replaced the need for libraries, a private company might have eliminated libraries since they are unnecessary, at least in their current form. Would that be bad? *"Oh my god, he just proposed the elimination of the cornerstone of our community. Where will children learn to read?"*

Would fraud increase under M4A relative to Medicare today? Some suggest the fraud would be worse since those covered under Medicare today are Baby Boomers and are "past the peak age of running a con" (Brett Arends, MarketWatch, July 1, 2019).

And how often do you hear ads touting, "Medicare will pay for it"? Would this be considered fraud? Scammers are now openly advertising the loophole they exploit. Isn't this a sign of the potential fraud under M4A? Won't the attitude that exists today, the *"I deserve this,"* be even greater with the government under M4A?

CLAIMS ADJUDICATION

As a potential solution to the cost problem, large groups have been created to share costs. It's true that adding costs to a larger base makes things cheaper in that everyone in the group can share fixed costs (for example, administration, rent, or fees). But credibility for rating purposes can be achieved with fewer numbers of enrollees than most people realize.

Claim amounts do not form a normal bell-shaped curve. You can think of a bell-shaped curve as having an average, with half of the claims above that average and half below. Healthcare claim amounts (measured per claim or per year) are skewed since large claims are nearly unlimited, with a significant portion of the population (perhaps 15 percent) having no claims at all (I say "perhaps" because of a lack of information about those claimants who never file their claims because their claims are below the deductible).

That health insurance requires large pools is an overstatement. Yes, pooling all 325 million US citizens' claims is a positive, but how large must a pool be to be credible? The Society of Actuaries mentions a rating formula that assumes full credibility at 10,000 life years. Since claims data over three years is often used, full credibility would be achieved for groups of just 3,333 lives. That's not to say that budgeting for a group this small would be very accurate, and subgroups may be too small to be analyzed with credibility. But the drive toward creating the largest aggregation possible is unnecessary for credibility.

Insurance companies have enough lives in which to have credible pools. As do individual states. The piloting of ideas has been part of the landscape for years, through state-run insurance pools or even through insurance companies. The aggregation being considered with

M4A, that everyone in the whole country needs to be included under one plan, is a red herring. It has more to do with control.

Concern over the government adjudication of claims reminds me of the old joke, *"How many government employees work here? About half."*

Another red herring is the supposedly high administrative cost in the marketplace, sometimes described as 20 percent of claims dollars, as if 20 percent is wasted on administration. Not only is this perception untrue (the average has been measured at 12 percent), it makes sense to have higher administration cost for important, high-cost services, such as what doctors provide. Would it make sense to transact procedures that cost thousands of dollars with little oversight?

Some say to look at the efficiency of Medicare, for instance, where claims are paid with just 3 percent administrative costs. Government is cheaper, these oft-reported figures show. But efficiency is only one part of the desired outcome.

The government doesn't include rent or any of the costs of its buildings, and there are other issues connected with Medicare's low cost:

- Medicare covers the most expensive group (over age sixty-five and the disabled); claim amounts are double that for other groups, so administrative costs are half of what they would be as a percentage.
- Some complain that Medicare passively pays claims with little intervention.
- The IRS, Social Security Agency, and other agencies help Medicare administer its program, but those costs are not counted.
- Medicare doesn't pay tax like insurers do, and that includes income tax and excise taxes such as premium taxes (2–5 percent paid to each state).

If healthcare administration savings would be so high, why not convert every industry to the government? One analysis from 2005 showed actual Medicare administrative costs per person were $509 verses $453 for private insurers, or over 10 percent higher! What if we switched to government administration only to find out it costs more? Then what? We try to switch back, only to find the market has dissolved? There would be no options.

The bottom line is that a consolidated M4A claims payer will have some economies of scale advantages, but the real savings would need to come from less regulation. But the amount of regulation needed would be higher, considering the need to prevent fraud.

Where could M4A government efficiency versus the market possibly come from?

- Employee Salaries and Benefits—not likely since costs would likely increase versus the market since employee salaries and benefits are higher for the government
- Efficiency (and economies of scale)—savings would be low
- Information Technology—not likely if government controls incentives to innovate
- Fraud—most potential for additional cost, offsetting any efficiency (For relative size comparison, Medicare fraud recoveries were estimated at sixty billion dollars per year, more than Medicare administration costs today.)
- Upcoding—like fraud but specific to physicians with legitimate claims that Medicare pays for, with upcoding for services and diagnoses that ultimately lead to higher payments made by Medicare
- Profit—would be eliminated, 2-5 percent of premium

The US government is not known for streamlining administration. So it's best to let the market administer billions of transactions each year, with the government paying for a few million large claims (or many fewer if CAT4ALL applies only to the individual market).

TECHNOLOGY

Technology is vital to life. Computers have revolutionized our lives in many ways. In healthcare, we have incredible innovation that improves our lives beyond just extending them. The private sector sparks innovation if the government encourages it without getting in the way. You can think of innovation as the opposite of regulation. The two must be balanced—an increase in regulation leads to a decrease in innovation, and vice versa.

Allow me to introduce an oxymoron—government innovation. As an example, when the only choice of product is the government, we get the DMV (Department of Motor Vehicles) solution to slow lines. A solution they developed is the system of assigning letters and numbers (like B284) to make it *seem* like customers are closer to getting called. Under the old system, a customer could tell their wait would be long (e.g., number 284 was just called, so 334 is still fifty away). With the new system, the number B294 seems like it's just ten away (but the DMV just added A through E in front of the number). That's a "divide and conquer" solution that obfuscates the real problem (slowness of the system). Applying that type of solution to healthcare is unacceptable.

A key to innovation is the drive for profits. Profit is the best incentive that society has ever found to get things done. While profits became a partial motivator for Apple and Steve Jobs, were there no profits to be had, would Apple have been created? Desire to benefit (whether through profits or merely to make a wage) has motivated everyone in the history of the world. Desire to improve one's position is a motivating force to get up in the morning.

The desire to create a life-saving drug is invaluable. Should we expect people to be motivated to find the cure for cancer for esoteric motivations? What if someone found the cure to cancer, but society would have to pay that person a billion dollars? Should we? I think there is no question, yes. And, therefore, we should tell people ahead of time that we will pay for them to profit from finding those cures so that they are motivated to find them. That's called for-profit, and that will continue to be vital in the future as it has been in the past.

We quickly adjust to the latest in technology. For example, in 1903, the Wright brothers first flew an airplane. We now fly commercially and complain about the snack. We are quick to move on to the next laurel, not recognizing how far we've come. Medicine is like that, where we now have a multimillion dollar machine that can take pictures of the inside of our body in 256 slices in just one minute. But we complain about the cost. Would we rather forgo the information that these slices provide?

Can the US afford to be the technology creator for the world where other countries benefit from US investments without paying the cost? But can we afford not to?

For example, about 5,000 heart transplants are performed every year in the world of which 2,000 occur in the US. Today, breast cancer kills 40 percent fewer women than thirty-five years ago, and prostate cancer kills 50 percent fewer men (per the American Cancer Society). Technology has been a vital part of that success.

There are myriad ideas that need to be investigated for their potential, which will require innovation spurred by profit:

- Insulin that doesn't require needle injections (early potential with an inhaled version)
- EKGs and X-rays performed on a smartphone
- Bioabsorbable stents
- Microbes in treating and preventing disease
- Cellular treatments and liquid biopsies
- DNA sequencing by person
- Curing Alzheimer's, termed by some doctors as "Type 3 Diabetes"

There are a multitude of avenues to pursue, and government agencies like the National Institutes of Health (NIH) cannot study every possible approach. Companies are more likely to find solutions along with incentives.

REGULATIONS

Regulation of the healthcare industry is important to assure quality services and to protect patients. But healthcare is one of the most regulated industries in the US. In 2019, the GAO (Government Accountability Office) added ninety-eight new actions to its list of fragmented, overlapping, and duplicative federal agencies (over all industries including healthcare).

And healthcare is complex, such that 535 members of Congress can't keep up. Lobbyists are important conduits for understanding the effects of complex bills. As John F. Kennedy stated, lobbyists are "expert technicians capable of examining complex and difficult subjects in a clear, understandable fashion."

The result of the complex network of oversight is an array of regulations that can be daunting. While the patient may think: "Good, my doctor has to comply," that ultimately affects the patient either through fewer doctors being willing to play that game or higher costs overall in the system. It's easy to underestimate the unseen.

While no state regulator takes blame for their individual regulation decisions, collectively regulations add 1 to 5 percent or more to the cost of healthcare in each state. Each regulation likely is important in requiring companies to "do what's right by their customers." But these decisions have created a multitude of requirements that make national insurance difficult to administer for employers, and many small employers point to state-mandated benefits as the reason for not offering coverage to their employees.

There are a multitude of government agencies regulating healthcare. Many are national, but state (fifty) and local government (fifteen thousand or more) agencies are voluminous. Here is a list of national regulators:

- CMS
- FDA
- CDC
- NIH
- DOL
- IRS
- EPA
- USDA
- OSHA
- NLRB
- AHRQ

- JCAHO
- NCQA
- AHRQ
- AAAHC
- AAHCA
- ACHC
- AAASF
- CIHQ
- CHAP
- DNVH
- CCIIO

And just to annoy my readers and show how complicated healthcare has become, here is a list of legislation:

- ACA
- HIPAA
- COBRA
- ERISA
- MMA
- ADA
- FMLA
- EMTALA
- ADEA
- TEFRA
- DEFRA

- OBRA
- BBA
- CHIP
- GINA
- HCQIA
- PSQIA
- HITECH
- HMO Act
- MHPA
- MACRA
- CON State Laws

Healthcare providers face overwhelming regulations. At what point does someone say, "Enough?" Agencies focus on their organization and what additional regulations to promulgate. No one focuses on what healthcare entities must do to practice medicine, and the patchwork of regulations that they must navigate to bring products and services to market.

MALPRACTICE

"If a doctor cuts off the wrong arm, I should have the ability to sue. Tort reform gets in the way."

But it doesn't. Tort reform would include limits on non-economic damages and attorney fees. Under tort reform, patients could still receive just compensation in actual cases of medical error, while incentives for trial lawyers to file frivolous lawsuits would be reduced. Further, healthcare providers would be less inclined to order unnecessary tests.

Opponents of tort reform often quote that it would save only 2 percent of healthcare costs. A 2009 study, *The Impact of Tort Reform on Employer-Sponsored Health Insurance Premiums* by the National Bureau of Economic Research is one such source.

Did anyone actually read the study? In the first paragraph, the authors state, "we find that caps on non-economic damages, collateral source reform, and joint and several liability reforms reduce premiums by 1 to 2 percent *each*." So that's 1 to 2 percent for each of the three items listed, or 3 to 6 percent. The experts claim that the three items may offset each other (each is a dependent variable) such that the aggregation may limit savings—that means savings in total may be less than the sum of each factor. This makes sense. But analysis of these kinds of studies "divide and conquer" (i.e., showing pieces of the puzzle to make savings seem small, like "2 percent").

A Gallup poll in 2010 of doctors showed that they practiced defensive medicine such that an estimated 26 percent of all healthcare spending may be unnecessary. The study found that three out of four doctors prescribed defensive tests to avoid the risk of lawsuit. This poll was underreported. Further, there are estimates that one out of every three X-rays taken in the ER are for legal rather than medical reasons.

A 2014 study by the American Board of Internal Medicine found that 72 percent of doctors surveyed say that doctors prescribe an unnecessary test or procedure at least once a week. Another study in 2012 by the American Academy of Orthopedic Surgeons reported that

96 percent of physicians practiced defensive medicine. So the question is, are doctors influenced due to excessive court awards, or would they order these unnecessary tests anyway?

A counter-study by RAND showed doctors did not order fewer tests in three states where the level of proof for medical malpractice in the ER was raised to gross negligence. The study showed that doctors in those states did not order fewer tests than doctors in nearby states (measured for fourteen years through 2011). However, the threat of malpractice has become ingrained in the practice of medicine such that changes may not be measurable in such studies.

That means with the possibility of limited liabilities in the future, will physicians change the practice of ordering unnecessary tests enough to be worth it to make changes? And how many years would it genuinely take to change practice patterns? It's difficult to know.

Regardless of studies, an easy-to-measure finding is that malpractice insurance for OB-GYN doctors is $250,000 to $300,000 per year. The first $250,000 in revenue for an OB-GYN goes to malpractice insurance, adding to the prices she must charge. And that cost is born by all, not just the doctor.

That there are a lot of commercials for injury lawyers proves there's a lot of money being made by attorneys suing providers. Yes, there are judgements that pay back the injured, and those judgements caution providers from doing wrong, but should there be so much advertising? As best as I can tell, no other country has as much attorney advertising. Prior to 1977, the American Bar Association prohibited lawyers from marketing for various reasons, one of which being that it would tarnish the dignified public image of the profession. That obviously isn't a concern today.

Innovative solutions have been proposed on many fronts. Single Payer proponents often point to what other countries are doing in healthcare. But loser pays litigation costs (sometimes called the English rule) in other countries is often ignored. Another unique idea is a no-blame model where patients can get awards from an independent medical board outside of the legal system, effectively replacing the malpractice legal system.

Medical malpractice reform is the change that we should stop talking about and just do. The savings will result at whatever the level. If the savings are small, the awards are small to individual court cases (either small awards or small in the number of awards). If they are large, that's why change is needed, and preventive medicine is unquestionably impacting healthcare costs.

FAIRNESS

"It's not fair." We've all heard and said this. A common desire of every person is to have fairness in everything we do. We appreciate an umpire's correct call even when our baseball team loses, for example. There is a sense of right in the world when someone gets fair treatment.

But fair is not always equal. Is it fair that someone can eat whatever they want and never gain weight? Is it fair that someone never studies, but always gets an A? Is it fair that someone's idea blossoms into Facebook?

Socialism dictates fair outcomes such that everyone gets an equal share. Capitalism dictates fair opportunity to get a fair outcome.

Healthcare is similar in that "fair" is fair access to healthcare, not equal healthcare. And what one individual pays in premiums plus copays is never the same as what another individual pays. One possibility is to have an individual pay the same percentage of income as a copay, but that could never happen. So since healthcare isn't ever going to be fair, should we even try?

Because of Obamacare, everyone's afraid of what they may have to pay in premium net of subsidies because they won't know until April 15 following the year when they file taxes. Think about that. In the guise of fairness, Obamacare requires a complicated formula that few understand to lower someone's net premium if their income is below 400 percent of poverty, but everyone is afraid (including those who qualify). H&R Block reported that 52 percent of all customers underestimated what they had to pay (on average they owed $530).

There is an odd phenomenon that exists in our nature that we like fairness in inputs and outcomes, so much so that we like to see the downfall of people we perceive as having an advantage. Because the English language doesn't have a word to describe this phenomenon, we borrow the German word *schadenfreude*. The *Merriam-Webster Dictionary* describes the word as "enjoyment obtained from the troubles of others."

At the core of this desire is fairness. When someone is successful who we think didn't put in fair effort (or didn't have talent in our estimation), we relish in their downfall. So, we like when the rich go bankrupt. Or the famous get divorced. Or the politician loses. Or the schoolmate voted the most likely to become whatever doesn't.

FOR-PROFIT

The key to preventing gouging is competition.

Most Blue Cross Blue Shield (BCBS) plans are not-for-profit. Their margins allow for similar profit, but that margin is required to be put back into the business, which may ultimately lower premiums, all other things being equal. One-third of all individuals in the US are BCBS beneficiaries, so the for-profit red herring is even more red. And yes, Blue Shield of California lost their nonprofit status in 2014 because their reserves (i.e., margins from prior years) were more than necessary to stay in business—according to the state of California.

If profits were the issue, nonprofit companies should be able to lower their prices and run the for-profit companies out of business (or at least obtain more business and save buyers millions of dollars). Why doesn't that happen?

Profit motivates the owner to enter the market and the employee to work for the employer because the profits allow the job to pay more, all other things being equal. But those who espouse an M4A system would do away with profits because any profit is just kept by the owner (or the independent doctor). That's true in any industry, but a socialistic approach to conducting business is desired because owners "just keep the profits." They argue there isn't any more pay because the employee never benefits from ownership.

What convoluted thinking! What's never measured under socialism is that owner would never create the company in which the employee benefits through employment. And then the patient doesn't benefit because the company doesn't exist.

Some say profits motivate people for the wrong reasons. There are a multitude of cases where the desire to profit is counter to the desire of the consumer. For instance, a car salesman wants to sell a car at as high of a price as possible to maximize their income, to the detriment of the buyer. A for-profit hospital wants to charge as much as they can, to the detriment of the cost of the healthcare system. A doctor wants to charge as much as possible, both to cover costs such as malpractice insurance and to personally make more money.

"Instead of personal gain through profits and wages, we should limit profits so that motivations are more benevolent. And we've seen benevolence work, whether it's the quality of the not-for-profit hospital that takes good care of patients, or people who donate their time to work for free in a nursing home. There are countless examples of people doing good deeds, even companies which create innovative healthcare for the benefit of society."

"Under M4A, the company does exist, but it is 'socially' owned by the government, which is all of us. The employee makes a living, and the patient gets treated as well. And often better because decisions aren't just based on 'greed.' They're based on the care for the patient. And the world is better off."

Really? The government forces the transaction to occur; it cuts out the owner and forces the employee to serve the patient. But is the government good at running any of these?

- The Post Office
- The DMV
- Department of Education
- CMS
- The FDA
- The VA
- The EPA
- The IRS
- The Secret Service
- The TSA
- Amtrak

The public has a propensity to get angry with middlemen who offer services at high prices. For example, we blame insurers for exorbitant premiums as if they're the cause. Our surface analysis goes something like this: 1) Healthcare premiums are high; 2) Insurers have luxurious offices; 3) Insurance company CEOs make, like, $20 million a year; 4) "They take my premium then make me jump through hoops to get my claims paid"; 5) Conclusion: insurance companies are a big part of the healthcare cost problem.

Further, Obamacare is losing competition due to losses in the individual market for insurers. Actuary Kurt Giesa of Oliver Wyman put the healthcare insurance losses at $4.7 billion in 2016. That's why insurers have left the market, not greed. By this thinking, insurers should stay in Obamacare markets because they can afford to, because they make so much money in other insurances. Under that line of thinking, General Motors should continue selling Oldsmobiles even though they weren't selling very well (they shut down the unprofitable line in 2004).

Meanwhile, there will be no US market-driven healthcare innovation. We will see stagnant growth (or none) in technology such that what we have today will be an improvement for some, but we will languish in healthcare and never know what could have been.

IDEAS THAT WON'T WORK

Giving Medicare the ability to negotiate drug prices for Medicare beneficiaries. Reason: cost shifting. The government doesn't actually negotiate; it controls. Price controls the government has employed since 1965 in Medicare and Medicaid shifted costs from the government to the private sector, with no effect on total cost (and great harm to everyone else not benefiting from those price controls, similar to rent controls). Lowering costs for the elderly and disabled through Medicare controls with drug manufacturers led to increased prices for the non-Medicare market. The bottom line is that lower costs need to create incentives, which is what competition does.

Paying the same amounts on prescriptions that other countries pay. Reason: with no R&D, there will be little to no advancement in prescription drugs. Nearly half of all drug R&D is performed within the US market. The US can either buy old, cheap drugs or expensive, new drugs. This is like *"cutting off your nose to spite your face."* (Whatever that means!) The idea is that if we follow what other countries do with price and demand that drug makers give us the same price as in, say, Canada, there will be no innovation, for the US or for the world.

Offering insurance across state lines. Reason: it would do nothing to help, and I'm a proponent of more competition, so if anyone would be in favor of this, it would be me. Why? Because the lack of competition in insurance is due to the attainment of top discounts. That's why we buy insurance from one insurer versus another. The reason more insurers don't enter a given marketplace is the incredible cost due to needing to achieve the best discounts. Differing discounts would have to be eliminated for competition to work, and that would be disastrous. So allowing insurers to cross state lines is like expanding the size of an internet cable when the bottleneck is further upstream. The result is no effect.

Allowing Obamacare plans to exclude certain coverages that aren't needed, like maternity. Reason: if one person's rate goes down, rates for others must go up to offset the cost of coverage. If costs are unaffordable when everyone pays for the same health plan (and the required Ten Essential Health Benefits—EHBs), eliminating one or more coverages for some means higher rates for everyone else, unless the change in coverage lowers the total spending.

By definition, insurance blends everyone's costs together. Put differently, if costs are too high, overall costs need to be reduced rather than lowering costs just for some. I recognize that risk allocation is appropriate (rates should cover actual risk, so rates should vary and not be limited, for example, to the three-to-one ratio for age), but allocation of high rates will not alleviate the problem for most. That's not to say people shouldn't be allowed to buy what they need.

Transparency menu boards. Reason: too much complication—it would be like a car dealership posting the cost of one of ten types of hubcaps (something you may need but peripheral to the main purchase). As of 2019, hospitals are required to post their chargemaster prices online under CMS Inpatient Prospective Payment System rules—certainly, the right direction, but will it work? Most people aren't even aware of this.

It isn't easy to compare prices. Once a comparison is made, it may not be accurate relative to the cost ultimately paid. That means if I calculate savings of X percent by going with one provider versus another only to find the cheaper prices are offset by either more or more intense services—not to mention unknowable elements like complication rates—savings may be lost. Any comparison I make would represent one service of perhaps 30,000 services listed on a chargemaster, coded something like NUC MED STUDY W/ CT SKULL-THIGH (and coded differently at another hospital). One example: Hospitals have posted price increases in newspapers for years for major categories of services with little notice by patients.

Vote directly on healthcare provisions. Some people claim there should be a different political system because politicians don't represent their beliefs. They claim that the system of representation (the House and Senate) is antiquated and unnecessary with the ability to vote on specific issues directly via the internet, rather than voting on representatives to vote on one's behalf.

I disagree. Perhaps more than ever, representation is important in healthcare decisions because of the complexity of the issues. While most people have an opinion about the high-level approach to changes in the healthcare system, few people truly understand all the elements that go into making well-informed legislation. It's true that individuals know more about various topics today and can read about them on the internet. But even the person who's most well read on a topic may not know details like how the government handles the issue today.

Imagine trying to read bills to decide how to vote. Kind of like voting on referendums today, where you decide on issues based on the one-line referendum at the bottom of a ballot, having no idea about the details. Choosing representatives to immerse themselves in bills and the knowledge they have about how healthcare works is vital to making the best decisions.

Politically, there is a bell-shaped curve of thought. I believe 80 percent of the population already have their minds made up. There's just 20 percent in the middle, and that may actually be 10 or 5 percent, or even just five people. While I'm joking, the point is, there may be few people in the middle, and these are the truly important people to the debate. Yet both sides spend their time focusing on the ends of the spectrum. The Single Payer debate may come down to the thoughts and beliefs of a few. Here is a classic distribution from which you can think about how many people are in the middle.

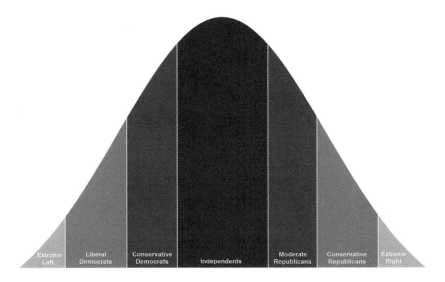

Decisions such as who should be elected to office may be made by just five people in the middle. People use issues to decide on a candidate, so if a candidate is for or against something, if that something is counter to that person's belief's, they would vote against that candidate. Even if that idea is opposed by, say, just one-eighth of the population. But if there are five similar issues with one-eighth being opposed, that's five-eighths against the candidate, and that person won't win. The same can apply to an idea, such as in healthcare: "Let's improve the status quo" could lose support one-eighth at a time. If one-eighth have preexisting conditions, and one-eighth have had to pay high copays, and one-eighth are frustrated by complexity, and one-eighth have had large claims, and one-eighth have had a bad outcome, then the right idea may fail. That's part of the attraction of M4A—unfortunately, to try something new.

BUT COSTS ARE STILL INCREDIBLY HIGH FOR HEALTHCARE!

I can already hear opponents to my idea, exclaiming that I'm ignoring every point ever made about the cost of healthcare in the US. *"The cost is unsustainable. How can I claim otherwise?"*

I'd like to bring back my literary device, continuing the Left-Right debate:

Costs are still way too high and are one-sixth of the economy.

> What should they be? Is one-sixth of GDP too high? Who says?

But it grows, so one-fifth, then one-fourth, then someday one-half will be the norm.

> But what is the norm? Who says? If people want to spend one-half on healthcare, that's what they want to spend. That becomes the norm, according to the people.

But the people don't have the ability to control how much they spend. Look at healthcare spending today.

> Fifty years ago, one would have said that one-sixth of GDP is ludicrous. Are you saying that fifty years from now spending one-half on healthcare is ludicrous?

Yes, because clearly it is.

> Then what should we spend?

How about the current level, like one-sixth? At least it won't increase like it has been.

Why would we expect to stop the increase in percentage now?

See, you must plan to spend less or it will never happen. That's your problem.

Kind of like saying, "I will never spend more than one-fourth of what I earn on rent." Doesn't each individual deserve the right to make that decision?

But again, healthcare insurance is expensive, and the normal person can't afford it. Are you even normal?

You'll have to define normal. Healthcare insurance is very expensive for the average person in the US. But if it's so important to most, then it should be the first thing they purchase, as important as food and shelter.

See, there you go again, healthcare insurance is just an annoyance that you can't claim is as important as food and rent. And when I spend more on food and rent, at least I get something like a nicer place in a better neighborhood and higher-quality food.

You get better insurance and better healthcare the more you spend. And it's not an annoyance, it's vital, as we've discussed.

"If you put the federal government in charge of the Sahara Desert, in five years there would be a shortage of sand." -Milton Friedman, 1980

OBAMACARE
ALREADY FAILED

"The [government] is that great fiction by which everyone tries to live at
the expense of everyone else."

–Frédéric Bastiat, 1848

FAMOUS QUOTES

'll start this chapter with some famous and not-so-famous quotes
about Obamacare from those who proposed the public should
accept the legislation:

"That means that no matter how we reform healthcare, we will keep
this promise to the American people: If you like your doctor, you will be
able to keep your doctor, period. If you like your health-care plan, you'll
be able to keep your health-care plan, period. No one will take it away,
no matter what." –President Obama

"Under my plan, no family making less than $250,000 a year will see any form of tax increase." –President Obama

"I will not sign a plan that adds one dime to our deficits—either now or in the future." –President Obama

"Lack of transparency is a huge political advantage, and basically call it the stupidity of the American voter or whatever, but basically that was really, really critical to getting the thing to pass." –Jonathan Gruber, ACA architect

"They proposed it and that passed, because the American people are too stupid to understand the difference." –Jonathan Gruber

"We just tax the insurance companies, they pass on higher prices that offsets the tax break we get, it ends up being the same thing." –Jonathan Gruber

"Strict youngest-first allocation directs scarce resources predominantly to infants. This approach seems incorrect. The death of a twenty-year-old woman is intuitively worse than that of a two-month-old girl, even though the baby has had less life. The twenty-year-old has a much more developed personality than the infant, and has drawn upon the investment of others to begin as-yet-unfulfilled projects . . . Adolescents have received substantial education and parental care, investments that will be wasted without a complete life. Infants, by contrast, have not yet received these investments . . . It is terrible when an infant dies, but worse, most people think, when a three-year-old child dies, and worse still when an adolescent does." –Dr. Ezekiel Emanuel, ACA architect

"FACT: Nothing in Obamacare forces people out of their health plans." –Valerie Jarrett, advisor to President Obama

"We all knew. The whole point of the plan is to cover things people need, like preventive care, birth control, pregnancy." –Sen. Kirsten Gillibrand (D-NY)

"[Obamacare] is the craziest thing in the world. [Americans] wind up with their premiums doubled and their coverage cut in half." –Former President Bill Clinton

OTHER QUOTES

The ACA was unnecessarily complex. No one would ever mistake "wordy" for "heady." That said, complexity is not smart; experts made the ACA complex, but not smart. It was designed in an echo chamber of ideas; what the designers thought would surely work on paper was bound to fail in reality.

And before changing the subject to M4A, we need to remain focused on the flaws with the current law and the promise-to-fix-what-ails-healthcare program called "Obamacare."

Other quotes:

- "We'll have the negotiations televised on C-SPAN."
- "Same way you'd shop for a TV on Amazon."
- "The servers crashed due to overwhelming demand."
- "These 23 health insurance co-ops will expand access to care."
- "If you misrepresent what is in this plan, we will call you out."
- "The millions who had plans cancelled on them had junk plans."
- "The penalty is not a tax."

WHERE WERE PEOPLE ENROLLED IN 2017?

Let's look at people's enrollment in 2017 versus in 2013 (before Obamacare):

PLAN	2013	PERCENTAGE OF TOTAL	2017	PERCENTAGE OF TOTAL
MEDICARE	49,000,000	16%	56,000,000	17%
MEDICAID	55,000,000	18%	62,000,000	19%
MILITARY	14,000,000	4%	16,000,000	5%
EMPLOYER	174,000,000	56%	181,000,000	56%
INDIVIDUAL MARKET	16,000,000	5%	8,000,000	3%
OBAMACARE	0	0%	12,000,000	4%
UNINSURED	42,000,000	13%	29,000,000	9%
TOTAL	313,000,000		323,000,000	

Sources: US Census Bureau, Kaiser Family Foundation. Numbers shown exceed 100 percent because the Census Bureau counts all coverages an individual may have during the year (coverage is not mutually exclusive). The total of individuals in the US is correct, but the categories are over-represented—this could have been avoided by counting only the main coverage an individual enrolls in, but that wasn't the case. So the percentages require mental adjustment.

Let's isolate the number of uninsured, since this number was the main purpose behind Obamacare. I chose to show the number of uninsured per the chart in the last chapter, which was estimated at fifty million individuals in 2010 when Obamacare became law. This is a huge number, and was higher than in any year before or after. There were forty-two million uninsured in 2013—the year before Obamacare went in place—and twenty-nine million in 2017.

Did the decrease from fifty million to forty-two million from 2010 to 2013 occur because of anticipation of Obamacare and the effect of certain provisions that went into effect immediately, such as coverage for students to age twenty-six? Or because the economy recovered from the 2008 recession such that more people had jobs and therefore healthcare insurance? We may never know, but recovery from the recession was a major influence, no question. So Obamacare solved one-third (actually, 31 percent) of the problem, and there's still twenty-nine million people without coverage. As I stated in the prologue, "So the ACA-level of complexity covered just one-third of the uninsured. It should have had one-tenth of the level of complexity to fix 75 percent of the problem."

Why is this the first time you've seen these before and after numbers? Because either it's hard to pull the right numbers together to compare, or certain writers would not want readers to know the facts. It's ridiculous to think that these numbers have never been shown.

So Obamacare created such upheaval for thirteen million participants in Obamacare? Even including those covered under Medicaid expansion (seven million more in the chart, although separately this number was estimated to be thirteen million new enrollees), the total new enrollment would be twenty-six million enrollees, or just 8 percent of the total population.

PLAN DESIGN AND PREMIUMS

I'll illustrate four situations that highlight the pros and cons and show the types of individuals who support and oppose the law. Here are four types of people that represent many of those impacted by the ACA:

- a subsidized ACA buyer
- an unsubsidized ACA buyer
- a Medicaid recipient
- a non-ACA participant in an employer plan

There are many others, of course (those outside of the ACA—for instance, those covered under Medicare, the VA, active duty military on TRICARE, those who benefit by having children covered to age twenty-six, those with and without preexisting conditions, retirees under age sixty-five, and so on). The bottom line is there are myriad situations, and I'm not attempting to deduce a composite for everyone, but just to highlight these four situations:

1. A subsidized buyer: Assuming a subsidy for someone in a reasonable cost community who buys a Silver plan, the premium for family coverage would be about $12,000 (annual) offset by an $8,000 subsidy (assuming a $50,000 family income) equals $4,000 in net premium. The Silver plan, due to the person being below 250 percent of the Federal Poverty Limit (FPL) in income, would have an out-of-pocket maximum of $5,000.
2. An unsubsidized buyer: Assuming income above 400 percent of FPL, the same Silver plan would cost $12,000 with an out-of-pocket maximum of $15,000.
3. A Medicaid recipient: A Medicaid recipient would receive free coverage with small copays for services.
4. A non-ACA participant in an employer plan: Annual premiums of about $4,000 for family coverage (pre-tax) with an out-of-pocket maximum of $10,000.

TYPICAL	NET PREMIUM	DEDUCTIBLE	OUT-OF-POCKET
SUBSIDIZED ACA	$4,000	$3,000	$5,000
UNSUBSIDIZED ACA	$12,000	$8,000	$15,000
MEDICAID RECIPIENT	LIMITED BY LAW	SOME STATES	SMALL COPAYS
EMPLOYER PLAN	$4,000	$4,000	$10,000

I won't draw any conclusions since details are incomplete. Suffice it to say that those with better coverage at a lower cost are typically in favor of Obamacare, and vice versa (especially those who fare much better or much worse).

One of the important factors that affects rates is the decision to cap rates to a ratio of three-to-one for older versus younger enrollees. The actual cost difference is more like six-to-one. That means the true cost for the oldest enrollees (age sixty-four) is about six times that of the youngest enrollees (age eighteen). This decision raises the rate for younger enrollees and lowers it for older enrollees.

Then, as we all heard, the success of the program hinged on younger people enrolling in Obamacare, which when they didn't, added to insurers losing money and ultimately leaving the market. This decision alone may have led to the downfall of Obamacare, all other things being equal, because the young and healthy didn't buy into Obamacare. This is an interesting point to learn from: that small decisions may become vital to the success of a program.

Also, there are elements that no one could have predicted, for example, like how Obamacare and Sarbanes-Oxley (SOX—the 2002 legislation that was a reaction to the Enron failure) would interact. Both affected businesses with many hours of analysis in compliance. Specifically, Obamacare added an estimated 150 million hours of work to employers (equivalent to 80,000 employees working full-time) besides the compliance hours SOX caused. Both laws encouraged small businesses to stay small to avoid compliance with further regulations required of larger, publicly traded firms. In other words, complexity on top of complexity leads to noncompliance.

BUT, BUT, BUT

Some say Obamacare didn't work because it wasn't allowed to work. What wasn't allowed to work? Which of the following would have made the difference?

- **"What if the fourteen states that did not expand Medicaid (thirty-six did, plus DC) had expanded Medicaid from 100 percent of FPL to 138 percent?"** Really? So under one-third of the population (population in those fourteen states versus the other twenty-six) not expanding Medicaid was important to the success of Obamacare?

The government initially offered to cover 100 percent of the cost of expansion, but that amount is now 90 percent, so the states who chose not to expand coverage were taking into account the 10 percent ongoing cost they would incur. Part of the reason they cared about "just 10 percent of the cost" is that they had to balance state budgets. These fourteen no-expansion states left $8 billion per year on the table. Had these states expanded Medicaid, Obamacare would have been responsible to cover $8 billion more in cost. The Supreme Court ruled that states could decide whether to expand their Medicaid populations, and the states which chose not to spent less. But these states' decisions did not cause high prices in the marketplaces.

- **"What if the individual mandate wasn't eliminated?"** Really? The elimination of the individual mandate occurred in 2019. The CBO had estimated, mistakenly, that the individual mandate elimination would lead to fifteen million people losing coverage, while the number is now expected to be just a few million. So this provision was not key to Obamacare's failure.

- **"What if insurance companies didn't leave markets?"** Really? Insurers left ACA marketplaces due to losses. So insurers leaving markets was a symptom of the actual problem of cost versus revenue. Any fix to this symptom fails to get at the root cause of the problem.

- **"What if the Trump Administration hadn't been so adamant about repealing Obamacare?"** Really? As if Obamacare ills weren't already having an impact before 2017.

- **"What if the Texas judge who found the law unconstitutional did not?"** Really? The law remains in place, pending the Supreme Court decision in 2021. This ruling has not affected Obamacare so far.

- **"What if more young people enrolled?"** Really? That many of the uninsured remained uninsured indicates the reason for being uninsured—that insurance wasn't important enough to pay the premiums required under Obamacare. The only way to change that is to either subsidize coverage (which Obamacare did), or provide it for free. And even if subsidized, many still didn't participate. Free may be the only way to get them covered, and the unintended consequences of offering free coverage already rules that out as a plausible solution.

- **"What if the newly insured didn't use the ER more than before?"** Really? Isn't the continued ER usage a better indicator of a portion of the population who view the convenience of ER care (available twenty-four/seven) as the reason for their healthcare use? There is no simple way to change that, and making coverage free would likely make things worse.

- **"What if the Obamacare markets weren't eroded with skinny plans, association health plans, and short-term plans?"** Really? These plans weren't even available in the first five years of Obamacare, and competition in plans is a positive. Only those who think "one size fits all" would fear such competition.

- **"What if enrollment hadn't been cut in half from ninety days to forty-five days?"** Really? The complaint claims that many individuals weren't aware of the deadlines to enroll. As if the entire US population needs to understand every aspect of social programs for the programs to be successful.

- **"What if Obamacare advertising hadn't been cut by 90 percent, or the navigator program hadn't been undermined by cutting their budget?"** Really? Early on, navigation of the new healthcare system was instrumental to its success (in 2013 through 2015). No program should continue spending at the same level as during its introduction.

- **"What if Cost Sharing Reduction (CSR) payments to insurance companies hadn't been eliminated for 2018?"** Really? The CBO estimated that rates increased an estimated additional 10 percent due to elimination of CSRs. Put differently, rate increases from the beginning of Obamacare would be 10 percent less than the 177 percent increase otherwise. So that's not significant.

SUPREME COURT RULINGS

Decisions of the Supreme Court have been vital to Obamacare since its inception. The law hinges on Supreme Court findings, to the point that people wait for rulings and are paralyzed until decisions are made whether to continue (or not).

But why isn't every Supreme Court decision 9-0 (or 0-9)? Chief Justice John Roberts said, "Supreme Court Justices are like umpires in that they call 'balls and strikes.'" So how does one judge see a ball when another sees a strike? How can that be?

We get upset when a baseball umpire errs in calling a ball a strike and vice versa. As fans, we get very upset if an umpire's call is wrong, especially if it's against our team. The organization Pitch F/X analyzed major league home plate umpires and found incorrect calls were made on 1.6 pitches per inning versus an electronic strike zone. My point isn't to replace umpires with electronics—only an umpire can determine where best to stand to see plays at each base and at home plate, and they are remarkably accurate in their calls, as proven by video review—but to make the point that umpires are fallible. We understand if their mistakes are arbitrary. But if they always favored one team, we would be outraged.

Such seems to be the case with Supreme Court justices, as they are "known" to make decisions that typically fall one way or the other (left or right). Since 2000, Supreme Court rulings have made the following decisions:

9-0: 36 percent
8-1, 7-2: 15 percent
6-3: 30 percent
5-4: 19 percent

Regardless of one's individual decision (and what a justice or even an individual deems is the "correct" decision), that five justices ruled one way and four the other suggests that either five or four are wrong. Understandably, Supreme Court decisions are not simply "right" or "wrong" like whether a pitch is a ball or a strike, but instead the cases they rule on are nuanced.

However, that one justice disagrees with another justice often occurs because politics affects the Court. Justices take an oath to be impartial in their decisions. Instead, justices often make their decisions based on politics, then craft arguments to support their position. Those decisions impact real life and are decided about 20 percent of the time by 5-4, meaning we must abide by laws that easily could have swung the other way. How is this good decision-making?

Regarding healthcare, the Supreme Court has already made rulings on Obamacare and will continue to make constitutionality rulings that will determine the future of healthcare in the US. So, programs like Obamacare, M4A, and even my CAT4ALL plan will live or die based on the political leaning of the court. Not ideal, but the way legislation works.

THE UNINSURED

Some people claim the calculated decrease in the uninsured population should start from the high point of the number of uninsured: 50 million people in 2010. The problem is that unemployment was approximately 10 percent that year, then 5 percent in 2015, so about ten million more people had jobs. It is unclear how much of the decrease in the number of uninsured prior to 2014 was due to employment, so I measured the effect of the ACA on the uninsured from 2013 to 2015, which is the same time period the Obama administration measured in 2016. The goal is to choose a long enough time period in which to measure the impact of Obamacare but short enough to not include some prior-to-the-law impacts that were due to gains associated with higher employment.

At least four million people paid the tax penalty in 2016, and about seven million went without coverage. They paid a tax penalty of $695 per year (per uninsured adult), or just $60 per month. The penalty buys nothing but is cheaper than a premium of $10,000 per year (or whatever the premiums were on the Obamacare Exchange), which many perceive as worth nothing because of the high deductibles. The penalty is a draconian alternative to buying into Obamacare. Further, many tax filers didn't answer whether they had healthcare coverage for all twelve months of the calendar year (although in 2018 the IRS began rejecting applications for lack of response, and the penalty didn't apply in 2019).

Many more people were exempt due to hardship than those who paid the penalty. The CBO stated in 2014: "CBO and JCT (Joint Committee on Taxation) estimate that twenty-three million uninsured people in 2016 will qualify for one or more of those exemptions. Of the remaining seven million uninsured people, CBO and JCT estimate granting exemptions from the penalty because of hardship or for other reasons."

However, the number of uninsured increased in 2017 because Obamacare premiums were so expensive—meaning, coverage cost so much that people perceived it was better to go without coverage. This prompted Michelle Obama to say on *Late Night with Jimmy Fallon* in 2014, "Well, thanks to the Affordable Care Act, young people can stay on their parent's insurance until they are twenty-six. But once they hit twenty-six—they're on their own. And a lot of young people think they're invincible. But the truth is, young people are knuckleheads. They're the ones who are cooking for the first time and slice their finger open; they're dancing on the barstool."

COVERAGE UNDER AGE TWENTY-SIX

Insurers were glad to cover kids to age twenty-six because this Obamacare feature lowered rates (rates per individual) but raised overall premiums. Many children under age twenty-six (those who were adults under age twenty-six) may have signed up under Obamacare as an enrollee. This is an example of two provisions leading to unintended consequences.

So support came from many factions who planned to benefit, including large insurers, pharmaceutical manufacturers, special interest think tanks (like Families USA), and several organizations with acronyms: AARP, AMA, AHA, etc. It's important to consider why a group supported Obamacare as it wasn't because, "It was the right thing to do," but instead was often, "What's in it for me?"

THE SUBSIDY

Eighty-seven percent of people in the Obamacare marketplace are receiving subsidies. That hints at the real reason people are willing to pay to get Obamacare: that it's relatively cheap (after subsidies), and a good deal versus what they get. Like anything else, people will buy something for a good value.

Plus, the deductibles in Obamacare plans are high. For a single person, a $5,000 deductible adds to the $6,000 premium such that coverage begins at $11,000 out of someone's pocket. So deductibles are like premiums (although only paid by someone with medical claims, perhaps 85 percent of a population). That means it behooved the designers of Obamacare to split the difference, such that premiums and deductibles are equally high. That way, complaints are divided between high premiums and high deductibles.

In Chapter 3, I highlighted that no payment can be made (or attempted to be made) that is perfectly fair. To do that, one would have to have perfect information about income at time of service, be it premium payment or copay payment. The attempt is fraught with new problems that sometimes make things less fair (for example, income doesn't take into account wealth).

Another fairness issue is that the subsidy doesn't vary enough to account for cost differences in healthcare by geography; but the premiums do. So if two people get an equal dollar amount of subsidy according to formulas, is it fair that the subsidy in Iowa pays 90 percent of the premium while in New York it pays 50 percent? The subsidy varies by geography, but not enough to make it fair.

TAXES

I imagine you're getting sleepy as you read the section title Taxes. I'll keep this section short only to mention that any change from employer plans to Obamacare is a net positive to the government through the amount of taxes collected. That means if someone takes Obamacare versus their prior employer plan (the whole concept of avoiding job lock, as Speaker Nancy Pelosi claimed), the premium previously paid by the employer (and any employee contributions which were pre-tax) becomes post-tax through Obamacare. For example, a $10,000 premium that previously was pre-tax would become post-tax, and therefore the government would net about an extra $2,500. This was a hidden windfall to the government, all other things being equal.

CBO SCORING

Obamacare was front-loaded with benefits and back-loaded with costs; several benefits went in place immediately:

- Coverage for children to age twenty-six
- Elimination of preexisting condition limitations
- Premium subsidies (and cost-sharing subsidies for those below 250 percent of FPL)
- Minimum Medical Loss Ratio (MLRs required to be 80 or 85 percent of premiums)

Other more controversial provisions applied later:

- Tax penalty—phased in, eliminated in 2019
- The Cadillac Tax—originally effective in 2018, later delayed to 2022, now eliminated
- Funding of the cost of Medicaid expansion by the federal government at 100 percent for 2014–2016, winding down to 90 percent in 2020

The early positives helped Obamacare to be perceived positively, with funding for those benefits occurring later. The bottom line is that we now are paying the full cost of Obamacare, plus the payment for early enactment of many benefits. Perception has thus eroded.

CBO scoring of Obamacare in 2009 showed a deficit reduction of $143 billion over ten years; then, a year later, the CBO revised that to just $28 billion; then, in 2014, the CBO declared they couldn't update the effect on the deficit. So the current "cost" of Obamacare is now unknown.

CBO scoring that underestimated the ultimate cost of Obamacare reflected the broader problem of estimating any new program. Projections of the cost of every new program in the US have underestimated the ultimate costs of programs. Here are a few examples:

- In 1913, the income tax was implemented at the top rate of just 7 percent of income. Today, the top tax bracket is 37 percent. Yes, changes perceived negatively are often phased in, but this is an example of "the camel's nose in the tent" if there ever was one. Implementing something that's perceived as draconian today started as "It's just a small program to help finance the government."

- In 1935, Social Security was intended to cover people in retirement. In 1939 came the addition of survivor benefits, followed by disability benefits in 1956. Social Security added Medicare in 1966. The bottom line is that Social Security coverage was meant to cover one element, but over time now covers more (and previous recipients received more than they paid into the system, such that there is no Social Security reserve). Depletion of the Social Security trust fund reserves is estimated to occur in 2034.

- Medicare cost just $3 billion in 1966. Today, annual expenditures are over $700 billion per year. Facing demise, Medicare payments have been ratcheted back, so it reimburses healthcare providers at approximately 70 percent of their costs; yet depletion of the trust fund reserves is still estimated to occur in 2026.

- Medicaid has squeezed the balloon such that it reimburses healthcare providers 50 percent of their costs, on average. Medicaid reimbursements are so low that 30 percent of healthcare providers won't even accept Medicaid patients.

- When the CBO claimed they could not update their Obamacare estimate in 2014, others claimed the reason for the CBO punting this estimate is that the CBO did not want to show an increase in the deficit; that the result would be an embarrassment to both the CBO and to Obamacare supporters. The bottom line is: the CBO has lost the public's confidence.

Further, CBO projection methods are limited in the answers they can provide. Often, frustration comes from the legislative mandate that the CBO not value changes dynamically, but that they reflect only status quo effects.

For instance, in estimating the impact of Obamacare rules that only apply to employers with over fifty employees, the CBO was not allowed to conjecture how employers might react to the fifty-employee threshold. So, frustration reflects the CBO's lack of anticipation for unintended consequences, but they aren't allowed to anticipate those consequences.

Some say it is good that there are limitations on the CBO because it's hard to hit a moving target. But a problem results when unintended consequences are so obvious that cost estimates are often nowhere close to reality. There are also unintended consequences that are nonfinancial, such as Obamacare legislation leading to more monopolies and higher compliance costs. While these should have been likely outcomes of the legislation, the CBO was not allowed to pontificate about the degree to which they would occur.

PASSAGE OF THE ACA

There were several "last-minute" deciders in passing Obamacare:

- Sen. Ben Nelson, NE: The infamous "Cornhusker Kickback" gave federal money of $100 million to the state of Nebraska to cover Medicaid expansion under the law (the only state to receive such a promise). The provision did not survive, as a week later the Senate voted to remove the Nebraska wording in the law. But the affirmative vote was already achieved—a bait and switch.

- Sen. Mary Landrieu, LA: The infamous "Louisiana Purchase" gave federal money of $300 million to the state of Louisiana to provide Medicaid funds for disaster relief to achieve an affirmative vote.

- Sen. Bill Nelson, FL: The infamous "Gator Aid" protected one million Florida Medicare Advantage participants from benefit cuts.

- Sen. Chris Dodd, CT: The infamous "Unnamed Health Care Facility" provision allocated $100 million for a new facility in Connecticut.

These deals were the most notable, but there were other backroom deals that secured votes both in the Senate and the House. Politics at its worst.

THE WEBSITE

It's easy to remember the failed Obamacare website and the troubles that caused. Will this have a long-term impact? It's difficult to know.

What we do know is that $2.1 billion was spent on a website that had many problems:

- Only six people got the website to work correctly on the first day.
- CMS built the site; they collected more information than was necessary for enrollment, making the system needlessly complex (according to the Inspector General in 2016).
- The realization of the website's insufficient capacity occurred four days prior to launch. The website crashed repeatedly (including two hours after launch, and at another point for sixteen days).

EMPLOYERS

Obamacare's impact on employers is immense, through rules and penalties that affect manpower and coverage. These rules were necessary despite Obamacare's focus mainly on the individual market (the Obamacare Exchanges), but the government legislation impacted all healthcare plans. Here are some impacts:

- Penalties apply to employers for not offering adequate coverage of either $2,000 or $3,000 per employee per year (indexed). This affected both the companies that did not offer adequate coverage, and every company that did who needed to be concerned about meeting the threshold. A report estimated that companies paid as much as thirty-one billion dollars in Obamacare penalties in 2016.

- The Cadillac Tax (tax on high-cost plans) originally applied in 2017, then 2022, then never, but employers needed to analyze the potential impact since Obamacare's inception.

- Penalties apply to employers with over fifty employees, so employers were incentivized to keep their full-time staffs below fifty—not an impact for employers well above or below that threshold, but something to consider if close.

- Penalties apply for employees working more than thirty hours per week, such that all employers must question how long employees were slated to work.

- Employers were forced to track who had coverage, by month, and to produce notices of coverage for tax purposes.

- Employers needed to consider whether to maintain grandfather status with their health plans (to avoid penalties).

- Employer costs increased to cover dependents to age twenty-six.

- Employer coverage had to be affordable to employees. This required employers to determine if the employee share is more or less than 9.56 percent of the employee's household income.

- Employer costs increased for many Obamacare taxes: Insurer tax for insured plans (typically 2 to 3 percent), one-half of the Medicare Part A Payroll tax, plus other taxes passed through to consumers, such as prescription drug taxes.

These Obamacare rules were so complex that many employers had to hire consultants to model the law. For example, "The penalty for each month the employer fails to offer coverage is $3,480 divided by twelve, for each full-time employee receiving a premium tax credit that month (up to a maximum of $2,320 divided by twelve, times the number of full-time employees [minus up to thirty])." What a waste of resources that never should have happened!

And most of these costs (penalties, and even the threat of penalties, which led to other actions) were passed along either to employees or customers. The fallacy that Obamacare penalized employers was wrong—it affected everyone downstream. None of these hidden costs actually provided healthcare; it was administrative gobbledygook that just added cost to the system.

UNINTENDED CONSEQUENCES

As with any legislation, the law of unintended consequences affected Obamacare. Some consequences of Obamacare were unexpected, but some were expected and ignored. Laws may backfire, and the worst laws cause so much backfire that the net-net is negative. That's the worst outcome, where laws make things worse. Here are a few examples:

- Employers close to the fifty employee threshold attempted to stay below fifty employees by not growing their business, finding other ways to get the work done without hiring employees (like electronic kiosks), and attempting to split their companies into smaller units (for which Obamacare needed to create complicated rules on how to count the number of employees).

- Obamacare defined "full-time employment" as "working over thirty hours per week." This led to employers wanting to keep the number of hours worked by employees below thirty and considering whether to hire two part-time employees instead of one full-time employee.

- Hospitals merged to avoid some of the compliance costs of Obamacare. Hospital monopolies have resulted in less competition and less choice in many markets.

It's difficult to determine the net-net of some of these changes. How does something get measured when it doesn't happen, such as jobs that never materialize? Obamacare led to many unintended consequences, according to articles:

- Elimination of healthcare coverage for retirees and spouses, because they can get Obamacare:
    - IBM
    - Time Warner
    - UPS

- Limiting employees to under thirty hours per week to avoid penalties:
    - SeaWorld
    - Carnegie Museum
    - State of Virginia

- Cutting benefits for part-timers:
  - Home Depot
  - Target
  - Walmart

- Downsizing in the healthcare industry:
  - Cleveland Clinic
  - Numerous smaller hospitals

Other impacts are less-known and must be estimated. For example, the National Bureau of Economic Research studied the impact of Obamacare and found that employers with fewer than fifty employees increased from 37 percent of all businesses in 2012, to 45 percent in 2016; obviously due to penalty avoidance.

HADN'T THIS BEEN TRIED BEFORE?

Hillarycare (the Hillary Clinton attempt to revamp healthcare) had been tried in 1993. It is insightful to see how the provisions of Hillarycare led to Obamacare provisions, suggesting that government takeover of healthcare has been in the works for twenty-five years.

The Obama Administration learned from the results of Hillarycare, a program doomed even though Democrats led Congress. While there are mechanical differences, the goals are the same: to have government-involved universal coverage, which would ultimately lead to Single Payer coverage.

As the website for Obamacare Facts recognizes, Hillarycare led to Obamacare. Obamacare and Hillarycare had many similarities:

PROVISION	OBAMACARE (2010)	HILLARYCARE (1993)
INCREASED GOVERNMENT INVOLVEMENT	Y	Y
MANAGED COMPETITION/EXCHANGES	Y	Y
EMPLOYER MANDATE	Y	Y
ALLOW PREEXISTING CONDITION EXCLUSIONS	N	N
UNIVERSAL HEALTHCARE COVERAGE, INCLUDING THE UNINSURED	Y	Y
GOVERNMENT-DECLARED MINIMUM BENEFITS PACKAGE	Y	Y
INDIVIDUAL MANDATE TO PUR-CHASE COVERAGE	Y	Y
NUMBER OF UNINSURED COVERED	13 MILLION PEOPLE	37 MILLION PEOPLE (PROPOSED)
FUNDING	NOT CONSIDERED A TAX	TAXES
ULTIMATE GOAL	SINGLE PAYER	SINGLE PAYER
PASSAGE	PASSED WITH ALL DEMOCRAT VOTES	FAILED DUE TO LACK OF DEMOCRAT VOTES

Source: Author's Analysis

THE MARKET

We all like to complain about the market. We tell others about situations where such-and-such company dissed us. I've complained about it too.

The focus of our complaints includes insurance companies, where the people who work for them make decisions that may deny our coverage. There are many annoyances in insurance companies that deserve our complaints:

- Denial of coverage
- High insurance rates
- Charging more for services after the fact
- Denial of in-network coverage
- Paperwork to sign up for coverage
- Paperwork to get paid for coverage

- EOBs in the mail/online that have lots of details, yet little "information"
- Mind-numbing number of EOBs
- Waiting on hold to even talk to someone
- Having to punch buttons to answer inane questions about coverage, when either the insurance company does/should know the answers

(Probably the most annoying thing is punching buttons with my account number, only to be asked for that number before the person on the phone can even talk to me.)

But what if the market didn't exist? That's what is proposed under M4A: that insurance companies wouldn't exist. We would cut out the middleman. Would we have the same (or similar) complaints about how the government does things? I know that Medicare EOBs are just as (if not more) mind-numbing.

Plus, Obamacare has already been devastating to the market:

US COUNTIES WITH:	2016	2017
1 OR FEWER INSURERS	2%	21%
2 INSURERS	13%	21%
3 OR MORE INSURERS	85%	58%

The market eroded when insurers left the market in 2017, based on poor financial results in 2016 and prior years, and has recovered little since then—the number of counties with three or more insurers in 2020 is just 67 percent. What is the best way to fix problems the customer has with any industry? The answer is competition. What we really want is a stable marketplace with stable insurers that conduct business fairly. This result is more of what we want:

- Being able to choose an insurance plan or insurer that we like
- Reasonable rates
- Reasonable rate increases

- Broad networks (that include my current doctors and a local hospital)
- Reasonable phone wait times

Obamacare has devastated the market, and it may never recover.

If I didn't have to spend so much on health insurance, I could buy other things.

Like what?

I could pay bills.

Which would give you more disposable income, which could then be spent on better food and shelter.

Exactly. Now you're getting it.

And that's more important than vital-to-life healthcare?

There you go again. Healthcare isn't vital to life; it's just something you have to buy, like car insurance.

Buying car insurance allows you to drive. You could argue that buying health insurance allows you to live.

That's silly. I don't need health insurance to live!

Not now, but at some point, yes. Health insurance, in some cases, saves people from dying, and in others, allows them to get back to being pain-free.

Then you don't need it to live today; only someday.

Didn't you say you like to plan? That's what insurance is, planning for that rainy day.

But I should fork over one-sixth just for a rainy day? I'd rather spend just 10 percent.

So would I. And keeping that percentage as low as possible is part of the management that needs to continue.

So why not set a goal of never spending more than one-sixth?

Because I can tell you that we'll collectively spend more than that someday. I can't pretend to manage that aspect.

Well, I can. So I implore my politicians to develop unique ways to manage to one-sixth.

Who?

Democratic Socialists.

What's the likelihood of that happening?

Well, at least they have a plan and are trying. You have no plan because you're not even trying.

My plan is competition, just like in other industries. But healthcare has been the most over-regulated industry. As Milton Friedman says, government intervention has led to most of the cost increase in the past fifty years.

Oh, give me a break! I've never heard that!

Exactly. And why not?

Because it's not true. Look at what's happened where competition has just led to people being greedy and gouging the market. That costs me!

You've read my analysis in Chapter 1, and I'll continue on the topic of "It's the Rich" in Chapter 7. Suffice it to say that we're all richer than people in all of history, but are just complaining about what someone else has.

We should just agree to disagree.

"It's not tyranny we desire; it's a just, limited, federal government."

–Alexander Hamilton, 1787

5

LET'S TRY M4A!

"Democracy is the road to socialism."

–Karl Marx, 1848

THE M4A SOLUTION

Why do people think M4A is a good idea? They see the current system as, "The glass is half-empty."

Like everything in life, there is a bell-shaped curve in thinking no matter the topic: some people only see the negative, and some only see the positive. But some people wake up every day looking for something to complain about. They won't accept anything short of perfect, already thinking Obamacare failed so they're ready to try something even more outlandish—as if the rest of us can allow them to keep trying things until they find something they like.

Democratic Socialists (and others) propose M4A as a solution to all the problems of the current system. How could abdicating authority to someone else be the goal? You can't promise to cover all people, provide

100 percent coverage that's free (including dental and vision), and pay for all of this without pain. Promises such as these will fail, just as a balloon that's squeezed causes another part of the balloon to stick out.

Democratic Socialists' logic follows along these lines: "Cover everyone and everything, and because we already spend so much on healthcare, the tab will be less than today, because the rest of the world has lower costs than in the US. And the system will continue as it has, with no unintended consequences."

The problem with that thinking, however, is that we have to insure the US population with all of its current needs, which are more than in other countries (whether due to our relative lack of health, accidents, lack of adherence to preventive medicine, stress, and so on). So M4A costs would start from our current costs and may even cost more because of increased utilization due to 100 percent coverage, as the Mercatus study suggests. Other studies performed by RAND and The Urban Institute show low savings potential.

Sometimes I get so frustrated with politics that I think, "Just do it! Get it over with and just enact your crazy ideas!" Let's pontificate about that with M4A, and rather than enact it to see what's in it, we can contemplate what the future would look like. I mentioned in the prologue that an actuary can't predict the future; the best we can do is mention the exit after we pass it. That doesn't mean I shouldn't try. After all, 0 percent of people predicted the cell phone revolution, but 100 percent know that it happened after the fact. And the person who claimed in 1995 that we would all be walking around with a brick phone in our pocket would appropriately have been ridiculed.

Simple math can predict the future under M4A. Today, the current healthcare system is 42 percent paid for through Medicare and Medicaid, and 58 percent through other means. We could say that 58 percent of healthcare transactions over-pay to cover the under-pay by the government. Studies have shown that Medicare pays seventy cents on the dollar, and Medicaid pays fifty cents. With simple math (ignoring different percentages for hospital, doctor, other, and geography reimbursement rates), that means private healthcare must pay 125 cents on the dollar (assuming a dollar is what the system needs).

As the portion paid by government increases toward 100 percent, the need to charge the private sector higher rates increases astronomically toward infinity. This scenario is silly, as the system falls apart well before reaching infinity. The point is, the government cannot increase its percentage of healthcare spending without ramifications: the private sector must pay an ever-increasing bill to maintain the system, then the government takes over, and the market dissolves. No more healthcare system.

Medicare and Medicaid have already disturbed the healthcare market for fifty years. Because of it, there is no one who actually knows what it costs to provide care. Even if an accountant performed the calculation to determine a provider's true cost for a service, it wouldn't matter because charging that amount to any entity (Medicare, Medicaid, insurance, consumers) never happens.

Maybe we can go slowly, like we have since 1965: turning up the heat while boiling the frog. I'm not suggesting such a thing, but referencing a familiar story where the frog jumps out when confronted with boiling water, while it doesn't when the water increases in temperature more slowly. And for those contemporary biologists who have studied this phenomenon and found that frogs jump out of water that increases in temperature more slowly, turning this story into a fable: quit spending our money researching such dumb things. The point is still warranted.

I'm not saying that all discounts should be eliminated so that market signals work again. But Medicare and Medicaid underpayments are so large that the accounting system is false. And it's only getting worse by the day, where purchasers chase discounts that are higher and higher: "Yes, I'd like a 55 percent discount instead of a 50 percent discount. But why are we bargaining with the price of something so vital to life? What does it really cost? Stop telling me I'm getting a good deal!"

What else is likely to happen under M4A? One obvious outcome is a lack of innovation. Why innovate when the system forces sharing in that creation? What if we had moved to M4A in the 1970s? Where would healthcare be today? Would we even have the technology of CAT scans or MRI machines? Perhaps not. Imagine the US if the internet and cell phones had never come about. Would we want to take that risk?

"But we shouldn't be the world's engine in development of ground-breaking medicines. The world benefits and we pay the cost!" What's the better alternative? Since we don't control prices in other countries, what's the solution? Take our ball and go home?

People who think M4A will provide an idyllic solution—free insurance for everyone—don't realize the demand that comes without a corresponding increase in supply. They think they'll be first in line; that their doctors will see them like they do today. But when there are fewer providers due to underpayments by the government, and with more demand because it's free, we will likely have ER-like wait times for routine services.

SCANDINAVIA

One should wait about fifty years before claiming their approach works. For example, growth in Denmark and Sweden has been slower since they've become more government-driven, as this chart shows:

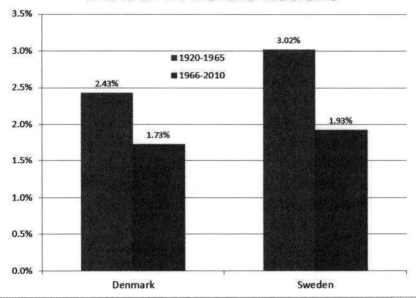

Welfare State Leads to Slower Growth in Nordic Nations

- 1920-1965
- 1966-2010

Denmark: 2.43%, 1.73%
Sweden: 3.02%, 1.93%

As the author and economist Daniel Mitchell describes, the first bar shows when Denmark and Sweden were less government-run and taxes were lower; more recent results are the second bar. As expected, taxes increased much more than in the US, as shown in the chart on the next page.

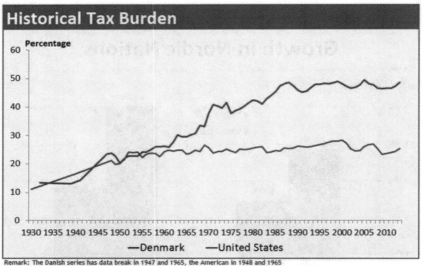

Historical Tax Burden

Percentage

Remark: The Danish series has data break in 1947 and 1965, the American in 1948 and 1965
Source: OECD Tax Databse, "Flora consolidated govt revenue", Whitehouse.gov, taxfoundation.org, "Økonomisk vækst i Danmark" - Svend Aage Hansen,"Beskatning i Danmark" - DST 1987 and own calculations

Democratic Socialists say, "I'm not talking about Venezuela; I'm talking about Denmark." In essence, they're saying: "I'm not a dummy. I'm very smart. I'm embracing a modern definition of socialism to change your focus. I can't admit that you're right."

Democratic Socialists think they won't fall into the socialism/communism trap because they're smarter than those before them—they haven't read *This Time Is Different: Eight Centuries of Financial Folly*. They think the problem is with those who tried socialism in the past but that they won't succumb to the forces that led to failure. "Who in their right mind would choose to be like the USSR, like Communist China, like the Nazi party, like Hugo Chávez?" Yes, it all comes down to choices, that "when progressivism doesn't work out quite like what's in my head, I'll choose better."

Adding the adjective "democratic" to "Socialism" doesn't change the basic definition of socialism. Socialism is more than just being kind. This wording is even being used with the new term, "democratic Capitalism." Terms such as "democratic" don't change reality, similar to using the full name for the Democratic People's Republic of North Korea.

SIXTEEN DUMB IDEAS

The ideas coming from Democratic Socialists are amazing:

- The Green New Deal
- Expand the Supreme Court
- Universal Basic Income
- Slavery reparations
- Wealth tax
- Abolish the Electoral College
- Free college and forgiving current loan debt
- Lower the voting age to sixteen
- Prisoners can vote
- Abolish ICE
- Sanctuary cities
- Post Office becoming a bank
- Tax the rich
- Penalties for companies who pay women less than men
- Right to affordable housing (rent control)
- Medicare for All

Let's see: Ideas-16, Good Ideas-0. Imagine a world where all sixteen schemes are enacted. That's the idyllic world proponents promise. If you think about it, each of the solutions above solve problems that are declared emergencies by their proponents. They focus on one issue, with blinders on, so that all they can see is the issue they attempt to address. Socialism is a great idea, just not a great reality.

Further, every bad argument in support of a bad idea is enough to lose credibility. For example, the argument that "all people should be able to vote" is enough to make one question whether anything that person says is worthy of consideration. Or "People coming out of college shouldn't be burdened with debt for the rest of their life." Or "The Rich don't pay their fair share." Or "Medicare works for the elderly; it will work for everyone."

It makes you ask the question: When is enough, enough? Obviously, never. So Obamacare wasn't enough. Nor will M4A be enough. It's time to stop. If you could get $20 for free, but a friend would have to pay $20, you would say no. But if you didn't know that person, you might say yes. Actually, people don't want free, they want freedom.

SOCIALISM

I can't even believe we're talking about this. While Venezuelans are eating zoo animals instead of starving, socialism is being considered in the US! And Single Payer is socialized medicine. Here is one Venezuelan's claim: "There is a human catastrophe in Venezuela. There is a resurgence of illnesses that were eradicated decades ago. Hundreds have died from measles and diphtheria. Last year, more than 400,000 Venezuelans presented malaria symptoms. Up to now, there are over 10,000 sick people from tuberculosis. People have been doomed to death. More than 55,000 cancer patients don't have access to chemotherapy. Every three hours, a woman dies due to breast cancer."

And we're worried about healthcare here.

I'VE STOPPED LISTENING TO THE "EXCUSE MAKERS" WHO JUST "CRY WOLF"

- "Our proposal [Medicare for All] will save the average middle-class family thousands of dollars a year in healthcare."
- "Let us wage a moral and political war against the billionaires and

corporate leaders, on Wall Street and elsewhere, whose policies and greed are destroying the middle class of America."

- "Medicare isn't the problem. It's the solution."
- "What the Bronx and Queens needs is Medicare for All, tuition-free public college, a federal jobs guarantee, and criminal justice reform."
- "Americans have the sticker shock of healthcare as it is, and what we're also not talking about is why aren't we incorporating the cost of all the funeral expenses of those who died because they can't afford access to healthcare? That is part of the cost of our system."
- "Both Medicare for All and Single Payer healthcare enjoy majority support in recent polling from the Kaiser Family Foundation."
- "No one ever makes a billion dollars. You take a billion dollars."
- "Denmark, not Venezuela."

In case you didn't know, Senator Bernie Sanders, Representative Alexandria Ocasio-Cortez, former US Secretary of Labor Robert Reich, and economist Paul Krugman uttered the aforementioned quotes. And because there's controversy about the following quote that Senator Sanders did not write, I quote directly from his Senate website: In August 2011, Sanders's official Senate webpage reprinted in full an editorial from the West Lebanon, New Hampshire *Valley News*, stating, "These days, the American dream is more apt to be realized in South America, in places such as Ecuador, Venezuela and Argentina, where incomes are actually more equal today than they are in the land of Horatio Alger. Who's the banana republic now?"

Excuse-makers are not just the people who said the things above, but those who make excuses for them, including the media. Such obfuscation serves to draw attention away from the real issues of socialism, like ignoring what's going on in Venezuela or forgiving Cuba. Nowhere in the world—including Syria, North Korea, the Sudan, or Iran—is life as bad as in Venezuela. Selling oneself into prostitution (including children) just to buy groceries is no way to live.

Every time some politician gets pinned down to their prior statements, they divert attention from Venezuela to Denmark—as if the two countries show the dichotomy of potential outcomes, and the path easily chosen will be the softer approach of Denmark; because who in their right mind would choose Venezuela? "No kidding, you'd pick the approach of Denmark before you'd pick Venezuelan Socialism. That's like saying you wouldn't pick the Great Depression-type of Capitalism."

VENEZUELA

The collapse of Venezuela is due to socialism. Back in 1999, Venezuela democratically elected Hugo Chávez as President (just twenty years ago). Socialists in the US claim that someone like Chávez could never get elected in the US, implying that Venezuela could never happen here. "We're a democracy," they argue (actually, a democratic republic, meaning we elect representatives democratically, so that 51 percent of the people cannot impose their will on 49 percent). But back then, Chávez was beloved, promising to take care of the poor and punish the rich. Many famous people in the US heralded his election as a model economic system:

- Michael Moore
- Sean Penn
- Danny Glover
- Oliver Stone
- Jesse Jackson
- Noam Chomsky

Noam Chomsky, an MIT professor educated in linguistics and a self-described Libertarian Socialist, is an interesting figure because he writes books espousing socialism. He is also the one person who has commented on the current Venezuelan crisis instead of being silent.

However, he makes excuses with statements like, "I was right" (about Venezuela, citing the success Venezuela had in reducing poverty ten years ago). He said that Venezuela was "quite remote from socialism." *"Yes, they didn't enact real socialism. Yes, more socialism is needed."*

There were countless others who foolishly praised Venezuela in the early days of their socialist experiment (as current president Nicolás Maduro and Hugo Chávez dubbed it "Socialism of the Twenty-First Century"). Names not everyone has heard of like Naomi Campbell, Courtney Love, and Joseph Stiglitz (an economist and professor).

Now that Venezuela has failed by running out of other people's money, Democratic Socialists move on to other countries and try to ignore the most recent and obvious example. Why is the burden of proof such that one must prove Venezuela is Socialist, but those who supported the country twenty years ago don't have to answer questions? How can Socialism even be considered as a realistic alternative to Capitalism? Moving on is an admission of failure.

Capitalism is the free market. When Capitalism impinges upon the consumer, the consumer has recourse to change companies or to sue. When socialism impinges upon the consumer, there are no alternatives and no redress available. The free market develops best practices. Individuals choose that best practice, helping to determine what is best. Socialism develops but one practice.

Capitalism provides an amazing array of products that fit the consumer's exact need at an acceptable price point. If not, the transaction doesn't happen. Yet Democratic Socialists want to focus on the profit someone benefited from in a transaction. That's a pessimistic way to view life and leads to a depressing existence of "everything I see around me is bad."

Let's talk about what "social democracy" means. Literally, it means "a Socialist government achieved by democratic means"—as when Venezuela first voted for Hugo Chávez in 1999 and then Nicolás Maduro in 2013. With the world's largest known oil reserves, Venezuela devolved from being the richest South American country to 90 percent poverty-stricken in just twenty years. They are the latest country to try socialism.

Academics have supported socialism for a hundred years in the classroom, heralding the likes of Marx, Lenin, and Stalin. They perceive that Socialism rewards individuals more fairly, unlike under Capitalism, where less-educated people can become rich (which they think is unfair). They complain that Capitalism is wrought with unfairness, where corporations dictate high prices and buyers lack control.

Democratic Socialists in the US suggest that others need to read more to better understand their ideology. They suggest that democratic socialism means libraries, museums, and parks. What? Talk about taking ideas out of context. Following this type of thinking, reading is good, so someone should read everything ever published. But that person would never get anything done.

Why is democratic socialism such a hot topic today? Is it because its time has come, or is it because it is a spectacle that warrants notice for its flawed logic?

Hugo Chávez wanted to take care of the poor in Venezuela through socialism. Venezuela began with social justice, then socialism, now poverty. Ironically, it's the poor who suffered the most. Think about what 90 percent below the poverty line in Venezuela means. Assume the middle class is above the poverty line, and let's assume they represent 5 percent of the population (at the most, 10 percent). Who's above the middle class? Just 5 percent of the population who happen to be in a good position (relative to everyone else); and the government itself, which can't be in poverty. For example, Hugo Chávez's daughter, María Gabriela Chávez (age thirty-five), is reportedly the richest person in Venezuela, with four billion dollars in wealth. *"Makes perfect sense."*

Why is it that Socialists claim Venezuela was caused by something other than Socialism—like authoritarianism, as if that's the problem, and a non-authoritarian government would do the trick? Instead, the opposite of Socialism—in other words, Capitalism—would solve many problems in Venezuela today. Some economists even say that if Venezuela went back to Capitalism, Venezuela would recover relatively quickly. But that solution wouldn't be advisable for President Maduro,

Senator Sanders, and other Democratic Socialists because if it worked, that would be the end of any discussion about this failed idea.

Inflation in Venezuela is 10 million percent! By comparison, inflation in the US is below 2 percent. Just to joke about what inflation brings, Dan Aykroyd played President Jimmy Carter on *Saturday Night Live* in 1978, saying, "Wouldn't you like to own a $4,000 suit, smoke a seventy-five dollar cigar, drive a $600,000 car? I know I would! Everyone will be a millionaire!"

Compare Venezuela and the US: in Venezuela, the question is where to find the next meal, be it the zoo or a garbage heap. In the US, there are grocery stores that are the envy of the world. Memes have even cropped up on the internet talking about "first-world problems" and the irony of complaints like, "My local grocery store doesn't have ripe kumquats available."

Here are some classic quotes:

- "I am convinced that the path to a new, better and possible world is not capitalism; the path is socialism."
- "We must reduce all the emissions that are destroying the planet. However, that requires a change in lifestyle, a change in the economic model: We must go from capitalism to socialism."
- "We must be aware of consumerism! That's our tendency. It's the capitalistic curse that we were poisoned with. We should spend only what is necessary."
- "The capitalist model, the developed model, the consumer model which it has forced on the world, is falling apart on Earth, and there is no planet nearby that we can emigrate to."
- "The only way to save the world is through socialism, but a socialism that exists within a democracy; there's no dictatorship here."

I know these quotes sound like Democratic Socialists in the US. They're all quotes from Hugo Chávez.

And lest we forget:

- "Why do some people have to go barefoot so that others can drive luxury cars? Why are some people able to live only thirty-five years in order that others can live seventy years? Why do some people have to be miserably poor in order that others can be extravagantly rich? I speak for all the children in the world who don't even have a piece of bread."
- "The revenues of Cuban state-run companies are used exclusively for the benefit of the people, to whom they belong."
- "I think that a man should not live beyond the age when he begins to deteriorate, when the flame that lighted the brightest moment of his life has weakened."
- "I am a Marxist Leninist, and I will be one until the last day of my life."
- "One of the greatest benefits of the revolution is that even our prostitutes are college graduates."
- "I find capitalism repugnant. It is filthy, it is gross, it is alienating . . . because it causes war, hypocrisy, and competition."
- "Venezuela, given its extraordinary educational, cultural, and social developments, and its vast energy and natural resources, is called on to become a revolutionary model for the world."

These are all quotes from Cuban socialist leader Fidel Castro.

What does socialism have to do with it? Socialism just failed in Venezuela, adding to the many other Socialist failures from history: Cuba, the USSR (Union of Soviet Socialist Republics), China, Vietnam, North Korea, Nicaragua, Zimbabwe, Cambodia, Laos, and more. How many times do we have to learn this lesson? Socialism has worked in but one place: a textbook.

ECONOMICS

Economists are questioned about their ability to predict the future. For instance, CBO analyst Gloria Chen stated in 2018: "Consumers' expectations have generally outperformed professional forecasters' expectations in terms of explaining and forecasting the dynamics of inflation over the past two decades." This finding points to the challenge inherent with all economists in looking at the past to project the future.

Capitalism. Capitalism was best illustrated by Milton Friedman. In a classic description, Friedman described something as simple as a pencil in 1980:

> Look at this lead pencil. There's not a single person in the world who could make this pencil. Remarkable statement? Not at all. The wood from which it is made, for all I know, comes from a tree that was cut down in the state of Washington. To cut down that tree, it took a saw. To make the saw, it took steel. To make steel, it took iron ore. This black center—we call it lead but it's really graphite, compressed graphite—I'm not sure where it comes from, but I think it comes from some mines in South America. This red top up here, this eraser, a bit of rubber, probably comes from Malaya, where the rubber tree isn't even native! It was imported from South America by some businessmen with the help of the British government. This brass ferrule? I haven't the slightest idea where it came from. Or the yellow paint! Or the paint that made the black lines. Or the glue that holds it together. Literally, thousands of people cooperated to make this pencil. People who don't speak the same language, who practice different religions, who might hate one another if they ever met! When you go down to the store and buy this pencil, you are in effect trading a few minutes of your time for a few seconds of the time of all those thousands of people.

What brought them together and induced them to cooperate to make this pencil? There was no commissar sending out orders from some central office. It was the magic of the price system: the impersonal operation of prices that brought them together and got them to cooperate, to make this pencil, so you could have it for a trifling sum. That is why the operation of the free market is so essential. Not only to promote productive efficiency, but even more to foster harmony and peace among the peoples of the world.

Capitalism is the entrepreneurial spirit that enables such amazing inventions to come to fruition. It unleashes all people to work together.

Friedman, who has been dead for ten years, was a proponent of long-successful Capitalism. He wrote in 2001, "A look at the data is instructive. The effect of tax exemption and the enactment of Medicare and Medicaid on rising medical costs from 1946 to now is clear. According to my estimates, the two together accounted for nearly 60 percent of the total increase in cost. Tax exemption alone accounted for one-third of the increase in cost; Medicare and Medicaid, one-quarter."

In 1850, French economist Frédéric Bastiat wrote, "There is only one difference between a bad economist and a good one: the bad economist confines himself to the visible effect; the good economist takes into account both the effect that can be seen and those effects that must be foreseen." Milton Friedman called this "the seen versus the unseen." A great example is the economic effect of free healthcare under M4A, where the good economist foresees the demand created by something that's free.

Socialism. I chose Paul Krugman to focus on in this section because John Maynard Keynes has been dead for seventy years (famous for "Keynesian Economics"), and Krugman applies socialist ideas when analyzing economics for the *New York Times* (*NYT*). He faults the free market system for unfairness (his irony helps sell books, grabs headlines, and ultimately attracts eyeballs on the internet). He looks to Socialism to fix the results of Capitalism.

Krugman claims Obamacare works and that the alternative is to "Get Sick, Go Bankrupt and Die" (a 2018 article he penned for the *NYT*), in which he states, "The GOP [Republican Party] can't come up with an alternative to the Affordable Care Act because no such alternative exists." *"Wow, an economist thinks there's no alternative to Obamacare! I guess that settles it."* He claims Obamacare is the only solution to covering the millions of people with preexisting conditions; otherwise, death is the result.

Students in economics learn how supply and demand works, what metrics such as GDP mean, and the effects of rational human behavior. But those pushing for Obamacare and M4A jettison the basics to argue for changes contrary to known human behavior. Facts are misused to justify spending more, such as ignoring the natural effect of offering free healthcare and claiming that the system will be cheaper in the long run.

There is no question that a market-driven economy is better than socialism. Some economist predictions are rooted in truth (Friedman) while other predictions are rooted in rooting (Krugman).

FREE MARKET IN HEALTHCARE

"Free market" means the market is free to meet evolving consumer needs, without price fixing or rationing from government. The free market in healthcare means that healthcare entities get bigger over time due to their success. Hospitals consolidate, doctors aggregate, device companies get larger. Would GE Medical be as big under socialism? Would they be building MRI machines without the profit motive?

One bad outcome of being big is that the company name can be demolished by one incident. For example, an HMO went out of business in the 1990s because of errors in detecting cancer. Had the errors occurred in separate companies, perhaps those companies could have survived. But because three cases happened under one roof, the company's press was so bad it couldn't continue to operate. That may have been a good thing, but we'll never know. We must understand the outcome of Capitalism leading to larger companies, who may then be brought down. The market reacts and fixes the problem.

INNOVATION AND GOVERNMENT SPENDING

No one can predict innovation. When the market gets an internal grant to study a problem and find a solution, if it doesn't work, they stop doing research. How do you know when the government is not successful? It gets bigger.

A great example of Capitalism is the company and product that Walt Disney built. Disney thought about what customers wanted, and the result was a remarkable company that most of us appreciate. Would Disney exist under socialism? Do we want to find out?

Under M4A, with no profit motive in the market, innovation would need to come from government agencies like the National Institute of Health (NIH). But examples of government spending include studying why nearly three-fourths of adult lesbians are overweight; what makes goldfish feel sexy; a study that showed rats on cocaine prefer to listen to jazz music versus classical; that adults who binge-drink tend to be less mature than those who do not; and that people who watch reruns of old TV shows are happier.

Senator Rand Paul (R-KY) released his fourth annual 2018 Festivus edition of *The Waste Report* that showed the government's expenditures:

- $76 million to soldiers in the Somali National Army
- $650,000 to develop a drama series to air in Afghanistan
- $250,000 toward teaching Rwandan special-interest groups how to lobby

- $874,000 toward studying the sexual habits of quails on cocaine
- $76,000 toward blowing leaf blowers at lizards to study the impact of hurricanes
- $375,000 toward studying horse and donkey hunting on the ancient Anatolian Peninsula
- $200,000 toward bringing British social activists to the US
- $2,488,000 toward studying daydreaming
- $50,000 toward teaching female entrepreneurs in India how to "vlog"
- $15,000 toward the National Endowment for the Arts for a play titled *Stoned Prince*, a fictional opera about Prince Harry

I can already hear the counterargument, "But these expenditures have nothing to do with healthcare." That's true, but they do have to do with government (and that someone requested the money, someone approved it, and the money was spent), and there's no way such a body should be in charge of something as important as healthcare.

The waste highlighted in the report amounted to nearly $115 million. I can't even fathom the explanation of these endeavors like, "We need to know how quails would react," or "Daydreaming is an important part of life." I felt sick reading through the report. There is no way the government should handle anything new.

MEDICARE AS A SOLUTION

Medicare is popular today because it's mandatory. But a Kaiser Family Foundation survey showed 56 percent support M4A when the question was posed without mention of cost. When cost was mentioned, support was just 37 percent. If you were to ask a Medicare beneficiary today what they want, they don't want M4A to ruin what they already have because they paid into Medicare all their lives.

What is M4A? The concept is simple—expand Medicare eligibility to all. But when Medicare was passed in 1965, the program was envisioned to cover only the elderly, since they didn't have coverage available and were no longer employed in a job with insurance coverage.

By no means is Medicare free (or inexpensive) in 2021. There are premiums, deductibles, coinsurance, copays, and other costs:

MEDICARE PART	PREMIUM (MONTHLY)	DEDUCTIBLE	COINSURANCE	OTHER
A (HOSPITAL)	$0	$1,484	$371/DAY	COMPLICATED DEDUCTIBLE "BANK"
B (PHYSICIAN)	$149 (INCOME BASED)	$203	20% (NO LIMIT)	NO OUT-OF- POCKET MAXIMUM
D (DRUG)	$35 (PLAN/ INCOME BASED)	$445	25%	"DONUT HOLE"

Further, to cover what Medicare doesn't, there are various plans available in the market, with premiums that vary from $70 to $400 per month per person. So, Medicare is currently not free, nor has it ever been free. If it were free, an estimated $5,000 per person per year would be needed to come from tax or other sources to replace supplemental premiums and out-of-pocket expenses not covered by Medicare. Plus, Medicare is funded by taxes paid over the individual's working lifetime—2.9 percent of wages, split 50/50 with the employer, such that the noticed tax rate is 1.45 percent.

If the doctor or hospital makes more money (albeit seventy cents on the dollar, because M4A would pay less), then the attitude will be, "We deserve to do one more scan because we're underpaid by M4A." But it wouldn't have happened under the old system. Is it worth it? No one can say, but we do know more services will happen, and this cost will be borne by the system.

TODAY'S THIRD-PARTY PAYER EFFECT

Milton Friedman famously chastised healthcare in the US as being paid mostly by a third party. In 2001, Friedman pointed out:

Two simple observations are key to explaining both the high level of spending on medical care and the dissatisfaction with that spending. The first is that most payments to physicians or hospitals or other caregivers for medical care are made not by the patient but by a third party—an insurance company or employer or governmental body. The second is that nobody spends somebody else's money as wisely or as frugally as he spends his own. These statements apply equally to other OECD countries.

A key difference between medical care and the other technological revolutions [in other industries] is the role of government. In other technological revolutions, the initiative, financing, production, and distribution were primarily private, though government sometimes played a supporting or regulatory role. In medical care, government has come to play a leading role in financing, producing, and delivering medical service. Direct government spending on health care exceeds 75 percent of total health spending for fifteen OECD countries. The United States is next to the lowest of the twenty-nine countries, at 46 percent. In addition, some governments indirectly subsidize medical care through favorable tax treatment. For the United States, such subsidization raises the fraction of health spending financed directly or indirectly by government to more than 50 percent.

We have become so accustomed to employer-provided medical care that we regard it as part of the natural order. Yet it is thoroughly illogical. Why single out medical care? Food is more essential to life than medical care. Why not exempt the cost of food from taxes if provided by the employer? Why not return to the much-reviled company store when workers were in effect paid in kind rather than in cash?

The revival of the company store for medicine has less to do with logic than pure chance. It is a wonderful example of how one bad government policy leads to another. During World War II, the government financed much wartime spending by printing money while, at the same time, imposing wage and price controls. The resulting repressed inflation produced shortages of many goods and services, including labor. Firms competing to acquire labor at government-controlled wages started to offer medical care as a fringe benefit. That benefit proved particularly attractive to workers and spread rapidly. Initially, employers did not report the value of the fringe benefit to the Internal Revenue Service as part of their workers' wages. It took some time before the IRS realized what was going on. When it did, it issued regulations requiring employers to include the value of medical care as part of reported employees' wages. By this time, workers had become accustomed to the tax exemption of that particular fringe benefit and made a big fuss. Congress responded by legislating that medical care provided by employers should be tax-exempt.

Employer financing of medical care has caused the term 'insurance' to acquire a rather different meaning in medicine than in most other contexts. We generally rely on insurance to protect us against events that are highly unlikely to occur but that involve large losses if they do occur—major catastrophes, not minor, regularly-recurring expenses. We insure our houses against loss from fire, not against the cost of having to cut the lawn. We insure our cars against liability to others or major damage, not against having to pay for gasoline. Yet in medicine, it has become common to rely on insurance to pay for regular medical examinations and often for prescriptions.

This is partly a question of the size of the deductible and the copayment, but it goes beyond that. 'Without medical insurance' and 'without access to medical care' have come to be treated as nearly synonymous. Moreover, the states and the federal government have increasingly specified the coverage of insurance for medical care to a detail not common in other areas. The effect has been to raise the cost of insurance and to limit the options open to individuals. Many, if not most, of the 'medically uninsured' are persons who for one reason or another do not have access to employer-provided medical care and are unable or unwilling to pay the cost of the only kinds of insurance contracts available to them.

One clue is my estimate that if the pre-World War II system had continued—that is, if tax exemption and Medicare and Medicaid had never been enacted—expenditures on medical care would have amounted to less than half the current level, which would have put us near the bottom of the OECD list rather than at the top.

THE REAL COST OF M4A

Opponents of M4A argue that the $32.6 trillion federal budget cost increase because of Single Payer over the next ten years (per the Mercatus Center at George Mason University) is too much.

This $32.6 trillion figure is sometimes quoted as the cost of Single Payer. It is not; it's just the increase in the government portion. Further review of the Mercatus study shows that the total National Healthcare Expenditure, regardless of who pays for it, is projected to be fifty-eight trillion dollars over ten years (midpoint). And this figure is before dental and vision coverages were added to the bill.

The study has been misinterpreted to claim that M4A spending could be two trillion dollars lower than current spending (implying savings of 3 percent). However, the Mercatus study author dispels this thought by saying that this finding is false (based on an errant reading of the study) and that spending could be more than if no change was made because of free coverage.

Even proponents of M4A claim this $32.6 trillion is the total cost. So, opponents use this number to say M4A costs too much, while proponents are using the same number to imply it's not that bad. Both are wrong; it's $57.6 trillion. And I don't think either side really understands what over ten years even means.

Also, the Mercatus study heavily caveats its assumptions and projections, such that savings could easily result in negative savings (additional costs), should hospitals and doctors decline to serve patients below their cost.

Senator Sanders is playing the same game of misstating the numbers. He said on the 2020 campaign trail in June 2019: "The number $32 trillion is roughly probably right. That sounds like a lot of money, but do you know what happens if we keep the current system, which is the most wasteful and expensive system in the world? Estimates of the cost will be $50 trillion. Medicare for All will be less expensive than continuing the current dysfunctional healthcare system."

Hmm . . . so it looks like we can save $18 trillion, or 36 percent. "Awesome, let's do that!" Nope, that's $32 trillion of increased government spending versus a total cost of $50 trillion. He's employing the apple-versus-orange argument.

And there's no excuse for distorting the numbers. The misunderstanding of the Mercatus numbers by some doesn't allow them to misrepresent the numbers to imply tremendous savings. Since this is Bernie's plan, he should be explaining the numbers as clearly as possible. *"This really adds to earning my trust."*

Proposals for Single Payer have failed in every state that considered it. Vermont considered Single Payer until its state taxes were estimated at 21 percent. California's price tag was $400 billion—more than double the current cost of all of California's government, such that taxes would need to triple. The concept died in Colorado, Hawaii, Illinois, Massachusetts, New York, Ohio, Oregon, New York, and Pennsylvania.

The real question is, why would anyone suggest adding to the cost of healthcare when it's too high to begin with? We cannot make changes just because a politician or a think tank says it will save money. For example, President Obama infamously stated, "The typical

American family will save about $2,500/year under Obamacare." I'm sure there was someone "typical" out there who saved $2,500. But the word "typical" was being used to imply "average," which it was not. There might have been someone out there receiving the subsidy who benefited by $2,500, but that was rare.

And any claim to saving money begs the question, savings versus what? Many studies have shown cost increases rather than decreases. A 2016 Kaiser Family Foundation report showed that premiums have increased almost $5,000 per person since Obamacare was enacted! And because we've heard the Obamacare lie before, we will never believe a lie again.

HEALTHCARE IS NOT A RIGHT

There are many rights. The Declaration of Independence declares inalienable (absolute) rights as "life, liberty, and the pursuit of happiness." The list of potential rights is voluminous. A quick Google search produced some surprising "rights":

- Digital rights
- Elderly rights
- Parental rights
- Migrant rights
- Patent rights
- Criminal rights
- Animal rights
- Child rights
- Worker rights
- Patient rights
- Privacy rights
- Housing rights
- User rights

These are all real rights, but obviously the word "rights" gets misused, which diminishes basic rights. Such is the case with declaring that healthcare is a human right, as if it's then okay to violate others' rights in the process. No one can declare healthcare is a right to the extent that it violates another inalienable right. For example, declaring healthcare is a human right violates others' rights to their private property, which includes their labor. Solving one person's rights leads to creating another person's lack of rights.

One cannot declare that healthcare is a right because of need. Otherwise, that leads to declaring food, clothing, and shelter as rights. All are needed to have life, liberty, and the pursuit of happiness. Does the government need to provide food? At what level? John Stossel famously showed what would happen if food were free at the grocery store, where everyone would stock up with the finest meats you could buy.

What would a right to healthcare look like? Would it include all healthcare, regardless of expense? Would that include organ transplants? Would that include convenience, such as using the ER on the weekend instead of seeing the doctor on Monday? Would that include using an expensive drug that helps with a symptom, but does not fix the root problem?

I argue the answer to the question: "No, healthcare is not a right. It is a right to purchase insurance."

And the media fosters similar messages, for their own benefit. The media have been described as the fourth pillar of government (meaning their power is equivalent to a branch of government). On certain topics, they are as important, if not more so, than the other three—the executive, the legislative, and the judicial branches. For example, "the 1 percent" is now a household term, but "the 1 percent" has existed since the dawn of time. Never has the animosity toward the über-rich been so pronounced, and the media has a lot to do with that.

HEALTHCARE SHOULD BE FREE

"Wouldn't it be great? Shouldn't everyone get needed care, such that they would seek help no matter the injury? If only the cost of that 'stupid' insurance didn't prevent everyone from buying it."

"But if the richest population ever to live are the elderly (which I will discuss in Chapter 7), then the poorest are the millennials. They have nowhere near the resources to be able to afford expensive healthcare. They're just scraping by."

According to a 2017 study by Bankrate.com and conducted by Princeton Survey Research Associates International, average millennials eat out three times per week, and 29 percent say they buy coffee at least three times per week.

By comparison, average Americans are not spending on such things. Here's a summary:

COFFEES PURCHASED PER WEEK	MILLENNIALS	ALL AMERICANS
AT LEAST 3X	29%	
NONE		59%

DRINKING AT BARS PER WEEK	MILLENNIALS	ALL AMERICANS
AT LEAST 1X	51%	
NONE		73%

EATING OUT PER WEEK	MILLENNIALS	ALL AMERICANS
AT LEAST 3X	54%	
AT MOST 1X		40%

The purchase of healthcare is a priority for some. Undoubtedly, there are some poor people who would purchase healthcare if they could afford it. That's not the point. Providing to those who can afford healthcare premiums but who prioritize their purchases such that they buy other things first doesn't make sense. And since every group and person is different, there is no way the government should decide what level of healthcare everyone should have. Individuals should have the ability to make individual decisions for themselves.

Would millennials want to take 10 percent off the top of earnings to pay for healthcare for which some wouldn't purchase on their own? If it were free, sure, but what if it cost 10 percent off the top? Their answer would be no, because they want to make the decisions as to what they buy.

I'll continue with another fabricated conversation, this time with a Democratic Socialist:

I'm not talking about Venezuela. I'm talking about Scandinavia.

> Of course not. You like what the Venezuelan dictators did; what you don't like is the outcome. I'd call you crazy if you proposed anything that Venezuela did. So, yes, divert attention to another country.

We could have the nirvana that Scandinavia has.

> Scandinavia is more "nationalist" than the US. Over 90 percent of their population is white. They're not Socialist countries. And no one in the US wants to pay their high tax rates.

Why not?

> People already go to great lengths to save a dollar on their taxes. No one wants to pay any more than they must. If they did, they could already voluntarily pay more. No one does that.

But if we just paid a little more, we'd all be happier.

> Would we? That's like saying if we all lived like monks in the happiest country in the world—Bhutan, which is next to Nepal—we too could be happy.

Well, they're doing something right.

Scandinavia or Bhutan? If Bhutan, I'd want "proof of concept" first. So, let's see an area of the US (Vermont?) take up the monk lifestyle and see if it's successful.

I'm not talking about becoming a monk!

Okay, then let's become Scandinavia. Double our tax rates, but flatten the income tax bands. Their tax rates are more regressive than in the US.

We wouldn't have to double taxes. That's too high.

Then how much?

They tax about 50 percent more than in the US.

Okay, so if the average tax bill is $10,000, we just need to write a check for another $5,000. Not gonna happen.

Why not? Do you know what we could do with another $5,000 per person?

Who's we? I think it's outrageous when the government "needs" 5 percent more next year, let alone 50 percent. And Scandinavia has VAT (Value-Added Taxes) that we don't.

Don't you want things to be better?

Of course. But your "better," isn't.

Why not? We could take care of the poor, and everyone would have healthcare.

Everyone could have healthcare coverage, but if that coverage cost 50 percent more, would that be good overall? There is a law of diminishing returns.

How so?

Spending more doesn't buy happiness. There is a certain level of happiness that a base level buys, but throwing more dollars at something doesn't increase happiness—or at least, throwing more dollars at the problem results in a lesser increase in value.

Sure it does; more spending buys more happiness. And the government is better at spending than individuals, because the government doesn't just exist to make a profit. Its spending can consider other aspects of the public good.

Your argument is basically that Capitalism is bad because individual owners profit from doing business, and do not consider other aspects of the public good.

Yes. There's no question that's true.

No, it is not true. All businesses must create value for the consumer, so they consider the whole picture (not just money), or else the transaction doesn't happen.

"The goal of socialism is communism." –Vladimir Lenin, 1917

WE'RE #37!

"I would predict that in less than seven years, we'll be in a Single Payer system."

–Charles Krauthammer, 2017

WHO RANKINGS

In 2000, the World Health Organization infamously ranked the US the thirty-seventh country in the world in healthcare out of 191 countries. That's incredible! Here are the top fifty, on the following page.

WHO HEALTHCARE RANKINGS 2000			
COUNTRY	RANK	COUNTRY	RANK
FRANCE	1	SAUDI ARABIA	26
ITALY	2	UNITED ARAB EMIRATES	27
SAN MARINO	3	ISRAEL	28
ANDORRA	4	MOROCCO	29
MALTA	5	CANADA	30
SINGAPORE	6	FINLAND	31
SPAIN	7	AUSTRALIA	32
OMAN	8	CHILE	33
AUSTRIA	9	DENMARK	34
JAPAN	10	DOMINICA	35
NORWAY	11	COSTA RICA	36
PORTUGAL	12	UNITED STATES	37
MONACO	13	SLOVENIA	38
GREECE	14	CUBA	39
ICELAND	15	BRUNEI	40
LUXEMBOURG	16	NEW ZEALAND	41
NETHERLANDS	17	BAHRAIN	42
UNITED KINGDOM	18	CROATIA	43
REPUBLIC OF IRELAND	19	QATAR	44
SWITZERLAND	20	KUWAIT	45
BELGIUM	21	BARBADOS	46
COLOMBIA	22	THAILAND	47
SWEDEN	23	CZECH REPUBLIC	48
CYPRUS	24	MALAYSIA	49
GERMANY	25	POLAND	50

The rankings were based on five weighted factors:

- Average Health—25 percent
- Distribution or Equality Health—25 percent
- Average Responsiveness—12.5 percent
- Distribution or Equality Responsiveness—12.5 percent
- Fair Financial Contribution—25 percent.

These rankings point out the flaw in the study since "Equality" and "Fair Financial Contribution" account for over 60 percent of the weight. Dr. Scott Atlas, Senior Fellow at the Hoover Institute and former Coronavirus Task Force advisor, wrote a book in which he debunks the WHO rating (and many others have done the same). WHO's results shocked many experts, leading to various articles regarding the study's questionable methodology.

Why has there been no update in twenty years to the study? Quoting the ranking of thirty-seven continues, even though WHO declined to update their findings in 2010 (presumably due to the controversial nature of the study).

THE COMMONWEALTH FUND STUDY

The Commonwealth Fund (a nonprofit foundation) reported in 2017 that US healthcare compares poorly with ten other nations that were all judged to be superior to the US based on various factors, including cost and quality.

Let's put the results of these two studies together relative to each other.

COUNTRY	COMMONWEALTH FUND 2017	WHO 2000
UNITED KINGDOM	1	18
AUSTRALIA	2	32
NETHERLANDS	3	17
NEW ZEALAND	4	41
NORWAY	5	11
SWITZERLAND	6	20
SWEDEN	7	23
GERMANY	8	25
CANADA	9	30
FRANCE	10	1
UNITED STATES	11	37

Correlation between the two study rankings is just 8 percent, according to my analysis. Close to 0 percent means the two studies' results are uncorrelated.

So how can France be the best in the world out of 191 countries, according to WHO, yet tenth out of eleven countries in the Commonwealth Fund Study? Perhaps one study points to a flaw in the other study. But which study is flawed? Or are both flawed?

The main conclusion drawn by others from the Commonwealth Fund Study was that it confirmed the poor ranking for US healthcare. However, French researchers never wondered how France could be #1 according to WHO, yet second to last according to the Commonwealth Fund. If a country reacted to each study, a whiplash effect would result. And I can hear the researchers reply, "But that's what the data shows! Our study is right!"

Rather than compare the US healthcare system to the whole world, the Commonwealth Fund chose ten high-income OECD countries. But none of the countries are close in size to the US, as their relative size based on GDP is comparable to that of individual states:

COUNTRY	HAS GDP THE SIZE OF:
GERMANY	CALIFORNIA + 40%
ENGLAND (UK)	CALIFORNIA + 10%
FRANCE	CALIFORNIA
CANADA	TEXAS
AUSTRALIA	NEW YORK
THE NETHERLANDS	ILLINOIS
SWITZERLAND	OHIO
SWEDEN	NORTH CAROLINA
NORWAY	INDIANA
FINLAND	SOUTH CAROLINA
NEW ZEALAND	UTAH

Source: American Enterprise Institute (AEI)

These WHO and Commonwealth Fund researchers should know better, as they are:

- comparing results using data that's inconsistently calculated across countries
- comparing countries' outcomes for what they know are different populations
- comparing small countries to larger ones
- ignoring results that don't really make sense
- ignoring innovation while weighing equality high
- using GDP as context
- ignoring cancer outcomes (where the US is #1, while both Canada and the UK are in the bottom half of countries' success rates, according to the American Cancer Society)
- using subjective patient satisfaction data

But what do the researchers care? They got the convenient results they were looking for, and they can claim that they performed academic studies. And the media got a story they liked to report: that the US spends the most and gets little in return.

What if the fifty states in the US were separately ranked using these ranking systems? One might expect equality to be the same across all the states, since the healthcare systems are the same, but would results vary because of demographics? (They would, of course, because of the flawed methodology.) Would longevity vary because of race and ethnicity? Would large-state data have more credibility than small-state data? There would be so many issues that one might laugh at such a study.

Why do people flock to the US to use the healthcare system? Do they realize the system is #37 in the world? If they did, they shouldn't come here. What do they know that apparently the researchers—and Michael Moore, whose movie *Sicko* claims Cuba's healthcare system is better than that of the US—don't?

I separately correlated the WHO rankings with the dollars spent by the 191 countries on healthcare and found that spending more dollars hardly correlated with the WHO rankings. In other words, for a country to rise on the WHO rankings, more spending doesn't improve a country's ranking much. The reason is that spending (and efforts meant to improve health) have little to do with the WHO ranking health systems.

REPORTING

The 2000 WHO study, while overwhelmingly panned when it came out and ever since, remains an oft-quoted study as if it's true. And the quotes aren't just those from 2000 when the study was first released.

Did the faulty study lead to passage of Obamacare? We may never know for sure, but Professor Atlas, who wrote an article titled "The Worst Study Ever?: Exposing the scandalous methods behind an extraordinarily influential World Heath Report," stated:

> In October 2008, candidate Obama used the study to claim that "29 other countries have a higher life expectancy and 38 other nations have lower infant mortality rates." On June 15, 2009, as he began making the case for his health-care bill, the new president said: "As I think many of you are aware, for all of this spending, more of our citizens are uninsured, the quality of our care is often lower, and we aren't any healthier. In fact, citizens in some countries that spend substantially less than we do are actually living longer than we do."
>
> In fact, World Health Report 2000 was an intellectual fraud of historic consequence—a profoundly deceptive document that is only marginally a measure of health-care performance at all. The report's true achievement was to rank countries according to their alignment with a specific political and economic ideal—socialized medicine—and then claim it was an objective measure of quality.

The *Wall Street Journal* wrote about the WHO study in 2009, "Among all the numbers bandied about in the health-care debate, [the #37 ranking] stands out as particularly misleading." They quoted Dr. Philip Musgrove, WHO's editor-in-chief of the 2000 report, as saying that the figures are made-up numbers. Musgrove later wrote for the *Journal of New England Medicine*: "The number thirty-seven is meaningless. Analyzing the failings of health systems can be valuable; making up rankings among them is not. It is long past the time for this zombie number to disappear from circulation."

Reporting of these and other studies since 2000 have added to the fodder. *Time* claimed in 2014, "The US ranks worst among eleven wealthy nations in terms of 'efficiency, equity and outcomes' despite having the world's most expensive healthcare system." (This reflects on the results from the 2014 version of the Commonwealth Fund study.) The Commonwealth Fund also ranked the US last among six countries in 2007 and last among seven countries in 2010.

The Commonwealth Fund study shows up as the first item when googling "US Healthcare Quality." "*Apparently, the UK has found the solution that should lead all countries to the 'promised land.' Or is that France?*"

LIFE EXPECTANCY

A second line of attack for proponents of M4A is that the US has lower life expectancy than in other countries. Proof of this goes back to the 2000 WHO study. The argument goes something like this: "If health-care is of such high quality in the US, why isn't life expectancy higher than for other countries?" One answer is that the US has a high level of healthcare quality, but life expectancy would be even worse without it because the healthcare system significantly improves longevity of very poor-health citizens. Imagine what US life expectancy would be without the world's greatest healthcare innovations?

This life expectancy comparison is just correlation, not causation. The thinking is that healthcare leads to (causes) longer lives, which is true, but to measure life expectancy across different populations and suggest one country has better healthcare than another is silly. A study would need to show the effects of healthcare, before and after, and there has never been such a study (nor should there be, as there would need to be a control group of people denied access to any healthcare in each country of the study).

Here are a few of the issues with using life expectancy as a crude indicator of health:

- Each country measures lives (and deaths) differently, so comparisons are flawed. For example, in the US, doctors attempt to save premature babies born under one pound while some other countries don't even count those cases as live births. So, this adds to US healthcare expense and lowers life expectancy.

- The US outperforms every other country in cancer and heart disease treatment. To be best in two major categories of care, yet to have lower life expectancy, shows that the average life span is not a good measure of the healthcare system but of many other factors.

- Life expectancy is not a measure of healthcare system efficiency, as not every healthcare intervention is intended to extend one's life. Many times, treating of symptoms becomes the focus (such as pain medication).

Dr. Atlas questioned the #37 WHO ranking in his book *In Excellent Health: Setting the Record Straight on America's Health Care*. The WHO's ranking was based on two flawed measures in the study: life expectancy and infant mortality. "Life expectancy at birth in 2003 was greatest in Japan at 81.8 years compared with 77.2 years in the United States; yet, the life expectancy of Asia Pacific Island Americans was 81.5 years (in 2001), even though those Americans have the same health care system as other U.S. citizens."

Further, "When combined with the far larger burden of smoking in Americans traced to the period between 1945 and 1985 when the United States had the highest per adult consumption of cigarettes of the OECD countries; the evidence of higher disease prevalence in the United States; the far higher rates of death from causes entirely unrelated to health care in the United States compared to other countries; and clear trends demonstrating that population obesity is also more adverse in the United States than in other developed countries."

The WHO study uses questionable weights to adjust each country's reported data, ranking US healthcare below Greece (#14) and Morocco (#29), with Slovenia (#38) and Cuba (#39) just behind the US. As Dr. Atlas sums up, "Garbage in, garbage out."

So the media readily compares life expectancy because it shows the US is poor by this measure. However, when adjusted for fatal injuries (deaths from homicides, suicides, car accidents), which have nothing to do with the healthcare system, US life expectancy is #1 (according to a study by Robert Ohsfeldt of Texas A&M and John Schneider of the University of Iowa).

Even though doctors have little ability to control the health of patients, the blame for America's health targets the healthcare system. If you think doctors should be measured on their ability to control behavior, think of their ability to influence patients in smoking, eating, exercise, stress, genes, air and water quality, and sex. There is no question the US life expectancy would be much lower without the successes of the US healthcare system.

INFANT MORTALITY

A separate WHO study ranked the US forty-first in infant mortality in 2011. But as Scott Atlas wrote in a 2012 article, "Infant and neonatal mortality rates are complex, multifactorial end points that oversimplify heterogeneous inputs, many of which have no relation to health care at all. Moreover, these statistics gleaned from the widely varied countries of the world are plagued by inconsistencies, problematic definitions, and gross inaccuracies, all of which disadvantage the ranking of the U.S., where accuracy is paramount."

Another major factor is the diversity in the US, as Dr. Atlas noted: "Throughout the developed world, and regardless of the health-care system, infant-mortality rates are far worse among minority populations, and the U.S. has much more diversity of race and ethnicity than any other developed nation."

The bottom line is that the comparison of infant mortality rates is so flawed as to be worthless, and infant mortality has little to do with the healthcare system.

But the government won't charge more for profit from something like, for instance, selling gas so cheaply that more use harms the environment. It can consider the big picture as a limited resource that is owned by all, not just one individual.

So what you're saying is that the government would not have allowed the sale of gas-guzzling cars in the past hundred years.

Exactly. That wouldn't have happened because the people running the government wouldn't have allowed decisions to sell big cars.

But would those government employees have had any more information than the actual sellers and buyers of cars in the past hundred years?

No, but they would care more. They would make different decisions.

But the consumer demand for those larger cars would be the same. So, something else would have to change—either the price would increase, or fewer/smaller cars would be purchased, both of which would negatively impact the economy.

There it is! Not everything should be measured by how it affects the economy. Money is only one aspect to consider, and government can consider other important factors. Look at where Europe is: they have high gas prices and smaller cars, including Smart cars.

But Europe has smaller cars not just because of the price of gas. Europe is more populated than the US, and Europeans choose smaller cars due to other factors, including culture. Had the US government either regulated gas prices or the size of cars to be sold in the US, consumers would have been dissatisfied. The result would have been bad both for the economy and for the happiness of the people.

But Europeans drive smaller cars and therefore have less carbon emissions. They care more about the environment and less about their own profit than Americans.

Do they really care more, or do they buy smaller cars because they have shorter distances to travel and less room for parking? And their gasoline taxes are through the roof. Culturally, they approach life differently.

But think of the efficiency of riding bikes like in Amsterdam, not to mention convenient public transportation, where there are lower emissions and much happier people.

Bikes are not efficient for traveling in most of the US, so that's a silly comparison. Any solutions you propose need to make sense, and not just for one city like New York in the summer, where one could travel by bike. The trade-off would be the lack of safety in "trying to be more like the Europeans." Culturally, Americans have larger cars because we drive more for longer distances and generally don't have convenient public transportation. And even if we did, would we use it?

Americans just need to get used to using public transportation. You already see it in large cities where some people don't even own a car.

Again, what a silly thought. Just because there are a few cities in the US where public transportation may make sense (due to cost to travel, store, insure, etc.) does not suggest this would work throughout the US. As I showed earlier, Denmark is four times denser than the US (population per mile).

But you must admit we could attain the same level of happiness as in Scandinavia.

No, I don't. You moving there would be less disruptive—try that first and report back. I'll take it under advisement.

You won't change. I know you.

Okay, you're right.

"If you think healthcare is expensive now, wait until you see what it costs when it's free." –P.J. O'Rourke, 1993

7

GREED IS GOOD

"Back in the thirties we were told we must collectivize the nation because the people were so poor. Now we are told we must collectivize the nation because the people are so rich."

–William F. Buckley, 1959

GREED

I must start with this classic quote from Gordon Gekko in the 1987 movie *Wall Street*:

"Greed, for the lack of a better word, is good. Greed is right; greed works. Greed clarifies, cuts through, and captures the essence of the evolutionary spirit. Greed, in all of its forms—greed for life, for money, for love, knowledge—has marked the upward surge of mankind."

Humans are all greedy. We desire to have nice things because they make life better (besides the basic elements of self-preservation and reproduction). Better wording would be "Self-interest is consistent." That doesn't have the same outrageousness to it, and it's not what Gordon Gekko said. But it points out that we are all greedy, or self-motivated, and "good" is a vague word that is more accurately, "consistent." "Self-interest" is not always "selfish."

"Greed" is a funny word, thrown around as being evil; yet it describes a basic human emotion. The *Merriam-Webster Dictionary* defines *greed* as "a selfish and excessive desire for more of something (such as money) than needed." We likely all agree that "more than needed" is excessive. But "excessive" is difficult to measure, and should be measured in the eye of the beholder. I'll add the term for those accusing others of greed as being jealous. A less charged word is "envious."

Here are some classic situations of greed, and my response with solutions:

- Wall Street is greedy. *Then invest in Wall Street stocks and benefit from it.*

- Stock ownership is greedy. *But as Ben Stein says, "Pension funds are owned by widows and orphans."*

- CEOs are greedy. *Boards of directors would pick a lower-paid CEO if they could, so the CEO must be worth it.*

- Doctors are greedy. *Then go see someone else.*

- The pie is limited, so the more you take, the less there is for everyone else. *Then expand the pie.*

- Martin Shkreli, the CEO who increased the price of the EpiPen by 500 percent, should be in jail. *Different company, same issue.*

Shkreli, CEO of Turing Pharmaceuticals, is in jail for seven years for unrelated securities fraud. The EpiPen is made by Mylan Pharmaceuticals, whose CEO is Heather Bresch (daughter of Democratic Senator Joe Manchin). The company is public, so anyone could invest and reap the benefit of this overcharging. Unreported is the fact that generic alternatives have come on the market (albeit years later) for a discounted price of just ten dollars.

• Lottery winners are lucky. *Then don't play.*

Some claim Capitalism is "greed of the individual." I claim Socialism is "greed of the collective." *"I want to get something, but I don't want to appear to be greedy."*

Then there's economist Thomas Sowell's take: "Someone pointed out that blaming economic crises on greed is like blaming plane crashes on gravity. Certainly, planes wouldn't crash if it wasn't for gravity. But when thousands of planes fly millions of miles every day without crashing, explaining why a particular plane crashed because of gravity gets you nowhere. Neither does talking about greed, which is constant like gravity."

IT'S THE RICH

We envy the rich and pity the poor. Some who claim, "It's the rich," think a rich person takes their money. But a rich person creates their money, and that improves the lives of all. If Warren Buffett creates a company that meets the needs of people, he benefits, and so do they. The consumer wins, the investor who invests in Buffett's company wins, Buffett's employees win. Should we be mad at Buffett for winning? For profiting? Why do some even think like this?

Should I be mad at the profiteer who thought of Uber? Of Airbnb? Of Expedia? Of Google Maps? Of Zoom? Of Amazon? Of Netflix? Of Facebook?

Mentioning Netflix reminds me of a hilarious connection made by John Stossel (Stossel cites Sean Malone): "Blockbuster's demise began when it charged a man named Reed Hastings $40 in late fees. That annoyed him so much, he started a subscription-based, mail-order movie rental company he called 'Netflix.'"

No rich person ever said, "Yes, I'm greedy." Others assigned that trait to the rich. Along the same lines, since I'm not part of the class of billionaires, I'll assign a trait to those who have made it: guilty. Not guilty in the normal sense of the word, but guilt-laden about being rich.

Income has always been taboo. No one wants to talk about how much they make, be it high or low. Along comes the government with their proxy rule for a company's annual report of the top five earners. Out trot the media commenting about someone who makes $20 million a year to help them sell newspapers (or TV airtime). But is this information ever put into context?

The guilt associated with all that wealth leads the rich to announce that they will "give it away" before they die. Don't get me wrong, I recognize their altruism. But I also recognize that part of their focus—after supposedly being greedy all those years during the accumulation stage, and after being beaten up for being rich for so long—their next endeavor is to cave to the demands of those on the left that they give it all back. That leads to philanthropic endeavors that provide positive feelings. *"Besides, what else should they do—continue to be greedy?"*

Some argue socialism changes these typically selfish people to be generous. But is it selfish that Socialists want what other people get from the healthcare system? And want it for free? Odd that those who espouse socialism live in capitalist countries.

Some argue about the broken market for executives. "It's mostly the Good 'Ol' Boys club (not necessarily boys, but mostly) who only keep their friends in high-paying jobs."

What happens in board rooms is secretive for reasons that go beyond executive pay (like direction of the company, products, and so on). But that doesn't mean the board is being secretive to spend more money on their friends. There are numerous pay-equity surveys that they review to make sure the company pays enough to attract talent, but less than necessary. Much research goes into the value proposition that the CEO generates for the company.

"There's the problem: surveys lead to all executives getting paid more!" Really? Why hire the three million dollar person if a one million dollar person could do the same job? Very few people are cut out to be executives who make speeches to hundreds or thousands of people, talk to investors (calls with hundreds of people, including the media), and make numerous decisions that make or break the company. Think about it: there's a reason one person is successful while another is begging for money on the street. You know it, but some want to vilify the rich and sympathize with the poor. Does that mean the poor person is more moral or worth valuing on this new scale they've created? That money is not the means by which to judge, but pity is?

Why do we look at the rich and poor with blinders on? Why can't we realize some no-name rich person was successful and deserved the money they accumulated? Why can't we realize the homeless person led an unsuccessful life that led to where they are? Do we have to be there every step of the way to be convinced of the success or failure of their whole lives?

GUILT

There are those who claim they are above others by claiming they aren't greedy themselves; that they have reached the pinnacle of Maslow's self-actualization. They chastise others for not achieving the level they claim to have reached.

There is no question as to praiseworthiness when the rich give away their wealth before they die. But when did they turn into Mother Teresa? Ten years ago? Does giving away your money mean you're above profiting and are now altruistic? What about those still profiting, even as they make these promises?

Some of the rich change once they have attained their wealth and feel guilty for being rich. They give their money away (think, foundations) and chastise those below them for trying to climb the rungs of the ladder they've already reached. Altruism becomes the code in which to value people.

But rich people who promise to give away their money really plan to give away 95 percent, providing first for their family and themselves. They have attained such a level of wealth that they can give away millions and still have enough to live well. But that doesn't put them at a level to tell what others should do, whether equally wealthy or less so.

In 1986, Warren Buffett told *Fortune Magazine* that he wanted to leave his children "enough money so that they would feel they could do anything, but not so much that they could do nothing."

Must we take altruistic direction from the rich? What about rich sports figures, who negotiate contracts for one hundred million dollars? Or entertainers who make twenty million dollars for one show (a two-thousand-to-one ratio of the highest-paid to the lowest-paid person involved in the show)?

The *Merriam-Webster Dictionary* defines *guilt* as "feelings of deserving blame, especially for imagined offenses or from a sense of inadequacy."

Further, people seem to think that money solves all problems. They think CEOs have it easy. CEOs may be "the boss" of their company, but ultimately "the boss" is always the customer. Every CEO—one way or the other—works for the customer. If they don't, the customer buys from another company, and uses that CEO's company.

WE LIVE LIKE KINGS

In the era of distinctly seeing ourselves, there's an awful lot of complaining out there. The complaint is that someone is doing better compared to someone else. What are we complaining about? The less there is to complain about, the angrier some people get, it seems. But comedian Bill Bailey says, "The way we live in the West, we live like kings."

Kings of the past had wealth due to heritage. We have wealth by working. And we have it better than, say, King Henry VIII, as we have more to choose from. Here is a comparison of what the average US citizen has versus this King:

	KING HENRY VIII	AVERAGE US PERSON
FOOD		
AMOUNT	UNLIMITED	LIMITED BY $
WHO	CASTLE CHEF	ANY RESTAURANT
VARIETY	LIMITED	UNLIMITED
SERVANTS	MANY	ONLY WITH MONEY
CLOTHING		
STYLE	COMPLEX	SIMPLE
VARIETY	LITTLE	MANY OPTIONS
SHELTER		
BUILDING	CASTLE	HOME
LOCATION	CASTLE	WORLD
ENVIRONMENT	POOR	HEATING, COOLING, INDOOR PLUMBING
HEALTHCARE		
WHO	KING'S DOCTOR	VARIETY
WHERE	CASTLE	CALL AN AMBULANCE
SUCCESS	MANY DISEASES	ELIMINATED MANY DISEASES
COST	FREE	PAY FOR INSURANCE
TRAVEL		
MODE	HORSE AND CARRIAGE	CARS, AIRPLANES
LOCATION	TYPICALLY WITHIN 100 MILES	THE WORLD

ENTERTAINMENT		
DRAMA	PLAYS	PLAYS, MOVIE THEATERS
COMEDY	COURT JESTER	TV, YOUTUBE, PODCASTS
GAMES	CHESS	APPS
LIFE		
LENGTH	55 YEARS	79 YEARS AVERAGE
OTHER		
INTERNET	NO	YES

Source: Author's Analysis

King Henry VIII couldn't drink the water, so he drank alcohol all the time (wine, ale). We have clean tap water (hot, cold), clean bottled water from below the surface of the Earth, and the ability to distill water even from the ocean.

And what if you wanted spices and produce today? Go to the grocery store. Back five hundred years ago? Go to war to get those things.

And what if the court jester wasn't funny? Off with his head. Today you go to a different show. Or you change the channel.

We don't die today from botulism. Or polio. Or smallpox. Just eighty years ago, people couldn't get body scans or chemo treatment. Somehow, those are now bad, because not everyone can afford them?

In addition, the whole world benefits from more wealth and higher incomes. This graph is so incredible, I repeat it here (from Chapter 2):

THE MOST IMPORTANT CHART IN THE WORLD

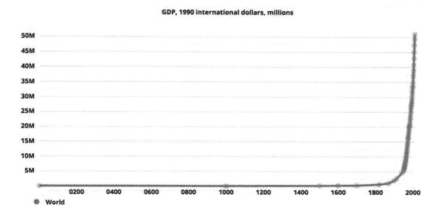

Source: Angus Maddison

As I've said, the key to statistics is context. Even if we have more prosperity than anyone in the world has ever had, but we compare ourselves to the next guy, we can find something to complain about. The chart above shows the "absolute" versus comparing to those nearby, the "relative." We have no contrast with the world—even though we have more information at our fingertips, few people watch the news to appreciate the differences between the US and other countries.

And it's amazing to see such narcissism at a time when "wokeness" is pervasive. One would think people living a hundred years ago would not understand what was going on around the world and would only appreciate the local world they see. Instead, it seems to be the opposite. How could that be? Is it possible that as we become more narcissistic, we divert attention to other traits so that we appear to be altruistic?

What if we questioned Capitalism in 1950 the way we do today? We would have missed out on the most amazing part of the curve. Just because we can't see the future, we again are asking ourselves whether Capitalism is the best way. We will know what the future holds in another fifty years.

What is it about being successful that people feel the need to compare themselves to, say, the Beverly Hillbillies who struck oil? *"I make a good living, but not as much as them."* We desire context for how we're doing, and instead of being satisfied with our position in life, we need to be #1. *"What, you won the second-place lottery prize of $250,000, and you're disappointed you were only one number away from winning the $100 million grand prize? So even though we make a good living, we declare our living could have been better?"*

And our inventions have helped everyone, more so for those with less wealth. Modern plumbing, television, clothing, supermarkets—those things benefit all of us, not just the rich.

And who says we should all have the same healthcare? Would that include that we all have the same shelter, food, everything in Maslow's chart? Where does the line get drawn?

Further, for those who move up the hierarchy to need something on a higher order, they should be more understanding of those who have not moved up to the same order. In other words, Mother Teresa reached a higher order beyond everyone, but she understood that no one else had the same values. That also exemplified the higher order of her need—something that many individuals appear incapable of, as if they need approval, saying, "Look at me!"

The richest population in the world are those over age sixty-five; they're richer than any other cohort. And they're richer than any generation in history. Median, too, not just mean. Does that mean we should envy the aged? Isn't it "too early" in our lives to compare to those over sixty-five when we won't have something to compare ourselves to for many years? What makes us so envious that some respond to the elderly, "Okay, Boomer"?

We have cell phones that can show video from the other side of the world; movies that stream on demand; stores that have countless options in what we call "convenience stores;" app stores with every game and music we can imagine—prosperity everywhere we look.

As Swedish Physician Hans Rosling famously said during a TED Talk, his grandmother was so amazed at her first washing machine that she watched it like it was a TV show "through the little window." Can't we realize that our lives allow us to do the things beyond what people a hundred years ago could only dream of? Somehow, we're mad that someone "took all that wealth" out of the economy, so there's none left?

One must wonder why such an incredible improvement in the world has occurred in the past two hundred years. Is it socialism, which led to control of the population for much of history? Or Capitalism, which has blossomed throughout the United States and some other countries? How is this even a question, with all the smart people we have today?

THE 1 PERCENT

"The 1 percent" has become the new term for the greedy group. People claim they don't belong to the 1 percent such that it's become a badge of honor to be part of the 99 percent.

Is it better to be altruistic, or to push others to be altruistic? Realize, though, that before pushing others to be altruistic one needs to be altruistic in one's own life; otherwise, hypocrisy results.

Most wealthy people are not greedy. It's important to realize this as the animosity toward the 1 percent is growing to such a ridiculous level and that only leads to damage, both mentally and physically. The 1 percent have worked hard to get where they are and will continue to work hard, which is important to helping others.

How can it be that the contemporary goals of giving to others have led to less giving? With giving heralded as a desirable trait, people are becoming more self-absorbed. Are we saying one thing and doing another?

And this categorization of the 1 percent is silly. There was a 1 percent group in the year 1000; there will be a 1 percent group in 3000 with no gains made toward this "made up" categorization of the 1 percent, because there will always be 1 percent of them.

There is likely little anyone can do to counter this thinking. Suffice it to say that we should all think a little deeper, that we shouldn't draw conclusions from what we hear in media, and that we should hold off judging until we have all the facts about a subject.

Do you view profits as getting something for nothing or what motivates every person in the world to produce? Profit motivates the market while creating work motivates the government. Which is better? Profit leads to wanting to develop solutions to people's problems. Government work leads to red tape.

Here's a favorite quote (from the song "I Wanna Be Rich" by Calloway):

"I spend my money on lottery, my fav'rite number is one, two, three."One more (from the song "I'd Love to Change the World" by Ten Years After): "Tax the rich, feed the poor / 'Til there are no rich no more."

There is a real problem in society with one side painted as worthy and the other vilified. Here are my examples of the "good" and the "bad":

THE GOOD	THE BAD
INDIVIDUAL	CORPORATIONS
POOR	RICH
THE 99%	THE 1%
SMALL	LARGE
UNDERDOG	OVERDOG
GOOD	EVIL
WORKER	EXECUTIVE
ALTRUISM	SELF-INTEREST

The problem with defining each group as either good or bad is that no group is black or white, but shades of gray. Just because a company is large doesn't mean it's bad; nor is a company good because it is small. With the application of this simplistic structure, the individual can do no wrong, yet corporations can do no right.

It's insightful to consider that half of all people work for large companies:

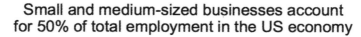

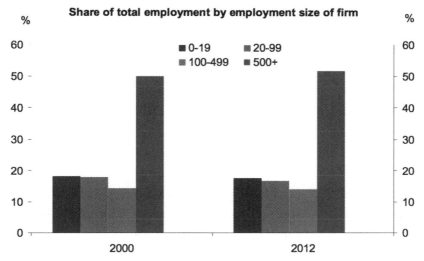

Source: Census, DB Global Markets Research

This means that half of all people work for small companies, half for large. Both are important to society (and are more of a continuum of size than implied by this chart that categorizes by company size). Large companies are important in that they bring economies of scale to the market that smaller companies cannot.

COMPANY SIZE AND GOUGING

No matter what large companies do, however, they're often perceived as gouging the market because the efficiencies they create are "not used to reduce prices and appear to only benefit their stockholders." Then they're vilified if they share the savings with customers through lower prices because they have lower prices with which the mom-and-pop shops cannot compete (think Walmart, placing them in the category of "damned if you do, damned if you don't").

Many states have enacted anti-gouging laws, which are meant to curb price increases during disasters. The premise is that it's heartless to charge someone in need an outrageous price. My complaint results from the unintended consequences that result from these "well-meaning" politicians.

But one positive of gouging is that it keeps the item available for those who really need it (besides eliminating long lines). If a flashlight's price doubles during a catastrophe, I may skip buying it because I already have one, so the flashlight is still available to someone who really needs it. If they're not willing to pay double, they may not really need it. That's a good thing, not bad.

Another positive is that high prices signal to the market to "bring more supply" to the disaster area, causing the high price-gouging to be temporary. Without it, no one would drive a thousand miles to bring generators to those in need (which happened during Hurricane Katrina with generators, among other items). Every summer, the price of gasoline goes up due to greater demand. Is this gouging?

The same is true with healthcare: for example, the EpiPen fiasco where prices were perceived by consumers to gouge. Patent law allowed the drug maker to get away with the gouging. So, laws should be written to prevent the problem, yet avoiding unintended consequences.

Equally unfair, there is a perception that large companies do not share efficiencies with their employees through pay and benefits. But chastisement of large companies happens when they compete for employees by paying more or offering benefits that smaller companies cannot afford. No matter what the situation, transactions (employees, customers) are segmented to use the arguments twice.

If large corporations are always deemed bad, that would mean individuals would win any lawsuit against a corporation, regardless of merits of the case. We see this thinking not only in court, but in the media when contemplating the merits of Single Payer. The result is that everyone must have coverage at all costs, and taxing corporations is a positive (even though the consumer ultimately pays the tax through higher costs). This suffers from the concept of the "seen" (bad corporations get taxed) versus "the unseen"—"good individuals" ultimately pay the tax.

WHY DIDN'T AMAZON PAY INCOME TAX IN 2018?

A classic example is the vilification of Amazon for not paying taxes. A major reason for Amazon not paying taxes is that they lost money in many years before 2018. Amazon made more in one quarter at the end of 2017 than it had cumulatively made since inception.

Why should a company pay taxes just because an arbitrary accounting measure is employed (the year), where, as an example, a company can lose money for four straight years, then make money in the fifth year? If that was my company, I'd be willing to pay taxes in year five if the government would pay part of my losses the other four years. Obviously, that isn't the tax rule because then I could get the government to fund my losing ideas.

The point is, there are rules that establish how much a company owes according to income tax legislation. Leave the analysis of those rules to professional tax accountants, not the media, and certainly not politicians. Unfortunately, numerous articles agreed with the politicians. My analysis is different from the knee-jerk reaction of, "It doesn't make sense that Amazon avoided paying any income tax."

The arguments that Amazon avoided paying taxes obfuscate what's really going on. Those arguments were:

- The Republicans' tax cut in 2017, where the corporate tax rate changed from 35 to 21 percent (which has been claimed to "slash Amazon's potential tax burden"—notice the word "potential" is meaningless, as the difference is 14 percent of income, so Amazon still would pay 21 percent)

- Tax credits for R&D investment
- Tax credits for stock-based employee compensation

The claim that Amazon got a "tax credit for stock-based employee compensation" is misleading. Had Amazon paid the $4 billion in cash (like regular pay) instead of stock-based employee compensation, they still would have received a credit as an expense of the business. Amazon employees would have been taxed on that pay immediately. No one would have chastised Amazon for paying employees more, but offering stock-based compensation helped their employees (647,000 of them).

Instead, the stock awards (which vest after five years of employment) encourage employees to be "owners" of the corporation. If they benefit by exercising those options and later sell them, the government taxes the income and ultimately receives what it would otherwise have received, plus taxes on any growth in the value of the stock. So, there is no difference in the taxes Amazon pays, and a small difference in what employees ultimately pay. Much ado about nothing.

CHARITY

I love when some billionaire says we should all pay more taxes. You first. What's stopping you from sending more into the government in taxes? And why do you take advantage of "loopholes" and spend tons of money on the best consultants to figure out how to do that?

Any billionaire's foundation's donation of billions pales in comparison to the billionaire's company's trillion-dollar benefit to the world, not to mention all the employees who benefited from the company. But we can't measure that, so we focus on the billions they plan to give away.

The US is the most charitable country in the world. According to the Charities Aid Foundation, the US population gave 1.4 percent of GDP to charity in 2016, while the second highest percentage was New Zealand at 0.79 percent. So what more needs to be given? The rest?

The rest that wasn't taxed? Some in government go so far as to call those "tax expenditures."

TAX EXPENDITURES

What the heck is a tax expenditure? Are politicians claiming that what didn't get taxed is an expenditure? According to that, the 50 percent I keep must be an expenditure. That's some pretty fanciful thinking!
Let's discuss tax expenditures:

- Employment-based healthcare deductions ($250 billion in 2012, per the CBO and Joint Commission on Taxation)
- Pension and 401(k) tax treatment ($160 billion)
- Home interest deductions ($70 billion)
- Earned income tax credits ($60 billion)
- Charitable contributions ($40 billion)
- Capital gains tax rates (included above)
- Obamacare tax credits (not measured)

There are those in politics who argue these tax expenditures cause much of the federal deficit, and their elimination alone would balance the budget—like saying, "If you just paid more, the deficit would go away." Only in Washington, DC.

Back by popular demand, it's a constructive discussion with a Democratic Socialist:

The rich are richer today than ever.

So are the poor.

But the poor could be better off. Do you not want to see them do better?

Of course; don't accuse me of that. As I pointed out earlier, John F. Kennedy stated that "A rising tide lifts all boats."

You just like the yachts to be raised. And the small boats that the masses live in are sinking.

That's not true. Haven't the poor always been poor?

So you don't want to help them?

I do. The system incents the poor to move up. Census Bureau data from 2018 showed this; as the middle class shrunk by 12 percent over the last fifty years, the lower class shrunk by 9 percent, while the highest class—households making $100,000 plus in constant dollars—increased by 21 percent.

That data shows there's still 28 percent of households making under $35,000 per year. How can this group afford healthcare?

By that thinking, how can they afford food, clothing, or shelter? They need Universal Basic Income to guarantee they're in the middle class. Let's see, that would only cost about a trillion dollars every year.

That doesn't sound like that much.

If it means a lot to each person, then it's a lot in total. You can't claim it means a lot to an individual but somehow that's not a lot in total. It's either a lot to both or neither.

But large corporations are the ones making all the money. It's not the poor.

Corporations are just people; they're not the devil. They're not the cause of people being poor.

Yes, they are. They make more, and people make less.

Under a fixed pie. Get all you can if the pie is fixed. But corporations are greater than the sum of their parts. They do more than the sum of what each individual can do.

That makes no sense. Every dollar a rich person makes comes from a poor person.

Maybe corporations shouldn't exist so that no one profits unnecessarily. That'll do it.

That's not what I'm talking about. The rich can get richer, just not at the expense of the poor.

They don't get richer at the expense of the poor. Do you even understand basic economics?

I do, enough to understand what's really going on. The rich get richer at the expense of almost everyone else. Three people own more than 50 percent of the population. Does that make any sense?

What should they own? Would you feel better if it were the top ten or twenty people? In 2016 you complained the top twenty people owned more than half the population. However, since 40 percent of the population had negative net worth, the average person also had more wealth than 40 percent of the population! What if one person owned more than 25 percent of the population? Would that be acceptable to you? What would be acceptable?

I can't answer that. But it's too high. I'm talking about Bill Gates, Jeff Bezos, and Warren Buffett. They're not Gordon Gekko types.

Does that matter?

The point is, there should be no billionaires.

So we need a floor and a ceiling? No billionaires, just everything happening the same without $250 billion in wealth being taken by three people. Instead, it's likely their companies wouldn't exist without them: no employees making money, no investors, no products. Thanks.

No, they can still make millions.

How could you possibly create enough rules for your idyllic world to happen?

I would just tax their wealth. My new plan covers it. See, problem-solution.

Let's see what unintended consequences would occur: billionaires move their companies to countries that don't tax wealth (most countries do not). Billionaires will be less incented to do well. We'll never be able to tell what impact this might have.

At least my plan will try to do something about the problem.

But it will make it worse. So much for trying. And confiscating wealth is a bad principle to start.

I'm not confiscating wealth. Why do you misname what my plan does?

Why do you misname what your plan does? It's like the name "Democratic Socialist:" an oxymoron. A wealth tax confiscates wealth.

It does not. It's just a tax.

A tax on what? We already tax consumption and income. What else can a wealth tax be called?

Why be so concerned about what something gets called? We have taxes in this country; it's just another tax. What do you care? You'll never pay it.

Nice. So, unless I'm part of the group who gets taxed, I can't have an opinion? Why not?

You can't be worried about what those bastards have to pay in tax, can you?

Brilliant. If we all just put on our blinders, we can do whatever we want to others.

Nice. So, now you're concerned for the billionaires?

I'm concerned for what it does to our economy. And what it does to fellow Americans. You can't just tax groups because they're too small to have a voice.

Are you kidding me? The Fat Cats control government decisions and have gotten fat from Capitalism. Their wealth was stolen and could be put to better use by the hard-working average citizens of this country.

Your name calling implies ill-gotten gains, as if certain people have taken from other people unfairly.

"We worship success, but we hate successful people."
–Michael Levin, 2018

HEALTHCARE JUST COSTS WAY TOO MUCH

"[Socialists] promise the blessings of the Garden of Eden, but they plan to transform the world into a gigantic post office."

–Ludwig von Mises, 1944

BASICS OF SUPPLY AND DEMAND

I don't want to provide an Economics 101 review course on supply and demand. Healthcare supply and demand forces are like those in other industries. There are some overriding themes helpful to consider in corralling healthcare costs through competition, though.

Some claim healthcare is different. They think healthcare

providers have some magical methods such that more providers cause more demand for their services. They argue that doctors can spend more time with patients, and that leads to higher charges. Today, this may be true where lack of competition doesn't encourage efficiency. It's true that more providers add to the number of mouths to feed—same as with any product or service. However, many doctors currently see too many patients to think about spending more time to charge more.

Shortage of supply is the biggest issue in countries with Single Payer. While Single Payer supporters make the claim that no country has eliminated their current system for the US system, those countries are moving toward market-based reforms to increase supply. When governments limit payments to providers, they lower supply, creating different problems. Some countries are attempting to alleviate those shortages by free market methods. For example, both Canada and the UK are implementing programs to entice providers to practice medicine.

So there's an increasing need for competition in the market, given the alternative: continued lack of competition by hospitals in various markets; insufficient numbers of doctors, nurses, and other professionals; and too few prescription approvals that take too long to approve. It is time to stop thinking healthcare costs in the US are too high (Chapter 1) so encouraging more competition is the goal. It doesn't help to vilify the "gouging by greedy providers," because providers are the key to the future of healthcare.

More competition is a sign of a healthy market. When there's less competition, oligarchy results (think OPEC) and prices increase. Ultimately, monopolies control the market, and demand the price that they want to charge. Government-run M4A would be a monopoly. The difference is that the government has the power to dictate lower prices, which consumers like. But the suppliers do not, and they either leave the market or become discouraged from innovating. Imagine the government attempting to hit the mark on twenty thousand items, where they either fail the consumer or the provider. The result may be the short-term elimination of the transaction and/or the long-term lack of innovation.

Supply. The market is as competitive as possible to keep costs low, with multiple options available. Some markets are monopolistic even where choices exist—such as in smaller communities or even suburbs where location is king and community hospitals really don't compete with other community hospitals. But there has been a decline in the number of hospitals in the US, as well as a limited supply of physicians, nurses, and other practitioners. Specifically:

- The number of hospitals in the US—about 5,000—has steadily declined over the past fifty years, partly due to inefficiency (leading to mergers) and inadequate margins (leading to closures) in the 1990s. Formation of new hospitals is unlikely, so competition among hospitals should be encouraged. Solutions to this issue are complex and need more time and study than I can devote here. Suffice it to say that competition in rural communities is problematic, and competition needs to be cultivated in unique ways (for example, urgent care centers that compete with emergency rooms, like "minihospitals"). Hospitals sometimes claim that consolidation saves money through economies of scale; a larger number of patients helps to defray fixed costs. While true in the short run, less competition impedes savings in the long run. There needs to be a balance of large hospitals that can perform complete services in which they become innovation leaders, and smaller entities that can both compete and perform specific tasks better. One idea is to change the Certificate of Need (CON) requirements that require verified need prior to acquisition, expansion, or development of new hospitals at the state level. CON requirements are very complex and may be an appropriate area of consideration.

- Medical schools that are not graduating enough physicians limit the number of physicians in the US—today, about 900,000. Plus, entrance exams are too rigorous. The American Medical Association (AMA) began in 1847 with the overall goal to improve public health.

Unquestioningly, public health has improved because of physician care and the focus on the quality of education, training, and practice of medicine. However, the AMA, along with state legislators, has helped to limit the number of physicians practicing in the US, and that has led to less competition and higher prices. Further, no one medical school focuses on the number of physicians needed overall, by specialty, or by geography. As a result, the US does not have enough primary care physicians, nor physicians willing to work in rural locations. A joke tells us something important about doctors: "The physician who was last in his class has a name: Doctor." In other words, there are good and bad physicians just like in any field, and the lack of competition has prevented the "purge" of poor doctors that would have otherwise occurred. So, in general, schools should expand the numbers of students admitted, and more licenses should be granted by the states.

• The number of nurses in the US has been an issue for fifty years; hospitals have had to attract nurses with pay bonuses and other perquisites because supply has been limited. The population of available nurses—about three million—is growing fast, but supply is not likely to keep up with demand. Nursing as a profession is demanding, and while improving the quality of nursing is a good thing, nursing schools need to ramp up their programs to handle increased volume instead of declining up to one-third of applicants (recently) due to insufficient program size. Also, there is pressure on nurses to attain higher degrees in the desire to attain higher incomes. There are downsides, though: Returning to school causes a lack of practical knowledge; school resources are costly; and pulling nurses out to teach may lower productivity, which means nurses must be pulled from other resources to fill vacated positions.

• There are other solutions to consider. With the proper education and a competitive price, Certified Nursing Assistants (CNAs)—who are not required to have a high school diploma—or Physician Assistants (licensed nurses) may be sufficient to provide some nursing care. Regardless, this "push me-pull you" issue has been going on for years, and only those in appropriate medical positions should make this call. Decision-makers should better analyze situations instead of "relying on the data" to justify their actions that more education is always better. For individuals, more education may be better, but for the general population, one could argue that too many people are taking too many courses chasing a better paying job, only to find that none are available. There is a practical reality that needs to set in (with student expectations, employer requirements, higher level institution profits) to balance education with work.

- The backlog of new prescriptions is enormous, caused to some extent by the Food and Drug Administration (FDA). While the FDA has recently increased its new-drug review (called "Fast-Track"), more is needed. Only in the US does the review of new drugs take twelve years on average. Plus, the average cost to bring a new drug to market is three billion dollars, according to a recent study by Tufts University (including the cost for drugs that are not approved). One way to increase FDA speed is to double the size of the US drug review group, which will increase costs. But to the extent that "time is money" and the slowness of FDA approval has cost the public both money and quality, faster approval speed is needed. For example, if a CEO of GM faced slowness in a line of cars getting built, she might double efforts to make it happen.

Why are drugs more expensive in the US versus other countries?

- FDA requirements make drugs safer, but at a cost. In some countries, drugs can sit on the shelf longer; drugs may include synthetic components banned in the US and are often available without a prescription.

- Some other countries won't cover a drug depending on its price. For example, in England, the National Health Service disallows therapies where the cost for a quality-adjusted life year (QALY) gained exceeds 50,000 British pounds (an arbitrary, non-indexed measure). This impacts the price requested by the maker of the drug, and in the long term, stifles innovation.

- "Free riding" is a concept where drug companies can pay for all their R&D costs through the US market while charging just the marginal cost of manufacturing pills in other countries. The US market represents 45 percent of pharmaceutical sales across the globe.

Another issue is patent length, which is twenty years for all drugs (although a few drugs have received extensions for up to five years due to testing time, or seven years for rare-disease drugs). In some cases, drugs get approved with just a few years left in which to recover the cost of getting FDA approval. In a world as complex and adaptive as the US, how is it possible that twenty years is applied to every drug? Why can't the FDA give approval for a variable length, depending on the circumstances; or ten years after FDA approval? I can't even get my head around the concept that the entity tasked with testing new drugs for efficacy can't be flexible in its determination that a drug is acceptable to the public, but that drug is only patented for a pre-determined twenty years.

A change to an automatic ten years after patent approval, for instance, would allow drug manufacturers to price their drugs more accurately. With variable years after approval, prices must be set to recoup costs with an assumption that the drug may only have patent protection for, say, five years. The drug maker then profits beyond five years until the end of the patent, if longer.

Another concept that is being debated is drug reciprocity—the idea that if a drug has been approved in Canada, US patients could access it. Congress should decide whether reciprocity should be allowed.

Finally, an idea comes from Germany, where Apothekes are as common as Starbucks. An Apotheke is a pharmacy, but with the ability to prescribe medicine without a prescription. For example, a pharmacist might prescribe a medication for pink eye without the need to make an appointment with a physician (saving, say, $200). If a pharmacist has had medication training and the potential harm is small, why does the patient need to make an appointment with a doctor, which only costs more time and money and impedes the doctor from doing more important work?

The bottom line: market supply reacts to demand over the long run.

Demand. Demand in healthcare drives costs higher, which it should. Markets for all products work efficiently because demand leads to higher prices, which signals to investors to add to supply, which stabilizes prices and ultimately stabilizes the market. It's the consumer who makes decisions of quality, quantity, and price through billions of transactions each year. The healthcare CPI (Medical Consumer Price Index, or M-CPI) has increased faster than general CPI by 1.8 percent per year over the past seventy years. That means nonmedical products have increased slower than the average CPI, such that the population desires more healthcare and less of other things.

Demand in healthcare will continue to increase demographically. It is difficult to isolate the effect of aging on healthcare costs, but a rule of thumb is that each year we age, healthcare costs increase by about 4 percent per year, prior to age sixty-five. That means costs increase by normal inflation plus additional costs due to aging.

Actuaries noticed that care increases as one ages and then spikes in the last year of life. While not extending one's life may be better for the greater good, the individual suffers. The decision to not provide care at the end of life is at the core of M4A savings. Obamacare architect Ezekiel Emanuel proposed consideration of what he called "The Complete Lives System," in which he argues that the value of one's life is a method of rationing healthcare.

Free healthcare under M4A increases demand. Economists claim that when something is free, demand is limitless (they use the term "inelastic"). Proponents of M4A claim that "free" doesn't mean the demand is limitless, because we're talking about healthcare, not an item to be hoarded. True, demand for healthcare reaches a limit because there's only so much that can be done to fix something (and the patient doesn't want more healthcare once they recover); but substitution occurs when something is free, such as using the ER for convenience rather than making an appointment with a doctor. In that case, cost increases because price has no impact on demand.

An oft-cited comparison why healthcare in the US is more expensive than in Canada is the number of MRI machines. There are three times as many MRI machines per capita in the US than in Canada. This reflects the demand in the US, where the market meets demand, versus in Canada, where the government manages the number of MRI machines. The average wait for an MRI machine in Canada is three months.

I've talked about increasing supply to help lower healthcare spending. Consistent with that is to reduce demand. Let's compare demand under the $100,000 CAT/Market plan versus M4A:

CATEGORY	CAT4ALL	M4A
PREEXISTING CONDITIONS LIMITATIONS	NONE	NONE
LIFETIME/ANNUAL LIMITATIONS	NONE	NONE
EMERGENCY ROOM	APPROPRIATE COPAY	FREE TO USE/MISUSE
PRESCRIPTION DRUGS	APPROPRIATE COPAY	FREE TO USE/MISUSE
AMBULANCE	APPROPRIATE COPAY	FREE TO USE/MISUSE
PREVENTIVE	FREE	FREE
DEDUCTIBLES, COPAYS, COINSURANCE	LIKELY, IN MARKET PLANS	NONE

Before you salivate over "free" in the M4A plan, know that costs must be paid regardless, so "free" means someone will have to pay to cover the cost. A market can be characterized as entropy (random), where it reaches equilibrium without a controlling force. Evolution of the market must be allowed to occur, as no one can predict its outcome. Great examples of entropy are the internet, cell phones, cities, organizations, social media, and even music. Governments can plan, but planning can kill the best evolution. Markets allow industries to evolve and develop products and services that no one can predict.

PRICE

Many researchers have claimed that price is the reason healthcare costs are so high. To reach this conclusion, they isolate components of spending and compare the pieces to those in other countries. Since the number of services is often the same or lower in the US, they argue, what sticks out is the price that's being charged. This conclusion fits with the narrative that the free market doesn't work very well in healthcare; providers charge too much, so Single Payer is the way to go.

However, comparing "units of service" across countries is flawed.

- As discussed in Chapter 1, an office visit in Canada isn't the same as an office visit in the US, so comparing "one unit of service" across countries does a disservice to the US system.
- More rural US hospitals must be staffed twenty-four/seven (including MRI scanners in emergency rooms) as compared to European countries.
- Hospitals are required to provide emergency care regardless of a patient's ability to pay (including noncitizen patients).
- There is higher use of emergency room care.
- There are lawsuit costs, both through direct payments and defensive medicine.

John C. Goodman, a healthcare economist, wrote in *National Review* in 2009 to question the analysis of prices since they were artificial—higher due to underpayments with Medicare and Medicaid and artificially lower in Single Payer systems due to lower reimbursements, which is equivalent to taxing providers. He instead analyzed country data by resources expended, in which case the US was average. "For example, we use fewer doctors than the average developed country to produce the same or better outcomes. We also use fewer nurses and fewer hospital beds, make fewer physician visits, and spend fewer days in the hospital. About the only thing we use more of is technology."

SCRIPT COST

"Now let me get this right. You're complaining that the cost of prescription drugs went from a $10 copay to a $30 copay? How is it possible that we don't appreciate what prescription drugs can do for us, but instead complain about their cost?"

For example, a drug developed to cure Hepatitis C—Sovaldi— was discovered in 2007 and came on the market in 2016 at a price of $84,000; it cures 95 percent of patients. Shortly thereafter, Harvoni was approved; it costs $94,000, with similar results. Is it better to have the drug available, or to not have it exist at all because it's so expensive? Undoubtedly, it's a good thing to have the drug available, but development of the drug was costly.

These drugs are just the "tip of the iceberg," in that many more drugs will come online in the next fifty years through incredible discovery, but at great cost. What is the world to do?

As a comedian once said, it's like "hurtling through the air in a piece of metal, but we complain that we only get peanuts on the flight." I understand it is human nature to "move on" from any discovery, understandably, but appreciation would partially balance such concerns. We've come a long way:

- In the 1800s, leeches were used to suck out toxins. Leeches must have worked (once) because someone recovered, so the practice continued for hundreds of years. Leeches were apparently better than direct "bloodletting," which had been used for thousands of years. The best and brightest minds thought of this.
- In 1854, a doctor in London pinpointed the outbreak of cholera to the water supply when others thought air was the cause.
- In the 1930s and 1940s, antibiotics were first developed on a grand scale.
- In 1950, lobotomies were still used to treat psychiatric diseases by boring holes in the brain.
- In the 1960s and 1970s, vaccines were first developed for the mumps, measles, rubella, chicken pox, and pneumonia.
- In the 1980s, drugs for mental health (Prozac) and cholesterol (Mevacor) were discovered.
- In the 2000s, biologics were being developed to treat cancer and other diseases.

In a perfect world, we would have a drug that cures disease with just one pill, no side effects, and at little cost. Sovaldi is close in that it's "just" a twelve-week regimen, but, importantly, Sovaldi can have side effects, and it isn't even close to being low-cost.

Congress has demanded proof of costs of drug manufacturers because initial prices have been so high. One could claim that oversight is a good thing because while competition is the limiting factor to drug prices, competition doesn't occur with single-source drugs under patent protection.

But with third-party payment, the patient has no reason not to use the drug. How do you create competition for a drug that only costs a patient thirty dollars (or zero dollars under M4A)? You can't; that's why the government thinks only more government can fix the problem. What needs to happen is for the government to get out of the way.

DRUG ADVERTISING

There are pros and cons to prescription ads, which I briefly mentioned in the prologue. While regulated by the FTC, are direct-to-consumer (DTC) ads necessary—especially if not everyone needs to learn about a drug that will not impact their lives? Since the industry spends $5 billion per year in marketing, one would assume elimination of this spend would lower healthcare spending by a large amount.

A 2011 CBO study described people's concerns: "Direct-to-consumer (DTC) advertising of prescription drugs has elicited various concerns. One concern is that DTC advertising may add to spending on drugs by consumers, insurers, and the federal government without providing enough benefits to justify that spending. Specifically, some observers worry that DTC advertising encourages broader use of certain drugs than their health benefits warrant. Another concern is that DTC advertising for newly approved drugs may lead people to use drugs whose potential risks were not fully discovered during the drug approval process."

The study concluded: "The magnitude of any effects of a moratorium on direct-to-consumer advertising for newly approved drugs would probably be small because a small share of drugs would be affected. Regardless, a moratorium would affect other marketing strategies used by drug manufacturers and the quantities and prices of certain drugs sold." The overall conclusion of the CBO report was to make no changes.

My general suggestion is to pare back advertising. There are facts on both sides of the argument, such that no action is action in this case. That's the problem with systems that have become so complex: there are reasons not to change anything because a faction of the population may be impacted. The problem here is that the FDA allows saturating ads that don't describe the real situation with the drug, such that drug companies can promise or simply improve results of another drug, but with risks that no one thinks will happen to them.

HIGH COST OF INNOVATION

A study by Precision Health Economics simulated removal of price controls in OECD countries and estimated that thirteen new drugs would be developed each year creating price controls in the US. So that becomes a measure of cost of creating price controls.

A new drug has been developed, but it costs $850,000 for the course of treatment. It prevents blindness, so there is an ethical dilemma whether spending this amount in resources is worth the outcome. To the patient it is. But should the system cover it? If all countries had price controls like OECD countries, perhaps the drug would not have been discovered. Would this be better?

The fact is that prescription drugs are very expensive to develop, while the cost to manufacture is small. Should a drug cost $500 to cover a portion of the R&D, or one dollar to cover the cost to manufacture? If the US approached prescriptions the way its neighbor countries did, prescription costs would decrease in the short run, but innovation would suffer, leading to higher costs in the long run.

LEGAL SYSTEM

I've already explored issues with the tort system, where there are lawsuits that cost the system money directly and indirectly. There are other oddities with the US civil court system.

- Proof of negligence is partial, such that just 10 percent warrants finding that a provider is liable.
- The jury only needs to find a majority who believe that the provider is negligent—not 100 percent, like in criminal cases.
- Class action lawsuits are prevalent, even more so because of the internet.
- The public has the attitude that someone must pay.

- Court costs are exorbitant such that providers and their malpractice insurers often settle to avoid court costs, even in baseless cases.

Estimates show that provider costs are one-fourth to one-third higher as a result. There are arguments that lawsuits are good because plaintiffs can receive compensation, and providers are more careful. There is a balance, though, and tort reform could help to reinstate that balance.

How can someone make $500,000 a year when someone else makes minimum wage?

Let's talk about that. Why is there a job that pays $500,000 a year and another that pays $20,000 a year? Aren't both jobs' wages fair?

Why isn't the high-paying job $480,000 and the minimum-wage job $40,000? That's just a 4 percent decrease for one and a 100 percent increase for the other.

Did you skip economics in college? You've ignored what the jobs actually entail to imply that one job should be paid more while the other is paid less. The market should determine what is fair, not some bureaucrat in Washington who doesn't know details about these jobs.

But $20,000 a year isn't enough for someone to live on, especially with a family.

Is that how a fair price for the job should be determined?

No, but that's why the minimum wage should be increased.

But what if the job is only worth $20,000 a year? Their job might be absorbed by automation, other people doing the job, or the job not getting done or the company going out of business—like some restaurants in Seattle and New York recently did, due to the new fifteen dollar minimum wage requirements in those cities.

They're going out of business due to greed. Their greedy owners made those decisions.

You can lament about what happened (or what should have happened), but the bottom line is fewer jobs because the government determined what the "fair price of labor" should be.

Well, how else do you keep people making enough to live on and prevent three people from making more than half of the population?

So, in your concern that a small group has more voice than you think they should, you would penalize them?

You want them to have more voice and not tax them? How could you?

How could you? Just because you can? How is a wealth tax not confiscation? What's next? Just like income tax started in 1913 as "just" a way to raise some revenue. The highest tax rate was 7 percent when it was first implemented. It was intended to be paid by those evil Robber Barons.

That's an apple and an orange.

Is it? You'll be gone from this Earth, and in ten years someone else will suggest "we just need to increase the wealth tax rate a little bit or make the wealth tax bracket a little bigger."

But this problem developed over years and years. We need to nip it in the bud now.

Who says it's a problem? You made that up.

How can you possibly argue it's not a problem?

If you would quit worrying about what someone else makes or has in wealth, you might actually notice how we live like kings today. Everyone.

The poor don't feel like kings.

I'm sorry, they don't? They can purchase any food they like, and it's fast and hot and tastes better than anything a king could have had. And they have a computer in their pocket that's as powerful as a human brain.

But they can't afford the monthly phone and text charges.

That's the reason they don't live like kings, because of cost?

Yeah, that's a real problem. And those three people who own more than other people could pay just a little more in taxes to help pay for those cell charges.

You've said the same thing for years: if only the rich could pay for the food, rent, clothes, and healthcare for others.

So what? It was true then; it's true now.

And it will be true in ten years. And one hundred years. It's selfish.

But doctors make too much in the US.

How much is too much?

Really? You're asking that question?

Yes, because I know you. If a doctor made $200,000 a year twenty years ago, you would have said that was too much. You'd say the same thing today.

And the best way to control that, you have to admit, is for the government to set the salary.

Like in the UK, where they can't attract enough doctors? So you want to restrict how much doctors make, yet the medical schools they must attend to get credentialed can charge whatever the market will pay?

We should control that, too. That way, the markets will produce the quality and number of doctors needed at more reasonable pay levels.

So because the balloon sticks out (doctor pay), you want to control everything in the system?

Why yes, that's the ultimate achievement to be expected under socialism. Doctors should make less and nurses more.

Seriously? What happens when you can't hire enough doctors? Or you get too many nurses? You think the government can determine the right levels of pay for millions of positions with billions of transactions, and do it "just right?"

But a socialistic system will make everything fairer.

Fairer according to whom?

Fairer according to everybody.

You mean you, not everybody. Because not everybody agrees as to what's "fair." You claim fair is just less in pay for doctors, so that in theory others can get more. Is that fair?

It's better than what we currently have.

What about other hospital staff? What about other clinic staff? What about drug researchers? Leave the market alone, or you'll screw it up!

"If we try to engineer outcomes, if we overturn tradition to make everyone the same, we ruin society." –Ben Stein, 2012

9

PROJECTIONS ARE COMPLICATED

"Socialism merely spends what capitalism creates."

–Dennis Prager, 2019

HEALTHCARE COST PROJECTIONS

Let's create an example to illustrate the difference in reimbursements between what M4A proponents propose and what competition would do. I'll create an imaginary healthcare product that, for simplicity and comparability, costs 100 dollars. I'll also pretend the market consists of three main entities—Medicare, Medicaid, and private. Private represents all nongovernmental payers and does not differentiate between the employer group and individual markets (nor direct-pay). The point here is to show how little the current government Single Payer plans (Medicare and Medicaid) pay today, relative to cost.

CURRENT HEALTHCARE PRODUCT		
SEGMENT	PRICE	TRUE COST
MEDICARE	$70	$100
MEDICAID	$50	$100
PRIVATE	$125	$100

M4A HYPOTHETICAL HEALTHCARE PRODUCT		
SEGMENT	PRICE	TRUE COST
MEDICARE	$70	$100
MEDICAID	$50	$100
PRIVATE	$70	$100

Source: Author's Calculations

Comments about M4A:

- The Mercatus Center at George Mason University estimate of $57.6 million in M4A spending over ten years highly depends on assumptions, so savings could easily be 0 percent. Also, the savings from insurance claim processing costs would not help a provider's product cost. I show the true cost to remain the same at $100, but the M4A payments' significant underpayments would continue even if the true cost were to decrease to $97. It is impossible for the true cost to decrease to $70, which would likely be the average reimbursement rate for this M4A Hypothetical Healthcare Product.

- M4A proponents claim that Single Payer would wring out the excess profits in both the insurance and healthcare industries. However, many insurers are already nonprofit today, and many providers are nonprofit—especially among the largest category of providers of healthcare: hospitals.

- Under M4A, all reimbursements would be below the true cost of the providers. So, low government reimbursement would force savings, causing providers to leave the market. Like with any product or service, increased demand with less supply and fixed prices leads to shortages—like in other Single Payer countries.

Instead, I propose a competitive market solution:

CURRENT HEALTHCARE PRODUCT		
SEGMENT	PRICE	TRUE COST
MEDICARE	$70	$100
MEDICAID	$50	$100
PRIVATE	$125	$100

COMPETITIVE MARKET HYPOTHETICAL HEALTHCARE SOLUTION		
SEGMENT	PRICE	TRUE COST
MEDICARE	$70	$90
MEDICAID	$50	$90
PRIVATE	$110	$90

Source: Author's Calculations

Comments about the Competitive Market:

- The Competitive Market Hypothetical Healthcare Solution would have a competitive market below $100,000 in charges per person, with CAT4ALL above $100,000. Medicare and Medicaid would likely exist as the two programs do today. Competition would drive down true cost lower than it is today (because today's market often lacks competition). Since Medicare and Medicaid already reimburse providers at below-cost levels, I assume those payments are unaffected by changes in the market; savings inure to the private market.

- This model doesn't address how either the below or above $100,000 mechanisms would work. Suffice it to say that below $100,000, market price would change as shown in the table; above $100,000, prices would change based on the federal government paying claims at prices like the current private market.

HISTORY OF MEDICARE

It's insightful to consider the history of Medicare to consider what it might look like under M4A. Since Medicare is part of the Social Security Act, let's start there:

- In 1935, Congress passed—and President Franklin D. Roosevelt signed into law—the Social Security Act, also known as the Old Age & Survivors Insurance (OASI). In 1956, disability coverage was added, becoming OASDI. The acronym added an "H" when it changed to OASDHI in 1965 with the addition of Medicare.

- Other groups were added along the way, including spouses and minor children of retired workers, government employees (about three in four), railroad workers, the self-employed, farm workers, domestic help, Puerto Ricans, and employees of nonprofits. In 1950 came the addition of Cost of Living Adjustments (COLAs).

- In 1983, Republican President Ronald Reagan signed a bill to increase the normal retirement age from sixty-five to sixty-seven and to tax SS benefits, helping to extend the SS Trust Fund.

- In 2000, President Bill Clinton signed a bill to eliminate the earnings test for employees above the full-benefit retirement age.

- In 2011 and 2012, President Barack Obama signed a bill temporarily lowering the payroll tax from 6.2 percent to 4.2 percent to alleviate strain on workers during the Great Recession, with federal revenues reimbursing the Trust Fund for the difference.

The latest report shows that Social Security will run out of money in sixteen years, while Medicare runs out of money in eleven years. "Run out of money" means the need to cut benefits, such that Social

Security can afford to pay just seventy-seven cents on the dollar, and Medicare will need similar cuts.

The Social Security eligibility age has gone up, not down, suggesting the Medicare eligibility age to follow suit by raising it from age sixty-five to sixty-seven, reducing Medicare costs by about 5 percent. People are living longer, so shortening the length of time in which someone receives Medicare should follow. Increases in life expectancy are the main driver for increasing costs of Social Security and Medicare.

Fraud has historically been a major concern—not only with the SS Administration tasked in 1993 to develop a new Social Security Card (still reportedly being developed), but in disability benefits with a revamping of proof of disability requirements.

One more discussion with my favorite Democratic Socialist:

The prices being charged for healthcare are too high.

> Define "too high." No question it's high, but "too high" implies you know what the price should be.

We could set prices to what they were in 2000. That would at least save money, and obviously prices in 2000 were enough for providers to live on.

> I see. Pick an arbitrary mark, which cuts out price inflation for the past twenty years. Sounds like rent control, like in New York City.

Good comparison. See? That worked.

> For those who benefited, but not for the renters who were not covered and who paid extra to cover for those who benefited. Nor for landlords, who couldn't make the low rents work, so they stopped fixing their buildings. The same thing would happen under M4A: innovation would stop.

First, you don't know that. And second, that's why everyone needs to be covered, so there would be no "renters" who have to pay extra.

I see. So, since it's free to all, all will be well—except for the pressure on providers, who would have to halt any innovation. And if that's not enough, they'll cut other corners.

What corners? Have you seen hospitals lately? There's tons that could be cut.

Yes, that's a good solution, to look around to determine where there appears to be extravagance and cut that out. Kind of like those billionaires.

Now you're getting it. Those billionaires have more than anyone could need in one hundred lifetimes.

By that approach, we would just retire all the billionaires; and I suppose their "seconds in command" would pick up where they left off.

Now you're getting it.

Would the price of anything change?

Of course it would. Those billionaires wouldn't get paid.

What about their "seconds in command"?

They would get paid less, clearly.

How much less?

Why do you worry about such things?

I'm not worried, I just want to understand your proposal to understand the savings. There are about five hundred billionaires in the US, so if they don't get paid anymore, and those under them get paid about half, that might "save" about fifty billion dollars, or about 0.3 percent of annual GDP.

Then we need to save more. A lower cap would do it.

But that just "squeezes the balloon," so something else sticks out.

Like what?

Well, either pay gets compressed all the way down the line, or companies don't innovate, or perhaps the companies never even exist. You'll never know what doesn't happen.

So let's just try it. Sounds like no harm—or none that we'll notice.

Yes, just ignore what happens. "It won't be bad, and we'll never even notice. We'll get to nirvana."

That's what I would say.

I was being sarcastic. Either we save such a small amount, like 0.3 percent, that we don't notice prices decrease, or we expand the impact beyond billionaires and live with fewer companies and no innovation.

That's a bit draconian, don't you think?

I agree things won't be that stark, but painting that bleak picture is the only way to get you to understand. Otherwise, you just claim it will all work with no unintended consequences. That's the dream of socialism; it works in your head.

We already have socialism. What do you think Social Security is?

So socialism is dependent on the name given to programs?

Well, at least the US has Social Security to rely on.

Does it? Where would we be without it?

See, I can't even believe you'd entertain such a thought.

A wise man once said, "You can't measure what didn't happen." But it's insightful to consider what would have happened so as to avoid the pitfall in assuming "all or nothing."

What do you mean?

Let's discuss the value of Social Security, and not grandstand that asking a question is scary, as if I want to take it away. It's not "all or nothing."

But you do want to take it away.

Says you. One of the arguments used in 1933 in favor of SS was that the market for retirement products was undeveloped, and people were unsophisticated about financial decisions. Today, neither is true.

So? That doesn't mean we should eliminate SS.

But it does mean that SS isn't as important as it once was and that people look at SS as a drag on their retirement. They often claim they could do better investing on their own.

They could not. Only the rich can afford the analysis needed to invest in today's complicated market.

That's why mutual funds and investment advisors evolved to provide expert advice available to everyone.

And they just gouge the little guy.

Says you. Anything where someone profits, you call it "gouging."

"The inherent vice of Capitalism is the unequal sharing of blessings; the inherent virtue of socialism is the equal sharing of miseries."
–Winston Churchill, 1945

I'M SO GLAD THE WORLD HAS FIGURED IT OUT

"The difference between a Nazi and a Communist is when you say how horrible Nazis have been, they don't say, 'Well, real Nazism has never been tried.'"

–Frank Fleming, 2017

WAIT, WAIT, WAIT

Many countries sacrifice waiting for cost. When the healthcare system is given over to the government, by definition, the government must allocate scarce resources based on what it considers most important. Think of triage in a hospital, where it's not uncommon to have to wait for someone else's more pressing health needs.

Further, Ron Bailey of *Reason Magazine* wrote, "Imposing price controls would lower prices, but at the cost of creating shortages, developing fewer new drugs, and—ultimately—compelling Americans to lead sicker and shorter lives."

COUNTRY COMPARISON

Using the same format from Chapter 1, here is a synopsis of the US compared to other countries' healthcare systems:

2015	US	CANADA	UK	AUSTRALIA	JAPAN
POPULATION	321 MILLION	36 MILLION	66 MILLION	24 MILLION	128 MILLION
RATIO	65	7	13	5	26
GEOGRAPHIC SIZE (MILLION MI^2)	9.1	9.1	0.2	7.7	0.4
RATIO	228	228	5	193	10
HEALTHCARE SPEND % OF GDP	16.8%	10.5%	9.7%	9.3%	10.9%
HEALTHCARE GDP	$3.1 T	$164 B	$285 B	$117 B	$478 B
RATIO	135	7	12	5	20
ADULT OBESITY RATE (2016)	36%	29%	28%	29%	4%
CAR ACCIDENT RATE PER 100,000	10.9	5.2	2.8	5.1	3.8
HOMICIDE RATE PER 100,000	5.0	1.7	1.0	1.0	0.3
DENSITY (PEOPLE PER KM^2)	36	4	272	3	351
MIGRANTS (NET)	+992,000	+248,000	+260,000	+198,000	+71,000

2015	US	FRANCE	GERMANY	SWITZERLAND	THE NETHERLANDS
POPULATION	321 MILLION	64 MILLION	82 MILLION	8 MILLION	17 MILLION
RATIO	65	13	16	2	3
GEOGRAPHIC SIZE (MILLION MI2)	9.1	0.5	0.3	0.04	0.03
RATIO	228	13	8	1	1
HEALTHCARE SPEND % OF GDP	16.8%	11.5%	11.1%	11.9%	10.3%
HEALTHCARE GDP	$3.1 T	$271 B	$378 B	$81 B	$79 B
RATIO	135	12	16	4	3
ADULT OBESITY RATE (2016)	36%	22%	22%	20%	20%
CAR ACCIDENT RATE PER 100,000	10.9	5.2	4.2	3.1	3.7
HOMICIDE RATE PER 100,000	5.0	1.6	0.8	0.7	0.6
DENSITY (PEOPLE PER KM2)	36	118	235	210	502
MIGRANTS (NET)	+992,000	+85,000	+388,000	+79,000	+13,000

Sources: Various, Author's Calculations

Undoubtedly, the US is unlike any of these countries. Of the countries listed, Canada is the only country that compares to the US with similar size; however, the population density of Canada is nine times less than in the US. The largest (and most tightly packed) population is Japan, with one-third of the population of the US. The adult obesity rate is about nine times higher in the US.

I'll compare the US system to that of Canada and the UK.

CANADA

It's useful to compare the healthcare systems of the US and Canada:

- Canada adopted its current system, called "Medicare," in 1984.

- Prescription drugs are not covered as part of Medicare; about two-thirds of Canadians purchase insurance for prescription drugs beyond the government plan, with employers providing many of the plans.

- The government pays the providers, collected through taxes.

- The Fraser Institute—a Canadian think tank—measured average wait times in Canada (2018):

  - 19.8 weeks (median) to see specialists—the longest wait was thirty-nine weeks for orthopedic surgery
  - Wait times varied by province from 15 to 45 weeks.
  - Eleven-week wait for MRI scans
  - 1.1 million Canadians are waiting for some type of health-care procedure (3 percent of the population)
  - Waiting is cumulative, in that there is waiting from the point of referral to see the specialist, then waiting for the specialist to perform the procedure

- Canada employs "loser pays" court costs, so no ambulance chasing, no limits on damages.

- Canada doesn't anesthetize like in the US, leading to longer recovery times.

Waiting for care often leads to deterioration of the condition such that, among other issues, the service doesn't even make sense anymore. One 2012 story tells of a boy with scoliosis; no surgery was performed for three years, leading to the boy becoming permanently disabled. Long waits have contributed to death in other cases—44,000 women died waiting for breast cancer treatment, according to the Fraser Institute, over two decades.

ENGLAND

In England, the National Health Service (NHS) is often described as the closest to a Single Payer system in the world. The government provides all healthcare services, from tax collection to distribution of healthcare. It has some of the biggest problems compared to other countries' healthcare systems:

- The most infamous story is that of Alfie Evans, a baby with a rare neurodegenerative disorder. The NHS had exhausted potential cures. When even Pope Francis offered to pay for experimental treatment in Rome, Alfie's parents took the NHS to court, where a judge denied the parents appeal. He died in 2018.

- Another infamous story is that of Charlie Gard, a baby with a rare genetic disorder. The parents wanted to try experimental treatment. While the parents raised funds to try treatment in New York, NHS denied the baby's transfer; British Courts agreed. He died in 2017.

- Another less-famous story is that of Ashya King. His parents rescued him and took him to Spain for light proton therapy, which cured the cancer that the UK doctors said was incurable.

- In early 2018, *The Guardian*, a British newspaper, reported: "16,900 people in a week were kept in NHS ambulances waiting for hospital care."

- Two people recently died at a British hospital after waiting for treatment for more than thirty hours in the hospital hallway.

- To cope with lack of funding and backlogs of patients, the NHS in 2019 proposed "group appointments," where doctors would see up to fifteen patients at the same time.

- Four million patients are waiting for care today.

- A study showed British hospitals have death rates 50 percent higher than in the US.

- There are seven thousand fewer doctors in the UK today than in 2005.

- The British Red Cross recently declared the UK health system a humanitarian crisis.

Britain's Florence Nightingale pioneered nursing, not only in the UK but through influence in all countries. Fortunately, gone is the Nightingale Ward concept of multiple patients in one room separated by curtains. Doctors finally recognized that transferring disease (even carrying from one patient to another on doctors' ties) was as important as treatment of the disease. So private rooms are the norm in the US, but not in the UK.

Too bad that the US media never covered the recent UK doctor union or nurse union strikes over low pay and bad benefits, not to mention poor access to services. To steal a famous saying, "If the media doesn't report on something, it doesn't make a sound." Put differently, just because the US media didn't cover the UK doctor and nurse union strikes, doesn't mean they didn't happen.

Other comparisons to the US:

- The UK has 39 percent higher rates of breast cancer for those aged eighty plus than in the US.
- The UK has 90 percent higher rates of breast cancer for those fifty plus.
- The UK has 72 percent more cataract issues.
- The UK has 89 percent more hip issues.
- The UK has 95 percent more knee issues.
- The US performs 300 percent more mammograms per person.
- The US performs 250 percent more MRIs per person.
- The US performs 32 percent more C-sections.

In the future, the UK has ordered the NHS to delay surgeries for up to a year for smokers and the obese unless they first change their lifestyles to the satisfaction of the government healthcare authority.

US WAITING TIMES AND FRAUD

In 2019, the Association of American Medical Colleges estimated that shortages in the number of physicians were 50 percent worse than anticipated prior to Obamacare. In 2016, the same annual study asked physicians why they were leaving the practice of medicine—the most common reasons were regulatory burdens and electronic health record requirements.

In 2016, the US Justice Department announced the largest finding of fraud in the US: 900 million dollars in false billings to Medicare and Medicaid. Is finding fraudulent activity good or bad? Some would say it's good, because finding fraud and charging those who commit fraud helps lower healthcare expenditures and deters others considering fraudulent activity. On the other hand, does finding fraud suggest the case is the tip of the iceberg and that there is a propensity among the population to commit fraud?

THE BOTTOM LINE

The US already struggles with shortages, wait times, and fraud. Adding to those issues hoping to lower costs would just exchange one set of problems for another. The US population's health is the starting point for healthcare needs, not a different homogeneous population in another country that is dissimilar. The US population has lower life expectancy, higher infant mortality rates, etc., as well as better-paid providers who are still incented to innovate. That should be the starting point for any analysis—not the "But we can just mandate costs and control the system like in the UK" approach.

We need Single Payer to control healthcare costs.

That's a nice theory. But in practice, if the government dictates prices, innovation will suffer.

It will not. The National Institutes of Health will provide more innovation.

So you're prepared to balance elimination of private innovation with public NIH innovation.

Well, the government must, if the private sector won't do it.

Because the government will squelch innovation!

Because costs are out of control!

So, you think there should be more government intervention. Are any of the countries I compare to the US healthcare system known for their innovation?

They're all much smaller.

Exactly. That's why they really can't be compared. And government controls with Medicare and Medicaid led to huge cost shifting that disrupted the market. The market just reacted to the underpayments from the government by charging the private payers more.

Had we done M4A years ago, we would have already overcome these issues.

That's not what you said in 1987. You said that Medicaid for All would bankrupt the country.

Well, then, let's do it in stages, like offering it as an option.

What's wrong with providing a service to people who are willing to buy that service at an agreed-upon price?

The government could do the same job without the profit motive. Wall Street makes their money by bilking the little guy.

Yes, someone less expensive can always "do the job." But can the government do it well? Name one service the government provides that the public actually likes. I thought monopolies were bad. Profit incents everyone to do their job well.

But investing has risks, while the government will always be there to provide payments.

At what cost, though? Annuities guarantee payment as well and provide better returns than Social Security. The market provides choice that the government either can't or won't. The authoritarian system known as "Social Security" has eliminated decision-making for everyone to the point where some people can't make decisions for themselves.

What do you want to do, then—fix something that's not broken?

I want to learn from it. Social Security and Medicare are similar, and since we've headed toward less reliance on Social Security, we should rely less on the government—not have Medicare cover more people.

Can't we just try it? Medicare for All will be cheaper than the current crazy system that only works for the insurance companies.

The crazy system evolved from other government interventions, like Medicare, Medicaid, state regulations, etc.

It did not. It started because insurance companies are greedy.

Are they greedy? Did you read the facts I unearthed—that insurers' profits are 3 percent of healthcare premiums, and half of insurers are nonprofits?

What, you'd let insurance companies continue their reign of terror over middle-class working people?

Knock it off. It's crying wolf that leads people to stop listening. And just a suggestion—don't comb your hair with a balloon!

"Urgent ends justify horrible means." –Matt Ridley, 2015

11

PLEASE, WOULD YOU STOP BEING WORRIED ABOUT GOING OUTSIDE?

"Of all the tyrannies, a tyranny sincerely exercised for the good of its victims may be the most oppressive. It may be better to live under robber barons than under the omnipotent moral busybodies. The robber barons' cruelty may sometimes sleep, his cupidity may at some point be satiated; but those who torment us for our own good will torment us without end, for they do so with the approval of their own conscience."
–C.S. Lewis, 1948

Note that this chapter was written in September 2020, so the data is dated.

WHY POPULATION DEATH RATE IS THE ONLY COVID-19 METRIC THAT MATTERS

How is it possible—if one were to conduct a Jay-Leno-Man-on-the-Street-type interview—that an average person would know how many people have died from COVID-19 in the US, but they wouldn't know the probability of an American dying from the virus?

They might answer that the death rate is 1 percent, or worse yet, a glass-half-empty-type might even say 10 percent.

Why so high? Because people can't do math! For example, as of this writing, there have been 655.2 deaths per million people in the US. To put this number in better context that a human could process, that means 0.06552 percent of the population has died. Yes, more will die, but there's a chance the death rate will be less than 0.1 percent, and definitely below 1 percent!

We've heard estimates of 1.8 to 3.4 percent death rates from the CDC (the Centers for Disease Control), and 3.4 percent from the WHO (the World Health Organization), which are both estimates of the rate of death per *case*. Instead, the actual death rate to date is 0.066 percent per person (healthy or not) in the US.

So the WHO and the CDC rates imply death is fifty times higher than reality! The key difference is context: Should the number of deaths be divided by an unknown number of cases (which can only be estimated), or the known population? I can hear complaints already about the comparison of an apple and an orange. But the "apple" from the WHO and the CDC is misleading in implying how deadly COVID-19 is, and intentional or not, that's the way the public perceived their findings. The "orange" is the actual rate of death in the US as a percentage of the population.

WHAT ABOUT THE UPTICK IN CASES?

There is a lot of hype about the recent increase in COVID-19 cases. No mention of the low number of cases previously—just the increase today.

No one has bothered to show the increase in cases together with hospitalizations and deaths in one chart, so I created this graph:

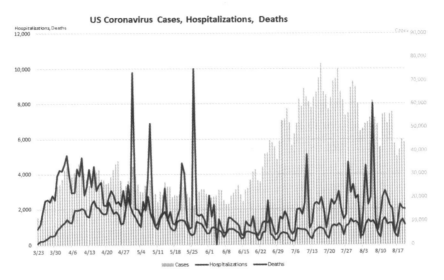

US Coronavirus Cases, Hospitalizations, Deaths

The "cases" bar values are shown on the right axis, while the "hospitalizations and deaths" line values are shown on the left axis (two axes allow for comparing relative increases). The data provided by the COVID Tracking Project shows the increase in cases beginning in June 2020, but there were no corresponding increases in hospitalizations or deaths through August 21, 2020.

Of course, there is a multiweek lag in the progression from cases to hospitalizations to deaths. But this graph puts to bed any concern about the uptick in COVID-19 cases leading to hospitalizations and deaths—it certainly hasn't happened yet, so how much longer must we wait for the data in "just two more weeks"?

Clearly, COVID-19 cases are related to hospitalizations and deaths but are not directly correlated. In fact, cases and hospitalizations are mathematically correlated equal to 0.18, assuming a two-week lag, which means the two data elements are not very correlated (correlation of 1.0 means two variables are perfectly correlated; correlation of 0.0 means two variables are not correlated at all). Cases and deaths are mathematically correlated equal to 0.04, assuming a three-week lag, which means the data shows the two are uncorrelated. All calculations were based on data from March 23, 2020 to August 14, 2020.

Cases are like the proverbial "canary in the coal mine." But if new cases are not as serious as previous ones—if younger patients with fewer preexisting conditions are those newly infected—there may be less cause for alarm. There's even new thinking that the latest strain of cases is not as severe as the first. Deaths have decreased since the early months—context that goes underreported.

The panic has led governors to issue stay-at-home orders, mask mandates, and continued school closings, frustrating residents. A friend said recently, in response to closing all non-essential businesses: "Please cancel my free trial of socialism!"

WHAT IS PROPER CONTEXT?

COVID-19 is the most concerning virus ever. Humans throughout the world have worried about viruses, so it's important to compare COVID-19 to other viruses in recent history:

PANDEMIC	YEAR	INFECTIONS	NUMBER OF DEATHS
COVID-19	2019–2020	8,000,000	220,000
EBOLA	2013–2016	29,000	12,000
MERS	2012–2019	2,600	900
SWINE FLU	2009–2010	1,000,000,000	500,000
SARS	2002–2003	8,000	800
HIV	1980–1990, MAINLY	75,000,000	35,000,000
HONG KONG FLU	1968–1969	100,000,000	1,000,000
ASIAN FLU	1957–1958	200,000,000	1,000,000

POLIO	1916–1955	1,000,000	50,000
SPANISH FLU	1918–1920	500,000,000	50,000,000

Source: CDC, NCBI, Live Science, Healthline, various others.

A first reaction one might have, and one that has been argued, is that "COVID-19 is worse than Ebola." It is, as cases and deaths are higher. If COVID-19 was like Ebola, where infection would be perceived as a death sentence, shutdown of the economy would be warranted—but it's not.

One could say that COVID-19 is "average" in the number of infections and deaths versus other viruses in the past one hundred years—not the highest, not the lowest. Much worse was Swine Flu, just a decade ago; plus, it's not as bad as the flus in the 1950s and 1960s.

This chart's purpose is to show that COVID-19 is not unprecedented, as there have been smaller and larger pandemics; of course, cases and deaths are just part of the picture, as hospitalizations and disabilities are not shown. This isn't Ebola either, where 40 to 50 percent of cases resulted in death. The death rate among children is negligible—yes, every death at every age is regrettable, but the death rate among those under age twenty, according to a Chinese study, was just 0.2 percent.

There are typically fourteen vaccines given during one's lifetime that can protect against up to 150 diseases, and four vaccines which are highly recommended. Without them, humans would suffer immensely, as they did in the past. We have developed vaccines to protect us from all types of diseases, and we will for COVID-19.

SKEWED RATES OF DEATH

The data is significantly skewed, as this chart shows:

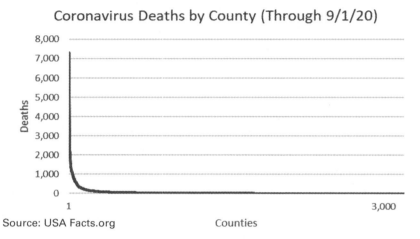

Coronavirus Deaths by County (Through 9/1/20)

Source: USA Facts.org   Counties

We knew this was true, but the visual was missing. The graph shows the number of deaths for every county in the US, sorted from highest to lowest. In fact, 80 percent of deaths are represented by 8 percent of the counties. In other words, just 250 counties out of 3,200 counties in the country represent 80 percent of deaths.

Those counties, of course, are the most populated counties, including the county with the most deaths in the US: King's County, which is part of New York City, with 7,300 deaths (through September 1, 2020).

Further, there are 700 counties without a single death, and another 1,300 counties with deaths in the single digits. That's 2,000 counties with fewer than ten deaths.

How else is the data skewed? Of course, by age. The age skewness is similar, in that 80 percent of all deaths have occurred among those over age sixty-five.

The CDC does not produce COVID-19 deaths by individual age and instead shows data in ten-year age bands (apparently, communicating that there were five children age ten who died would somehow compromise privacy). Since I'm an actuary, I took the liberty of taking their ten-year categories and interpolating to get death rates by year of age:

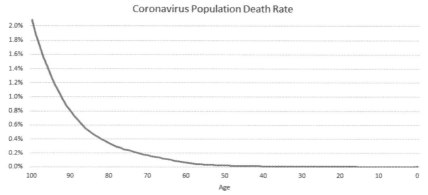

Source: CDC, smoothed by age

The similarity in skewness is obvious: deaths over age sixty-five represent 80 percent of all deaths, like the 8 percent of all counties. So, combining the two—the probability of death of the working-aged population (those under age sixty-five) in 92 percent of all counties—is even more miniscule. Multiplying these probabilities can represent the probability of death, but that would assume the variables are independent. Since they are not independent, I wouldn't want to multiply the probabilities together to declare what the probability of death would be, but the probability of death is at most the probability for those under age sixty-five, which is 0.013 percent.

What other data is this skewed? I thought about data that shows the number of preexisting conditions, knowing that data would be skewed such that the higher the number of conditions, the higher the rate of death. However, the CDC only provided enough information to create this graph, which doesn't look skewed because all that's known is that the rate of death for COVID-19-only deaths is 1.6 percent, while the rate with other conditions is 19.5 percent:

Case Death Rate by Number of Conditions

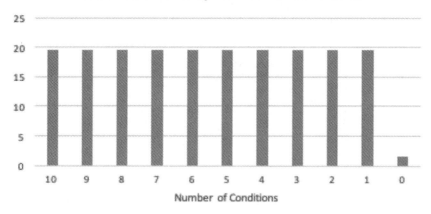

Source: CDC Morbidity and Mortality Weekly Report, June 15

In looking for this data, I noticed a big controversy about the data released by the CDC on September 2, 2020. The CDC reported various causes of COVID-19 deaths, and COVID-19 was the sole cause listed on just 6 percent of death certificates. A few people interpreted that to mean 94 percent of deaths were caused by other conditions, such that death figures for COVID-19 were falsely reported.

That led many in corporate media, including the CDC, to set up a "strawman" argument that *everyone* was misinterpreting their figures and that many people needed to be corrected that the death toll from COVID-19 was indeed as high as it is—not just 6 percent of that number. So many took to the media to "prove" the false interpretation was wrong. "*Way to beat a dead horse.*"

The rest of the population realized how common the 2.6 additional conditions were that existed for the deaths of 94 percent of the total. As some have said, there is a big difference between dying *from* COVID-19 versus *with* COVID-19.

The bottom line is that we know the graph above would also look skewed if the data were available, such that those with multiple pre-existing conditions would have even higher death rates. It doesn't matter; we know the death rate is quite skewed dependent on the number of conditions.

In fact, the number of conditions may explain the distribution by age (the middle skewed graph). In other words, if the number of conditions among the elderly is what leads to the higher death rates, it may not be age that's the real cause, but instead the number of preexisting conditions.

CITY DATA

COVID-19 data isn't tracked by city: it's tracked by zip code (too detailed) and by county (not specific enough).

Instead, I'll assume the main county represents the main city. In other words, the main county includes most of the main city population, although city and county geography are not correlated one-to-one.

The assumption works well for most cities, so the point I make is valid: cases and deaths are highest in a few large cities.

The table shows data by US city for counties with the largest number of deaths from COVID-19:

LOCATION	POPULATION	CONFIRMED CASES	POPULATION CASE RATE	CONFIRMED DEATHS	POPULATION DEATH RATE	RATIO TO REST OF THE STATE*	
						CASE RATE	DEATH RATE
NEW YORK CITY	8,200,000	233,969	2.9%	23,689	0.29%	1	3
LOS ANGELES	10,000,000	249,274	2.5%	6,036	0.06%	1	2
CHICAGO	5,200,000	132,072	2.5%	5,098	0.10%	2	2
PHOENIX	4,500,000	136,040	3.0%	3,093	0.07%	1	1
DETROIT	1,700,000	33,376	2.0%	2,897	0.17%	2	4
MIAMI	2,800,000	162,026	5.8%	2,666	0.10%	2	2

*Ratio to Rest of the State is the Ratio for the city divided by that city's state

Data through 9/8/2020

The chart is the first of its kind, remarkable in that it shows data by city. These six cities can be compared to each other, as well as the comparison I've added in the last two columns, where the case and death rates are compared to the case and death rates in the rest of their respective states.

For example, New York City has essentially the same case rate as New York State (outside of NYC), while the death rate for NYC is three times that for the state. That's a remarkable outcome—that while the NYC case rate is similar to the rest of the state (actually about 40 percent higher using decimals that are not shown), the death rate is three times higher. This measures what others have speculated: that COVID-19 has hit residents quite hard in the city.

Detroit also has poorer ratios than the rest of Michigan. In fact, the death rate in Detroit is second highest behind NYC, such that 0.17 percent of residents have died from COVID-19.

What is the cause of this? Of course, there is no formula that explains the situation in every location; but I'd like to analyze two key factors that the media has not: direct flights from Wuhan, and population density.

There were only two cities in the US with direct flights from Wuhan, China: New York City and San Francisco. San Francisco, interestingly, did not succumb to the same problems that New York City did; in fact, not even close.

But direct flights from Wuhan to European cities—Rome and London—seemed to have had an impact on the number of cases in those countries. Interestingly, Europe had no other direct connections to Wuhan, although, of course, many travelers had connecting flights.

As expected, population density varies greatly in the US. The average is ninety-four people per square mile (the world average is 129 per square mile, such that the US is below average). However, New York City averages 26,403 people per square mile! The least dense city of those in the table is Phoenix, with 3,126 people per square mile. Note that all US numbers shown here are per mile, whereas numbers shown earlier comparing to other countries in the world were calculated per kilometer.

So, to the extent that the infection is spread further in congested areas, cities are more likely to have cases, hospitalizations, and deaths as a result.

By contrast, South Dakota has suffered 167 total deaths and 10,000 cases among its 900,000 people (population density of eleven per square mile), which is a death rate of 0.02 percent.

The bottom line is that averages can be deceiving. State-based data, while useful to consider, "hides" what's really going on: that more-populated areas are suffering more from COVID-19.

FALSE DATA

Of course, all the data shown here should be accepted with a grain of salt. There are issues with each data type:

- **Cases:** The actual case rate is unknown, and testing may merely make us aware of less serious cases (because we already know about the more severe cases—a sampling bias problem, since known data implies that infections often lead to hospitalization and death). It is not known how much of the recent uptick in cases is due to additional testing and how much is due to communication of the disease. New cases tell us only about the potential for additional communication, not the severity of the case.

  Also, what if a patient tests positive, then subsequently tests negative. Does that case still count? Should negative tests offset prior positive tests? And what about multiple positive tests—does that imply two cases, where only one case actually occurred?

  And what is a case? A "case" used to describe when someone showed symptoms. The word has now morphed to describe even asymptomatic people.

- **Hospitalizations:** The hospitalization rate has come into question recently as hospitals started testing every patient, so all admissions are counted as COVID-19 hospitalizations, regardless of the reason for the admission. That has tainted this important statistic.

Hospitals are paid more for COVID-19 cases, so the incentive may be misaligned with the goal of accurate measurement of COVID-19 hospitalizations.

- **Deaths:** Death is easy to determine, however: On April 14, 2020, the state of New York added 3,778 to its rolls as it changed counting methods to include cases that were "likely" due to COVID-19 versus the prior method of counting only "confirmed" deaths. At the time, the change added 17 percent to the number of US deaths. So, we can't even consider death statistics—the one statistic that is a vital measurement, which should be reliable—as accurate.

  Another issue is determining the cause of death, since flu and pneumonia deaths are lower than normal in 2020; are flu and pneumonia deaths lower because COVID-19 caused death among the unhealthy, such that the patient would have died from flu or pneumonia in a more "normal" year?

LOCKDOWNS

More lockdowns continue to be considered to corral the virus. But detailed data is the only way to combat the misinformation that has panicked the US. Decisions have already been made, so any recommendations I propose should be based on the specifics of each locale and school or school district.

Schools could be kept open based upon a Red/Yellow/Green approach. The approach is applied based on risk level, and my findings show that risk level varies by density of the population. Urban schools tend to fall under Code Red, suburban schools tend to be Code Yellow (especially in suburbs with high numbers of cases/hospitalizations/ deaths), and other areas fall under Code Green.

Regardless of whether age or preexisting conditions leads to death from COVID-19, those at higher risk could be isolated such that the rest of society needn't. That means schools could open with appropriate social distancing to limit the number of COVID-19 cases, rather than remaining closed because, "Children could die!"

We should learn from the data by specific location. Most people in the US don't live in New York City. There are 125,000 schools and 15,000 nursing homes that are not in New York City. Government one-size-fits-all rules don't fit in most locations.

MEDICARE FOR ALL

Calls for M4A have been remarkable during this pandemic. Bernie Sanders and others claimed that M4A would alleviate many of the problems that have arisen during the pandemic; however, this is what has transpired:

- People have lost and continue to lose their health coverage because of job loss.
- People can't afford the cost of ill health.

So let's address these issues:

- **People have lost and continue to lose their health coverage because of job loss.** The problem, M4A supporters claim, is that coverage is employment-based. If health insurance wasn't tied to employment, people would still be covered. However, a major problem with providing health insurance for everyone is the cost. At what point in the process is the system able to generate enough to afford the cost? Employees generate enough value through their work to pay for insurance. No value is created without work, meaning $3 trillion per year is not affordable by the system to provide coverage through M4A. Such a scheme would necessitate a redistribution of wealth from workers to provide coverage for all 325 million people. That means some people would get something (and very rich benefits through M4A) for doing nothing.

Suppose that 80 percent of the population works to provide insurance for 100 percent of the population. In this simplistic example, an additional 20 percent needs to be created by those working, or 20 percent divided by 80 percent, which is an additional 25 percent. Without a sudden productivity improvement of 25 percent, the only way to create enough for everyone would be a 25 percent reduction in pay. And if fewer people choose to work such that 75 percent work to provide for 100 percent of the population, that's 25 percent divided by 75 percent, or a one-third cut in pay. As fewer people work, the ratio in this simple example increases exponentially, such that the system would, at some point, fall apart.

The system wouldn't likely reach this point of no return, because people work for reasons other than healthcare (rewards for doing a good job, etc.); but someone working harder to pay for the benefit of a non-worker is the crux of the problem. My CAT4ALL plan, which provides a safety net plan for all, but at less cost to the system, offers workers (and non-workers) a choice to buy coverage below $100,000.

Under M4A, while Senator Sanders would claim individuals are not "forced" to buy anything, the system would be "forced" to afford first-dollar coverage, which is essentially the same thing (and no, "taxing the rich" cannot create enough dollars to pay for everyone).

• **People can't afford the cost of ill health.** The real question comes down to cost, which would be zero dollars out-of-pocket under M4A. Conversely, under CAT4ALL, costs above $100,000 per year would be covered, as would costs below $100,000 for those who purchase coverage. As for cost-sharing, richer plans could be purchased for higher premiums, and vice versa. The bottom line is that individuals would get what they pay for.

One more conversation with my DS friend:

We'd be much better off with COVID-19 if we had M4A.

Why would that be?

Everyone would be covered, so that everyone could afford treatment, as well as the cost of the vaccine.

You mean treatment would be free. But would the vaccine ever have been developed?

We'll never know.

Exactly. What a risk to "try it" another way. COVID-19 has been the most impactful virus in the history of mankind. To speculate that "things could have been better" is so ludicrous that it makes all your logic seem corrupt.

It is not. We wouldn't have private companies profiting by billions of dollars.

But the cost to the world is in the trillions of dollars. Profit is not a big concern at this point.

But a quarter of a million people have died under the current healthcare system.

What would it have been under M4A?

Like you'd say, we don't know.

No, and we wouldn't want to find out. Free healthcare doesn't mean quality healthcare.

Are you implying the quality would decline with M4A?

Yes, certainly long-term innovation would suffer. And cost (not copays, but taxes) would be so high that we wouldn't be able to afford the same healthcare under a future pandemic.

Well, why did the US do so poorly compared to the rest of the world?

The answer is very complicated, but many reasons include mobility of the US population, age, obesity, and culture.

Exactly. And M4A would have already improved the population health, such that the impact would be more like that in other countries.

That sounds like your bad argument that we could be like Scandinavian countries if we would just enact the policies of Scandinavia.

What's wrong with that?

Because we're nothing like them. And you do know that Sweden did not lock down their country at all and has had reasonably good results with under 10,000 deaths. How do you explain that?

Their decision was unique in the world.

Exactly. Countries make decisions that reflect their population, government, situation, etc. The US has made a good decision with healthcare to not succumb to the pressures you incite.

"Capitalism: the rich make. Socialism: the rich take."
–Andrew Wilkow, 2018

WRENCH

IN THE WORKS

"Under the Truman administration it was proposed that we have a compulsory health insurance program for all people in the United States, and, of course, the American people unhesitatingly rejected this."

–Ronald Reagan, 1962

write this on November 30, 2020. How does the 2020 election impact this book? The answer is complicated, because many people are involved beyond just the president.

M4A is not likely to be passed given the election. As quoted in the *Los Angeles Times*,

"People were talking in a really cocky way before that Democrats were going to take the trifecta [the White House, Senate, and House], and we were not ever going to talk to Republicans about anything. We were going to ram all this policy down their throats," said Rep. Scott Peters (D-CA), a moderate. "Ambitious liberal policies like Medicare for All and the Green New Deal are likely to be pushed to a back burner, though Rep. Alexandria Ocasio-Cortez (D-NY) and other progressives have signaled they will continue to advocate for their movement."

And will those enrolled in Obamacare notice an increase in their premiums beyond the 177 percent increase they've already experienced since 2013? Since they've already accepted high increases in premiums, they likely won't complain much more—especially the 87 percent receiving subsidies to purchase Obamacare. If the people on Obamacare exchanges don't demand it, will there be change?

Not likely. A Democrat president with a Republican Senate likely means that healthcare will not change in a major way in the US. Obamacare will likely continue, with minor modifications. As a result, M4A will not progress. Nor will my CAT4ALL.

The best outcome as a result of this book is for context to change from, "We spend too much as a percentage of GDP," to, "We spend a high but acceptable percentage of HDI." Should this shift in opinion occur, more reasonable changes to the healthcare system will be likely, versus knee-jerk reactions that will destine the country to overhaul a system that currently works better than other proposed systems (Single Payer). If a change in attitude does not occur, a Single Payer system would spell the end of innovation and sacrifice the long-term for the short-term.

In other words, there may be lower increases in premiums for a time. Will a 5 percent increase in Obamacare premiums seem reasonable, versus the prior 177 percent increase? But under M4A, there would be a halt to innovation and a decline in the number of health plan options, the number of doctors and healthcare professionals, the number of new drugs, and the number of life-saving interventions (because the government option would move resources to those people with future production value). We would not be able to measure "what could have been," so it's possible we wouldn't even realize the loss or what would have been with no changes to the status quo.

Here is an attempt to describe what the healthcare system would look like under M4A. I'll pontificate as to what CAT4ALL would look like in the following section.

M4A

Proponents of M4A often extrapolate to suggest what the near term may look like. Anyone would agree that speculating about the long term is even more difficult (and likely to be wrong), but I should still try.

Short Term. Since M4A is based on original Medicare, is there a reason one might expect success? Original Medicare solved coverage issues for those over sixty-five in the early years, at great cost in later years. Today, Medicare is perceived successful by few because it's projected that it will run out of funds in 2034, it has been projected to run out of funding for at least half of its existence, it underpays providers for the quality work they perform, it is mind-numbingly complex, it creates EOBs that no beneficiary understands, and it invites fraud like no other program.

The only lesson to learn from the enactment of original Medicare is that even if the plan had been successful in meeting original intent, future legislative changes led to program expansion and cost increases. Another way to put this is, if there are two good ideas for a program, and either idea could work by itself, diluting one idea with changes from the other may spell failure. Of course, this is true of any governmental program that changes trajectory due to a new president, a new Congress, or even a new administrator of the program.

Since the huge increases in original Medicare costs are tainted with increases due to expansion and other elements of change, I will return to the original Mercatus study: "it is likely that the actual cost of M4A would be substantially greater than has been estimated from its legislative text." The reason for this statement is that the legislative text assumes payment of providers at current Medicare payment levels, which are below average provider costs. This means the $32.6 trillion increase in federal government spending assumes this "bottom" reimbursement level, so the range of increased federal government spending is $32.6 trillion to $38 trillion over ten years is more likely; therefore, potential savings may turn out to be actual cost.

Long-Term. Recent Medicare spending is about one hundred times greater than in the 1960s, and recent Medicare cost increases have been higher than for non-Medicare over the last ten years. However, I recognize these increases in healthcare costs have more to do with eligibility as well as the age of the group that's covered.

There are three areas of potential long-term cost increases:

- The Medicare Trust Fund is already projected to run out of funds in 2034. There's pressure to decrease Medicare reimbursements to meet current obligations, so there's no room to increase Medicare reimbursements in order to keep Medicare providers engaged under M4A.

- M4A spending could escalate due to demand if the plan provides care for "free." We know costs will increase; we just don't know how high. Because of price inelasticity, one could expect demand to cause a 20 percent increase in cost, versus the status quo (20 percent is made up to illustrate that the increase in cost due to demand is significant, and could easily offset any savings from, for example, administration).

- We know innovation will essentially stop. Since we can't measure what doesn't happen, the impact is unknowable. The bottom line is either shorter life expectancies or higher costs because innovative solutions never evolve such that end-of-life care is more prevalent (and ultimately more costly).

Another major issue is that M4A eliminates the insurance industry. Once that happens, there is no alternative, as the market will be gone, perhaps for as long as ten years even if allowed to grow again as an industry. Whether proposed as an option or a full replacement, M4A eliminates or leads to elimination of the private insurance industry market.

The long-term scenario appears to be the end of the healthcare system as we know it. One could not dream of a scarier scenario of higher cost, lack of innovation, and failing markets that lack providers. The bottom line is that M4A is destined for failure, either because it costs too much or it spends too little. There is no way to "thread the needle" to accomplish every goal, and the worst possible outcome—spending more than the status quo—is likely.

CAT4ALL

A better solution is obvious: catastrophic insurance (the very definition of insurance) that provides preexisting condition and bankruptcy security, while maintaining the market, allows the market and innovation to evolve to meet the public's needs. The 2020 election seems to make the chances of CAT4ALL coming to fruition less likely, but perhaps that's all the more reason to make it happen. Without it, Obamacare and the "choice" of a government option will lead to similar results as for M4A.

Short Term. No modeling exists that would show the impact of CAT4ALL; there is no reason for CBO to score such a change unless legislated. It is likely that the cost of the CAT4ALL plan would be similar to current catastrophic expenditures, both private and public. Such a comparison may not be as vital to the overall cost picture, since there is no comparison to current spending that is comparable, other than to assure providers of consistent revenues.

The bottom line is that costs should be similar to costs in the short term for the status quo, with major winners and losers, unfortunately. For example, those receiving Obamacare subsidies would lose them (potentially offset through lower taxes or higher pay). The goal may be more focused on getting past the upheaval and setting the stage for market competition to benefit in the long term.

Long-Term. There are three areas of potential long-term cost savings:

- Competition in the market, which cannot be measured or antici-pated until it happens. The savings has the potential to be, say, 10 percent, as assumed in my example in Chapter 9 (significant, but unknown how successful it may be). Savings from competition will, of course, be uneven by geographic area, by category (hospital, physician, drug, etc.), and by year (smaller in the early years until competition takes hold).

- Quality would improve in a similar fashion to the recent past. We won't be able to measure what could have happened, but quality of healthcare would likely improve like it has in the last twenty years. An example might be that hospitals compete for market share, where every encounter at the hospital improves. Quality should lower costs in the long run. And outrageous balance-billing may occur to a lesser extent where, for example, a $1,000 extra charge for out-of-network coverage may instead be $500.

- Innovation will hopefully continue similarly to the status quo. An example may be a vaccine for COVID-19, where incentives are aligned to find a solution. Another example is cures for rare diseases, where the potential to profit is more important than the esoteric desire to help a fellow person. Innovation ultimately leads to higher quality and lower costs.

The long-term scenario appears to be the only acceptable outcome with the healthcare system, such that CAT4ALL is a reasonable alternative. If the costs of the status quo system are unacceptable, keeping good parts of the current system makes sense to avoid upheaval that everyone regrets.

One more conversation with my DS friend:

The real problem is hospital chargemasters that are so complex, with like, 20,000 items, which no employee can even understand or explain. Nor can the patients. That leads to the real culprit: those greedy people who work there pushing paper and doing unidentifiable things, like "administration."

You're right that chargemasters are very complex and making them transparent will not likely change buying habits if care is free. The hospital struggles to even explain them.

Then why don't we hire cheaper and fewer people to do these jobs, like would be the need with the simpler M4A system?

Rather than killing incentives in the current system, why not simplify where possible? Of course, if other people could do these jobs and be employed for less, they would be so employed; if administrators make so much for doing so little, you, too, could be an administrator. Go ahead.

Okay, that's a life-long endeavor.

So just invest in one of the for-profit hospitals and share in those profits.

Okay, requires money.

Then I can't help you. You're insufferable.

You're just a healthcare apologist who takes up the side of high-charging entities.

No, I'm making counterarguments that never get made by anyone. I don't take the easy route by blaming everything I see just because I'm frustrated.

Well, something needs to be done.

Not if it sacrifices the long-term for the short-term, like M4A does.

It does not. Like you say, you can project costs long-term; so we should look at costs that can be projected, like in the short term.

That's smart. Let's save money today that costs us tomorrow, even if the net-net spends more in total.

It would not. You just said that future costs can't be predicted with any accuracy.

So, yes, being short-sighted in your world is a virtue. That's how Medicare got started in the first place. With hindsight, there's no way you could argue that spending one hundred times the short-term costs would be palatable.

Okay, what would you have done, Mister twenty/twenty visionary?

The same thing I'm proposing today: create a catastrophic coverage plan that provides bankruptcy and preexisting condition protection, without the "rent control" that Medicare employs today.

Something must change. We can't afford the cost of our health-care system.

Yes, we can. Our HDI is high enough.

"Communism has sometimes succeeded as a scavenger, but never as a leader. It has never come to power in a country that was not disrupted by war or corruption, or both." –John F. Kennedy, 1963

EPILOGUE

ENVY OF THE WORLD

I marvel at the US healthcare system. It is often described as the envy of the world, yet people castigate it as if it's poor. How ironic.

Healthcare in the US is so desired that the best and brightest want to practice medicine here, the population benefits as patients, we develop many amazing interventions and cures, and we are positioned well to tackle complex problems in the future. This is a great time to be alive and to benefit from the one system that hasn't succumbed to the pressures of cost and quality, to triage cases in the halls of hospitals, and to the falsehoods being promoted about an emergency in our healthcare system. We've already made the decision to pay for quality healthcare, including innovation that's second to none.

Healthcare is too important to declare an emergency, which leads to ideas like M4A. The US shouldn't overreact to the healthcare conundrum such that something, anything needs to be done. This drumbeat has been whittling away at society for fifty years.

WHAT DO PEOPLE REALLY WANT?

Healthcare costs may grow to 50 percent of GDP. So be it. Maslow's Hierarchy of Needs, along with the cost comparison to HDI, shows that we're in uncharted territory. In the whiniest voice you can imagine: *"But everyone should have healthcare!"*

My goal is not to be the most-read book, but to have influence on the discussion. That may mean merely that the reader talks more intelligently about healthcare, or that many politicians in the US read the book. (I'm sending a copy to Congress.)

There are some elements that I chose to highlight:

- I show lots of data. I did this on purpose to provide you with statistics. Many articles today are written under the premise that numbers bore readers, so numbers are avoided. A recent article mentions two responses in a survey, first a percentage of respondents, but then quotes "the majority of responses" for the second. I'm sure this was done because the author assumed that another mention of "52 percent" would make the reader's eyes glaze over. However, the wording "the majority of responses" implies that maybe 60 percent or even 70 percent favored something, while just 52 percent implies a less-riveting result. A classic approach to help the writer make a point, but an obfuscation of the data.

- I chose to show positive charts about Obamacare enrollment, rather than disparaging the law's enrollment as some have done (showing only enrollment figures from 2013 to 2015, for example). I felt I didn't need to hammer every point home.

- Expertise is not experience. There are many experts on all topics, but it takes experience to have common sense. Every reader has common sense, and it's the conglomeration of every experience that makes people who they are. No expert can change that. So experience leads people to think positively about the US healthcare system, despite what they are told.

- I'm exasperated that many articles highlight high costs in the US without proper context. For example, articles that highlight hospital bills that show how expensive treatment compares to other options—for example: aspirin tablets for $1.50, where the same amount buys a hundred pills at a drugstore. Hospital pricing is based on an allocation of costs such that the pill's ingredient price (variable) may be just ten cents, but the price charged reflects allocated fixed costs. Writers claim to have the head-shaking facts that "prove" their point, only to rile up a few readers. *"Yes, the hospital should create a new program to buy units of fifty aspirins from external pharmacies and then pass the savings on to patients for just, say, fifty cents. That'll do it."* Of course, the extra dollar must come from something else that the writer can then complain about costing too much. As if the hospital doesn't already purchase in bulk to keep costs down.

One more story: Panama suffered 365 deaths from toxic cough syrup in 2007, an event that was so widespread because Panama provided free medicines to its citizens.

HATFIELDS AND MCCOYS

"And the rich will exhaust all possible advantages to make money on a new program." This argument is akin to what I call a "Hatfields and McCoys" arguments. For those who may not know, the Hatfields and the McCoys were mortal enemies in the late 1800s—two warring families who would kill members of the other family in retaliation for killings of their own families. The killings emanated from one original sin: the stealing of a pig.

My point: Government complaining about how someone reacts to what the government does exacerbates the issue. No, legislation did not lead to the death of anyone; but legislation that causes a reaction that the government doesn't like and didn't intend, and then complaining that it's the individual's fault, is short-sighted.

Had either the Hatfields or the McCoys stopped retaliating, the feud would have ended. If the animosity toward rich executives would stop, the government would stop enacting laws that lead to other acts the government deems wrong:

- In 1993, legislation capped the deductibility of executive pay to the first $1 million for a company's top five executives. President Clinton heralded this change as the beginning of the end of executives being overpaid.
- Companies avoided the $1 million cap by paying performance-based pay. So CEOs got paid more due to stock options and the like. Today, stock options are deemed immoral because CEOs receive very high pay (think Jeff Bezos of Amazon). Executive pay may be higher than what it might have been, had the Clinton Administration not tried to fix the problem.

Other examples of "Hatfields and McCoys" arguments:

- **Preexisting condition limitations**: Insurance companies tried to limit customers' fraudulent claims, but Congress declared insurance companies are evil because of these limitations. *"Of course, we can't blame individuals who caused these limitations to be needed in the first place; the problem is how the insurance companies reacted."*

- **Obamacare changes:** Obamacare failed on its own, but some claim President Trump wanted Obamacare repealed, so his recent changes made it fail. *"We can't blame failure on the law itself."*

- **Obamacare design:** Obamacare rules have led to insurance company losses in the market, so some insurance companies withdrew from the market, while others went out of business. *"The lack of insurers available in certain markets is due to those greedy insurance companies."*

- **Provider charges:** Medicare and Medicaid underpay providers, but when providers offset low payments by charging private entities more, they're accused of gouging the market. Had they not charged the private market more, would they still be in business? If you think about it, private insurance has made Medicare and Medicaid viable. *"We can't blame Medicare and Medicaid."*

- **The uninsured:** Proponents claim that anyone against M4A must be evil since they must be against covering the uninsured, as if their idea is the only way to cover them. *"But everyone must be covered."*

One last conversation with my DS friend:

> With Single Payer, we'll be more competitive because our businesses won't have to shoulder the burden of our healthcare costs.

> That's a silly accounting argument that shifts the burden from companies to taxpayers. Costs will increase to cover those taxes, whether the taxes are directly paid by companies or individuals. That's like taking a gallon of water out of one part of the lake and putting it in another part, thinking that you've lowered the lake level.

> So what you're saying is that we shouldn't try Single Payer?

> Correct. It will fail, and we don't need full-blown revolution.

> And instead we should try catastrophic coverage for all?

Yes. It will eliminate medical bankruptcies while allowing the free market to cover what the government doesn't.

But people won't be able to afford coverage under $100,000. We'll still have medical bankruptcies.

Perhaps. But those cases, one could argue, will be self-inflicted.

That's not true. No one knows they're going to hit $100,000 in claims in a year, so they have no control.

That's why they should buy insurance.

But what if they can't afford it?

I thought healthcare insurance is the most important thing to purchase in life. So why don't those in need buy coverage?

Because the premiums are too high.

We don't know that until the new market forms. And that complementary market insurance will be purchased by, maybe, two-thirds of the population.

That would still be one-third who aren't covered.

By choice. Every purchase in life is an individual decision to either get something or to keep the money the individual chooses not to spend.

What will the US rank in the WHO study be?

It would move up, but I don't know how high. And I don't know that a debunked study's ranking will mean much.

But what will you do with the ACA?

It would need to be repealed and replaced with CAT4ALL.

But what about the gains from the ACA?

Which ones?

No preexisting condition limitations, which is the most important one.

Check. There will be no preexisting condition coverage under CAT4ALL, and the market will follow whatever preexisting condition coverage regulations are passed.

Well, I'll tell you right now: the market shouldn't have them.

Okay, the government can decide through regulation, either at the federal or state level.

What about coverage for kids to age twenty-six?

Coverage through age twenty-five can be an independent regulation and that would only need to apply in the market.

What about Medicaid expansion?

It wouldn't be a consideration with CAT4ALL. Each state could choose whether to expand Medicaid, without the current coercion from the federal government, where money to pay for expansion is available to the states only if they make the right decision.

So, you wouldn't encourage Medicaid expansion?

Medicaid is run by each state, so each state should be free to make that decision. If you think about it, expanding Medicaid would be such a simpler way to address the number of uninsured, instead of creating complicated Obamacare regulations that affect everyone. Why go through a process where everyone may qualify, but then don't because they don't qualify for a subsidy? It's more complex than it needs to be.

Won't your regulations need to be complex?

Probably. The CAT4ALL plan regulations will need to be about as complicated as Medicare regulations are today, and market regulations will need to cover specific issues like those that exist with the current individual market.

Won't the market premiums be high, like insurer premiums with the ACA?

Some will be high, but all will be lower than under the ACA. Over half of the cost is due to large claims, and the market won't have to bear that cost. If there is price-sensitivity to the new insurance, that's a good thing.

But that's a bad thing today—price-sensitivity.

Yes, but what options do people have today if there is only one insurer in their market?

But the new market will face similar problems.

However, incenting competition allows more plans to enter the market. Having options will benefit the consumer. And the decisions, right or wrong, will be smaller, because the premium will be $500 per month rather than $2,000 per month.

But competition still doesn't work when you're in an ambulance and need care immediately.

> There will still be market forces (both for the consumer choosing their insurance and for the insurance company to negotiate better deals with providers). All that will need to occur before you're in the ambulance.

Isn't cost control by the government better than the market?

> No. Providers will leave the market if they can't survive with government controls. That's happened everywhere government control is tried.

Why not control price first?

> That's moronic. Your fix with government control will lead to as many problems, if not more.

So, what would you do?

> Evolution, not devolution.

Nice. Devolution as in to devolve. But what if it doesn't work?

> As Matt Ridley wrote, no one can manage the unmanageable. Here's a shortened version of his quote: "The truth is that nobody is in charge. It is the hardest thing for human beings to get used to, but the world is full of intricate systems."

I'll ask again: What if it doesn't work?

The new healthcare market should work like markets have always worked.

But you can't just have companies deciding willy-nilly everything they want to do. There must be regulation.

It's not an all-or-nothing proposition. Regulations need to allow freedom in the market. And the market self-corrects when consumers don't like something.

That didn't happen with preexisting conditions.

Only because if a company chose to offer coverage without preexisting condition coverage, their price would have increased so much that they couldn't stay in business. So, yes, a market needs rules for commerce.

Well, why the heck didn't that happen already?

Good question. Regulators tinkered around the edges, but preexisting condition limitations continued to be allowed in the individual market. Don't blame the player; blame the game.

"There is nothing wrong with America that can't be fixed by what's right with America."

–Bill Clinton, 1993

ENDNOTES

PROLOGUE

p. 1 'as it has inviolably since the dawn of time'. "World Death Rate Holding Steady At 100 Percent." *The Onion*. January 22, 1997. http://www.theonion.com/article/world-death-rate-holding-steady-at-100-percent-1670.

p. 3 'Low Income: 63'. "Life Expectancy at Birth, Total (Years)." Accessed April 2020. http://data.worldbank.org/indicator/SP.DYN.LE00.IN.

p. 3 'Maslow's Hierarchy of Needs'. "Abraham Maslow." Wikimedia Foundation, April 4, 2020. https://en.wikipedia.org/wiki/Abraham_Maslow.

p. 4 'they are markets with decentralized, diffuse controls'. *Genome: The Autobiography of a Species in 23 Chapters*, Matt Ridley, 2006, HarperCollins, New York, p. 151.

p. 4 'Why are there twenty-three brands of underarm sprays?' Krayewski, Ed. "Bernie Sanders: Don't Need 23 Choices of Deodorant, 18 Choices of Sneakers When Kids Are Going Hungry." Reason.com. May 26, 2015. https://reason.com/2015/05/26/bernie-sanders-dont-need-23-choices-of-d/.

p. 9 'by puppet politicians such as Reagan and Thatcher'. K, Sammy. "Why Don't Some Americans Want a Universal Healthcare System?" *Medium*. Extra Newsfeed, November 16, 2017. https://extranewsfeed. com/why-dont-some-americans-want-a-universal-healthcare-system-a47e99f24496.

p. 10 'six to eleven bread portions per day'. Stampfer, Meir J. "Rebuilding the Food Pyramid." *Scientific American,* December 1, 2006. https://www. scientificamerican.com/article/rebuilding-the-food-pyramid/.

p. 10 'The 1992 food pyramid came from Sweden'. Smallwood, Karl. "Who Invented the Food Pyramid? Today I Found Out", August 24, 2014. http://www.todayifoundout.com/index.php/2013/09/invented-food-pyramid/.

p. 10 'Only the US and New Zealand allow direct-to-consumer prescription drug advertising'. Lee, Benita. "How Is Consumer Drug Advertising Regulated in the United States?" The *GoodRx Prescription Savings* Blog, June 18, 2019. https://www.goodrx.com/blog/prescription-drug-advertising-regulation-united-states/.

p. 11 'US healthcare is rated #37 in a 2000 World Health Organization study'. "The World Health Report 2000 - Health Systems: Improving Performance." World Health Organization, July 29, 2013. https://www.who.int/whr/2000/en/.

p. 12 'costly new drugs and diagnostic technologies'. McCaughey, Betsy. "Single-Payer a Danger for Cancer Patients." RealClearPolitics, January 10, 2018. https://www.realclearpolitics.com/articles/2018/01/10/single-payer_a_danger_for_cancer_patients_135970.html.

p. 17 'A 2,700-page bill with twenty thousand pages of regulation'. Weisman, Jonathan, and Robert Pear. "Partisan Gridlock Thwarts Effort to Alter Health Law." The *New York Times*, May 27, 2013. https://www.nytimes.

com/2013/05/27/us/politics/polarized-congress-thwarts-changes-to-health-care-law.html.

p. 17 '80,000 pages of regulations'. Crews, Jr., Clyde Wayne. "Obama's Legacy: 2016 Ends With A Record-Shattering Regulatory Rulebook." *Forbes Magazine*, December 30, 2016. https://www.forbes.com/sites/waynecrews/2016/12/30/obamas-legacy-2016-ends-with-a-record-shattering-regulatory-rulebook/#118bb2421398.

CHAPTER 1

p. 20 'Health Care Spending as % of GDP'. Drum, Kevin. "Chart of the Day: Health Care Spending as a Percentage of GDP." Mother Jones, June 23, 2017. https://www.motherjones.com/kevin-drum/2017/06/chart-day-health-care-spending-percentage-gdp/.

p. 21 'Countries allocate a markedly higher percentage of income to health as disposable income rises'. Random Critical Analysis, January 31, 2020. https://randomcriticalanalysis.com/.

p. 22 'higher GDP per capita than the US (2019)'. World Bank, "GDP Per Capita." World Bank. Accessed September 2020. https://data.world-bank.org/indicator/NY.GDP.PCAP.CD?most_recent_value_desc=true.

p. 25 'healthcare industry and its sixteen million employees'. "Healthcare Job Growth Outpaced Nearly Every Other Sector in 2018." HealthLeaders. Accessed April 2020. https://www.healthleadersMedia.com/strategy/healthcare-job-growth-outpaced-nearly-every-other-sector-2018.

p. 26 'Spurious Correlations by Tyler Vigen'. "15 Insane Things That Correlate With Each Other." *Spurious Correlations*. Accessed April 2020. https://www.tylervigen.com/spurious-correlations.

p. 29 'Denmark is a market economy'. Goldhill, Olivia. "Denmark Says It Isn't the Socialist Utopia Bernie Sanders Thinks It Is." Quartz, November 1, 2015. https://qz.com/538499/denmark-says-it-isnt-the-socialist-utopia-bernie-sanders-thinks-it-is/.

p. 29 'an extensive and expensive healthcare system'. "Finland's Government Resigns after Healthcare Reform Fails." CNBC, March 8, 2019. https://www.cnbc.com/2019/03/08/finlands-government-resigns-after-healthcare-reform-fails.html.

p. 29 'just 9 percent of Swedes call themselves socialists'. "Sweden's Lessons for America." Cato Institute, March 5, 2020. https://www.cato.org/publications/policy-report/swedens-lessons-america.

p. 30 'compare the US population to that of Scandinavia'. "Countries in the World by Population (2020)." Worldometer. Accessed April 2020. https://www.worldometers.info/world-population/population-by-country/.

p. 30 'compare the US population to that of Scandinavia'. "World Development Indicators." DataBank. Accessed May 2020. https://databank.worldbank.org/reports.aspx?source=2&series=SH.XPD.CHEX.GD.ZS&country=.

p. 30 'compare the US population to that of Scandinavia'. Central Intelligence Agency, February 1, 2018. https://www.cia.gov/library/publications/the-world-factbook/fields/400.html.

p. 30 'compare the US population to that of Scandinavia'. Central Intelligence Agency, February 1, 2018. https://www.cia.gov/library/publications/the-world-factbook/fields/367.html#DA.

p. 30 'compare the US population to that of Scandinavia'. "Homicide Rate."

Our World in Data. Accessed May 2020. https://ourworldindata.org/grapher/intentional-homicides-per-100000-people?year=2015.

p. 30 'compare the US population to that of Scandinavia'. "Transport - Road Accidents - OECD Data." The OECD. Accessed May 2020. https://data.oecd.org/transport/road-accidents.htm.

p. 30 'compare the US population to that of Scandinavia'. "Ethnic groups." Accessed May 2020. https://www.indexmundi.com/factbook/fields/ethnic-groups.

p. 31 'Scandinavian countries are the least corrupt countries in the world'. "United States." Transparency.org. Accessed August 2020. https://www.transparency.org/en/countries/united-states.

p. 31 'measures about half that in Scandinavia'. Ortiz-Ospina, Esteban, and Max Roser. "Trust." Our World in Data, July 22, 2016. https://ourworld-indata.org/trust#how-do-countries-around-the-world-compare-in-terms-of-interpersonal-trust.

p. 31 'while Scandinavian countries averaged 76'. "Country Rankings." Country Rankings: World & Global Economy Rankings on Economic Freedom. Accessed May 2020. https://www.heritage.org/index/ranking.

p. 32 '2018'. Small, Leslie. "HHS: Benchmark ACA Premiums to Rise 37% in 2018." FierceHealthcare, November 1, 2017. https://www.fiercehealth-care.com/aca/hhs-benchmark-aca-premiums-to-rise-37-2018.

p. 32 'Assistant Planning for Evaluation'. "Individual Market Premium Changes: 2013–2017." Health and Human Services, May 24, 2017. https://aspe.hhs.gov/pdf-report/individual-market-premi-um-changes-2013-2017.

p. 32 'we have no poverty either'. "If Sweden's Big Welfare State Is Superior to America's Medium Welfare State, Then Why Do Swedes in America Earn Far More than Swedes in Sweden?" Cato Institute, September 13, 2012. https://www.cato.org/blog/swedens-big-welfare-state-superi-or-americas-medium-welfare-state-then-why-do-swedes-america.

p. 35 'profits averaged about 17 percent of revenues from 2006 to 2015'. U.S. Government Accountability Office. "Drug Industry: Profits, Research and Development Spending, and Merger and Acquisition Deals." December 19, 2017. https://www.gao.gov/products/GAO-18-40.

p. 36 'revenues of $242 billion in 2019'. O'Brien, Jack. "UnitedHealth Group Ends 2019 With $242B In Revenues." HealthLeaders. January 12, 2020. https://www.healthleadersmedia.com/finance/unitedhealth-group-ends-2019-242b-revenues.

p. 39 'A rising tide lifts all boats'. "John F. Kennedy on the Economy and Taxes." JFK Library. Accessed May 2020. https://www.jfklibrary.org/learn/about-jfk/jfk-in-history/john-f-kennedy-on-the-econo-my-and-taxes.

p. 40 'The US develops more drugs because US patients use more drugs'. "Paying for Prescription Drugs Around the World: Why is the U.S. an Outlier?" The Commonwealth Fund. October 5, 2017. https://www.commonwealthfund.org/publications/issue-briefs/2017/oct/paying-prescription-drugs-around-world-why-us-outlier.

p. 40 'Four of the world's top ten hospitals for treating cancer are in the US'. Miller, Noah. "The 10 Best Hospitals in the World." Newsweek, March 29, 2019. https://www.newsweek.com/2019/04/05/10-best-hospitals-world-1368512.html.

p. 41 'We have the highest percentage of specialists per physician than any other country'. "U.S. Health Care Spending: Comparison with Other OECD Countries." Cornell University ILR School, September 17, 2007. https://digitalcommons.ilr.cornell.edu/cgi/viewcontent.cgi?article=1316&context=key_workplace.

p. 43 '2015 GDP'. "GDP by Industry." U.S. Bureau of Economic Analysis (BEA). Accessed May 2020. https://www.bea.gov/data/gdp/gdp-industry.

p. 43 'US Industry GDP Pie Charts'. Google Search. Google. Accessed May 2020. https://www.google.com/search?q=us+industry+gdp+pie+charts+2012&tbm=isch&ved=2ahUKEwi_wYmljJ3pAhUOQawKHZwNBv0Q2-cCegQIABAA&oq=us+industry+gdp+pie+charts+2012&gs_lcp=CgNpbWcQAzIECCMQJ1C1ywxYydcMYMXbDGgAcAB4AIABU4gB_QKSAQE1mAEAoAEBqgELZ3dzLXdpei1pb-Wc&sclient=img&ei=-Y2xXv_gNo6CsQWcm5joDw&rlz=1C1GGRV_enUS763US764#imgrc=wy97Fg2jMHCE6M.

p. 43 'Robert Kornfeld of BEA reconciled'. "Research Spotlight A Reconciliation of Health Care Expenditures in the National Health Expenditures Accounts and in Gross Domestic Product." BEA. September 2010. https://apps.bea.gov/scb/pdf/2010/09%20September/0910_healthcare.pdf.

p. 46 'This chart provides an amazing array of statistics never compared before'. Statistics Canada: Canada's national statistical agency / Statistique Canada : Organisme statistique national du Canada. Accessed May 2020. https://www150.statcan.gc.ca/t1/tbl1/en/tv.action?pid=3610043401.

p. 46 'This chart provides an amazing array of statistics never compared before'. "Gross Domestic Product (GDP)." Office for National Statistics. Accessed May 2020. https://www.ons.gov.uk/economy/grossdomesticproductgdp.

p. 47 'serving households (such as the Red Cross)'. "Nipa Primer." BEA. Accessed May 2020. https://www.bea.gov/sites/default/files/methodologies/.

p. 47 'free medical and dental treatment to Venezuelans'. The Associated Press. "Navy Hospital Ship Comfort Treats Venezuelan Migrants, Colombians." *Navy Times*, November 27, 2018. https://www.navytimes.com/news/your-navy/2018/11/27/navy-hospital-ship-comfort-treats-venezuelan-migrants-colombians/.

p. 49 'about two-thirds purchase supplemental coverage'. Kliff, Sarah. "Private Health Insurance Exists in Europe and Canada. Here's How It Works." Vox, February 12, 2019. https://www.vox.com/health-care/2019/2/12/18215430/single-payer-private-health-insurance-harris-sanders.

p. 51 'But the penalty was $700 per person in 2017'. "Affordable Care Act Tax Penalty Calculator." Medical Mutual. Accessed April 2020. https://www.medmutual.com/For-Individuals-and-Families/Health-Insurance-Education/Health-Insurance-Basics/Penalty-Estimator.aspx.

p. 51 'Many people submitted silent tax returns'. Keith, Katie. "IRS Round-Up: Inspector General Report And Guidance on Mandates." Health Affairs, January 31, 2019. https://www.healthaffairs.org/do/10.1377/hblog20190131.860755/full/.

p. 52 'Healthcare Expenditures per Capita as a Percent of US Expenditures: 1997'. Huber, M. "Health Expenditure Trends in OECD Countries, 1970-1997." Health care financing review. CENTERS for MEDICARE & MEDICAID SERVICES, 1999. https://www.ncbi.nlm.nih.gov/pmc/articles/PMC4194642/.

CHAPTER 2

p. 58 'Clinton—370, H. W. Bush—168, Perot—0'. 270 to win, 1992 Presidential Election. Accessed October 2020. https://www.270towin.com/1992_Election/.

p. 58 'most networks during prime time'. "Ross Perot Electronic Town Hall." YouTube. Accessed May 2020. https://www.youtube.com/watch?v=mPIVIOCbCmg.

p. 61 'but ahead of others'. "Judging Health Systems: Focusing on What Matters." An Ounce of Evidence | Health Policy, September 18, 2017. https://blogs.sph.harvard.edu/ashish-jha/2017/09/18/judging-health-systems-focusing-on-what-matters/.

p. 63 'Price Changes'. Perry, Mark. "Chart of the Day (Century?): Price Changes 1998 to 2020." Carpe Diem, blog. AEI. Accessed October 2020. https://www.aei.org/blog/carpe-diem/page/5/.

p. 64 'In a 2016 article, *Reason* Magazine'. Tupy, Marian. "The Most Important Graph in the World." *Reason*, December 13, 2016. https://reason.com/2016/12/13/the-most-important-graph-in-the-world/.

p. 65 'The above chart shows life expectancy'. Roser, Max, Esteban Ortiz-Ospina, and Hannah Ritchie. "Life Expectancy." Our World in Data, May 23, 2013. https://ourworldindata.org/life-expectancy.

p. 66 'Life expectancy at three points in history'. Roser, Max, Esteban Ortiz-Ospina, and Hannah Ritchie. "Life Expectancy." Our World in Data, May 23, 2013. https://ourworldindata.org/life-expectancy.

p. 70 'Population Statistics'. "Countries in the World by Population (2019)." Worldometer. Accessed May 2020. https://www.worldometers.info/world-population/population-by-country/.

p. 71 'Waiting Your Turn'. "Wait Times for Health Care in Canada 2019." *To Do Canada*, January 9, 2020. https://www.todocanada.ca/wait-times-for-health-care-in-canada-2019/.

p. 72 'Canadian Wait Times (2008)'. "Waiting Your Turn: Hospital Waiting Lists in Canada 2008 Report." Studies in Healthcare Policy. Fraser Institute. Accessed May 2020. https://www.fraserinstitute.org/sites/default/files/WaitingYourTurn2008.pdf.

p. 73 'The Golden Hour of Medicine'. "Golden Hour (Medicine)." *Wikipedia*. Wikimedia Foundation, March 9, 2020. https://en.wikipedia.org/wiki/Golden_hour_(medicine).

p. 74 'Sources of Waste in American Health Care'. Evans, Robert G. "Waste, Economists and American Healthcare." *Healthcare policy = Politiques de sante*. Longwoods Publishing, November 2013. https://www.ncbi.nlm.nih.gov/pmc/articles/PMC3999538/.

p. 75 'Growth of Physicians and Administrators'. Borders, Max. "The Chart That Could Undo the Healthcare System: Max Borders." Foundation for Economic Education, April 29, 2015. https://fee.org/articles/the-chart-that-could-undo-the-us-healthcare-system/.

p. 76 'Prevalence of Self-Reported Obesity Among US Adults by State and Territory, 2017'. "DNPAO Data, Trends and Maps: Explore by Topic." Centers for Disease Control and Prevention. Accessed May 2020. https://nccd.cdc.gov/dnpao_dtm/rdPage.aspx?rdReport=DNPAO_DTM.ExploreByTopic&islClass=OWS&islTopic=OWS1&go=GO.

p. 77 'Cost per Human Genome'. "The Cost of Sequencing a Human Genome." Genome.gov. Accessed May 2020. https://www.genome.gov/about-genomics/fact-sheets/Sequencing-Human-Genome-cost.

p. 78 'Ebitda Margins by Industry'. FT Alphaville. Accessed May 2020. https://ftalphaville.ft.com/2016/03/29/2157698/ranking-americas-industries-by-profitability-and-tax-rate/.

p. 79 'Number of Hospitals in the US'. "Fast Facts on U.S. Hospitals, 2020: AHA." American Hospital Association. Accessed May 2020. https://www.aha.org/statistics/fast-facts-us-hospitals.

p. 80 'Breakdown of community hospitals'. "Fast Facts on U.S. Hospitals, 2020: AHA." American Hospital Association. Accessed May 2020. https://www.aha.org/statistics/fast-facts-us-hospitals.

p. 81 'The chart above shows Medicare, Medicaid, and Private Insurance acceptance'. Boccuti, Cristina, Christa Fields, Giselle Casillas, and Liz Hamel. "Primary Care Physicians Accepting Medicare: A Snapshot." The Henry J. Kaiser Family Foundation, December 23, 2015. https://www.kff.org/medicare/issue-brief/primary-care-physicians-accepting-medicare-a-snapshot/.

p. 82 '2015 Consumer Expenditures'. "Consumer Expenditures in 2015: BLS Reports." U.S. Bureau of Labor Statistics, April 1, 2017. https://www.bls.gov/opub/reports/consumer-expenditures/2015/home.htm.

p. 83 'Medical CPI versus General CPI'. Kanopiadmin. "How Government Regulations Made Healthcare So Expensive: Mike Holly." Mises Institute, May 9, 2017. https://mises.org/wire/how-government-regulations-made-healthcare-so-expensive.

p. 84 'Poverty Rate Throughout History'. Rector, R. (n.d.). The War on Poverty: 50 years of failure. Retrieved August 2020, from https://www. heritage.org/marriage-and-family/commentary/the-war-poverty-50-years-failure.

p. 86 'Who pays Taxes?'. DeSilver, Drew. "Who Pays U.S. Income Tax, and How Much?" Pew Research Center, October 6, 2017. https://www.pewresearch.org/fact-tank/2017/10/06/a-closer-look-at-who-does-and-doesnt-pay-u-s-income-tax/.

p. 87 'Taxes on the Rich'. Greenberg, Scott. "Taxes on the Rich Were Not That Much Higher in the 1950s." Tax Foundation, January 2, 2020. https:// taxfoundation.org/taxes-on-the-rich-1950s-not-high/.

p. 88 'Company Size'. Kiersz, Andy. "The Impact of Small Business on the US Economy in 2 Extreme Charts." *Business Insider*, June 16, 2015. https:// www.businessinsider.com/us-employment-by-firm-size-has-a-fat-tailed-distribution-2015-6.

p. 89 'Inflation by Country'. "Inflation rate, average consumer prices."IMF. Accessed May 2020. https://www.imf.org/external/datamapper/ PCPIPCH@WEO/OEMDC/.

p. 90 'A Collection of Various Measurements'. "Research." The Institute of International Finance. Accessed May 2020. https://www.iif.com/ Research/Capital-Flows-and-Debt/Global-Debt-Monitor.

p. 90 'A Collection of Various Measurements'. Blahous, Charles. "The Cost of a National Single-Payer Healthcare System." Mercatus Center George Mason University. https://www.mercatus.org/system/files/ blahous-costs-medicare-mercatus-working-paper-v1_1.pdf.

p. 90 'A Collection of Various Measurements'. Blahous, Charles. "The Fiscal Effects of Repealing the Affordable Care Act." Mercatus Center George Mason University, n.d. https://www.mercatus.org/system/files/mercatus-blahous-repealing-aca-v1.pdf.

p. 90 'A Collection of Various Measurements'. "Trustees Report & Trust Funds." CMS. Accessed May 2020. https://www.cms.gov/Research-Statistics-Data-and-Systems/Statistics-Trends-and-Reports/ReportsTrustFunds.

p. 90 'A Collection of Various Measurements'. "The 2015 Annual Report of the Board of Trustees of the Federal Old-Age and Survivors Insurance and Federal Disability Insurance Trust Funds." The Board of Trustees, Federal Old-Age and Survivors Insurance and Federal Disability Insurance Trust Funds. Accessed May 2020. https://www.ssa.gov/oact/tr/2015/tr2015.pdf.

p. 90 'A Collection of Various Measurements'. "2015 Annual Report of the Boards of Trustees of the Federal Hospital Insurance and Federal Supplementary Medical Insurance Trust Funds." The Boards of Trustees, Federal Hospital Insurance and Federal Supplementary Medical Insurance Trust Funds. Accessed May 2020. https://www.cms.gov/research-statistics-data-and-systems/statistics-trends-and-reports/reportstrustfunds/downloads/tr2015.pdf.

p. 91 'A Collection of Various Measurements'. "Congressional Budget Office." Congressional Budget Office. Accessed May 2020. https://www.cbo.gov/topics/retirement/medicare.

CHAPTER 3

p. 93 'sideline business in national defense and homeland security'. "U.S. Department of the Treasury." Remarks of Under Secretary of the Treasury Peter R. Fisher to the Columbus Council on World Affairs Columbus, Ohio Beyond Borrowing: Meeting the Government's Financial Challenges in the 21st Century, May 7, 2020. https://www.treasury.gov/press-center/press-releases/Pages/po3622.aspx.

p. 94 '5 percent of the people have 50 percent of the claims'. Sawyer, Bradley, and Gary Claxton, KFF. "How Do Health Expenditures Vary across the Population?" Peterson-Kaiser Health System Tracker. Accessed May 2020. https://www.healthsystemtracker.org/chart-collection/health-expenditures-vary-across-population/#item-family-spending-also-is-concentrated-with-10-of-families-accounting-for-half-of-spending_2016.

p. 99 'Just 115,000 people enrolled in the new Obamacare risk pools'. Pollitz, Karen. "High-Risk Pools For Uninsurable Individuals." The Henry J. Kaiser Family Foundation, February 22, 2017. https://www.kff.org/health-reform/issue-brief/high-risk-pools-for-uninsurable-individuals/.

p. 99 'showed just 257,000 individuals were denied coverage in 2009'. Waxman, Henry A. "Coverage Denials for Preexisting Conditions in the Individual Health Insurance Market," October 12, 2010. https://oversight.house.gov/sites/democrats.oversight.house.gov/files/documents/Memo-Coverage-Denials-Individual-Market-2010-10-12.pdf.

p. 99 'just 500,000 individuals with preexisting conditions'. McCaughey, Betsy. "ObamaCare - the Myth of Preexisting Conditions." TheHill, December 7, 2016. https://thehill.com/blogs/pundits-blog/healthcare/309081-the-pre-existing-conditions-myth.

p. 99 'Here's a chart that shows prevalence'. "Income, Poverty, and Health Insurance Coverage in the United States: 2010." US Census Bureau, n.d. https://www2.census.gov/library/publications/2011/demo/p60-239/p60-239.pdf.

p. 99 'Here's a chart that shows prevalence'. "Health Insurance Coverage of the Total Population." The Henry J. Kaiser Family Foundation, April 23, 2020. https://www.kff.org/other/state-indicator/total-population/?-dataView=1&currentTimeframe=8&sortModel=%7B%22colId%22:%22Location%22,%22sort%22:%22asc%22%7D.

p. 100 '2017 McKinsey study estimated that elimination of preexisting condition limits'. "Premium Reconciliation and Pre-ACA Deep Dive." McKinsey & Company, May 10, 2017. https://www.ronjohnson.senate.gov/public/_cache/files/2c915f24-f868-4207-85ed-4d0d319c45e8/johnson-and-lee-dear-colleague-july-19a.pdf.

p. 101 'Some proponents of Obamacare claimed'. "Medical Bankruptcy in the United States, 2007: Results of a National Study." *The American Journal of Medicine.* Accessed May 2020. https://www.amjmed.com/article/S0002-9343(09)00404-5/pdf.

p. 101 'Other studies showed hospitalizations caused just 4 percent'. "Just 4% of Bankruptcies Are Caused by Hospitalizations, Research Suggests-Surprising Many Experts." Advisory Board Daily Briefing. Accessed May 2020. https://www.advisory.com/daily-briefing/2018/03/30/medical-bankruptcy.

p. 101 'Other studies showed hospitalizations caused just 4 percent'. Dobkin, Carlos, Amy Finkelstein, Raymond Kluender, and Matthew J Notowidigdo. "Myth and Measurement - The Case of Medical Bankruptcies." *The New England Journal of Medicine.* U.S. National Library of Medicine, March 22, 2018. https://www.ncbi.nlm.nih.gov/pmc/articles/PMC5865642/.

p. 103 'just 15 percent of known individuals who commit fraud are ever prosecuted'. "HEALTH CARE FRAUD Types of Providers Involved in Medicare, Medicaid, and the Children's Health Insurance Program Cases." GAO. Accessed May 2020. https://www.gao.gov/assets/650/647849.pdf.

p. 103 'There are 10,000 procedure codes'. "CPT Coding: A Look at What's Coming in 2019." HIAcode, November 19, 2018. https://www.hiacode. com/education/a-look-at-whats-coming-in-2019-for-cpt/.

p. 103 'There are 70,000 diagnosis codes'. Torrey, Trisha. "What Are ICD Codes and How Can You Look Them Up?" Verywell Health, April 2, 2020. https://www.verywellhealth.com/finding-icd-codes-2615311.

p. 103 'There are 20,000 drugs available'. Office of the Commissioner. "Fact Sheet: FDA at a Glance." U.S. Food and Drug Administration (FDA). Accessed May 2020. https://www.fda.gov/about-fda/fda-basics/fact-sheet-fda-glance.

p. 103 'a coding system with nearly 10,000 procedure codes'. "RBRVS Overview." *American Medical Association*. Accessed May 2020. https://www. ama-assn.org/about/rvs-update-committee-ruc/rbrvs-overview.

p. 104 'past the peak age of running a con'. Arends, Brett. "Four Massive Problems with the Democrats' Medicare-for-All Plan." *MarketWatch*, July 1, 2019. https://www.marketwatch.com/story/four-massive-problems-with-the-democrats-medicare-for-all-plan-2019-07-01.

p. 106 'the average has been measured at 12 percent'. Woolhandler, Steffie, David U. Himmelstein, Gilead I. Lancaster, Joseph P. Drozda Jr., Steffie Woolhandler, David U. Himmelstein, Ryan Crowley, et al. "Single-Payer Reform: The Only Way to Fulfill the President's Pledge of More Coverage, Better Benefits, and Lower Costs." *Annals of Internal Medicine*, June 1, 2017. https://www.acpjournals.org/doi/10.7326/M17-0302.

p. 106-107 'Medicare administrative costs per person were $509 verses $453 for private insurers'. Roy, Avik. "The Myth of Medicare's 'Low Administrative Costs'." *Forbes Magazine*, August 7, 2014. https://www.forbes.com/sites/theapothecary/2011/06/30/the-myth-of-medicares-low-administrative-costs/#58bc8a29140d.

p. 109 '2,000 occur in the US'. The Daily Beast. "Dick Cheney Surgery: 7 Essential Facts about Heart Transplants." The Daily Beast Company, March 26, 2012. https://www.thedailybeast.com/dick-cheney-surgery-7-essential-facts-about-heart-transplants.

p. 110 'ninety-eight new actions to its list of fragmented'. "2019 Annual Report: Additional Opportunities to Reduce Fragmentation, Overlap, and Duplication and Achieve Billions in Financial Benefits." Accessed May 2020. https://www.gao.gov/reports/GAO-19-285SP/.

p. 110 'complex and difficult subjects in a clear, understandable fashion'. Bhambhani, Dipka. "What Is a Lobbyist? The McCormick Group's John Hesse Says It's about Communication." PR Week Global, May 4, 2016. https://www.prweek.com/article/1393747/lobbyist-mccormick-groups-john-hesse-says-its-communication.

p. 110 '1 to 5-plus percent to the cost of healthcare in each state'. Cauchi, Dick, and Alise Garcia. "State Insurance Mandates and the ACA Essential Benefits Provisions." NCSL. Accessed May 2020. https://www.ncsl.org/research/health/state-ins-mandates-and-aca-essential-benefits.aspx.

p. 112 'reduce premiums by 1 to 2 percent each'. Avraham, Ronen, Dafny, Schanzenbach, and Max M. "The Impact of Tort Reform on Employer-Sponsored Health Insurance Premiums." NBER, September 24, 2009. https://www.nber.org/papers/w15371.

p. 112 '26 percent of all healthcare spending may be unnecessary'. "PHY-SICIAN STUDY: QUANTIFYING THE COST OF DEFENSIVE MEDICINE." Jackson Healthcare. Accessed May 12, 2020. https://jacksonhealthcare.com/media-room/surveys/defensive-medicine-study-2010/.

p. 112 'unnecessary test or procedure at least once a week'. "Survey: Physicians Are Aware That Many Medical Tests and Procedures Are Unnecessary, See Themselves As Solution." *Choosing Wisely – Promoting conversations between providers and patients*, May 1, 2014. https://www.choosingwisely.org/survey-physicians-are-aware-that-many-medical-tests-and-procedures-are-unnecessary-see-themselves-as-solution/.

p. 113 '96 percent of physicians practiced defensive medicine'. "Study Illustrates High Cost of Defensive Medicine Practices by Orthopedists." *Healio*, April 13, 2012. https://www.healio.com/orthopedics/business-of-orthopedics/news/print/orthopedics-today/{b3825420-573d-49c0-976c-99b0a9a63e53}/study-illustrates-high-cost-of-defensive-medicine-practices-by-orthopedists.

p. 113 'A counter study by Rand'. Waxman, Daniel A., J. Geleris, N. van Doremalen, and M. R. Mehra. "The Effect of Malpractice Reform on Emergency Department Care: NEJM." *New England Journal of Medicine*, January 8, 2015. https://www.nejm.org/doi/full/10.1056/NEJM-sa1313308?query=TOC.

p. 113 'tarnish the dignified public image of the profession'. "John R. Bates and Van O'Steen, Appellants, v. State Bar of Arizona." Cornell Law School, June 27, 1977. https://www.law.cornell.edu/supremecourt/text/433/350.

p. 113 'sometimes called the English rule'. Slater, Dan. "The Debate Over Who Pays Fees When Litigants Mount Attacks." *The Wall Street Journal*. Dow Jones & Company, December 23, 2008. https://www.wsj.com/articles/SB122999187816728533.

p. 115 'on average they owed $530'. "Following ACA Rules, Tax Refunds Take Hit: H&R Block Newsroom." Tax Information Center, February 6, 2020. https://www.hrblock.com/tax-center/newsroom/healthcare/affordable-care-act/tax-refund-hits-for-taxpayers-following-aca-rules/.

p. 115 'according to the state of California'. "With Billions in the Bank, Blue Shield of California Loses Its State Tax-Exempt Status." *Los Angeles Times*, March 18, 2015. https://www.latimes.com/business/la-fi-blue-shield-california-20150318-story.html.

p. 117 'healthcare insurance losses at $4.7 billion in 2016'. Wyman, Oliver. "Analysis: Impact of Market-Stabilization Proposals." Oliver Wyman Health. Accessed May 2020. https://health.oliverwyman.com/2017/08/analysis_impact_of.html.

p. 118 'similar to rent controls'. Britschgi. "New York's Progressive Rent Regulations Having the Exact Same Negative Consequence That Skeptics Predicted." *Reason*, January 28, 2020. https://reason.com/2020/01/27/totally-predictable-consequences-of-new-yorks-rent-regulations/.

CHAPTER 4

p. 125 'No one will take it away, no matter what'. "Obama: 'If You like Your Health Care Plan, You'll Be Able to Keep Your Health Care Plan'." PolitiFact. Accessed May 2020. https://www.politifact.com/obama-like-health-care-keep/.

p. 126 'will see any form of tax increase'. "The Obameter." PolitiFact. Accessed May 2020. https://www.politifact.com/truth-o-meter/prom-ises/obameter/promise/515/no-family-making-less-250000-will-see-any-form-tax/.

p. 126 'either now or in the future'. Jackson, Brooks. "Obama's Health Care Speech." FactCheck.org, October 6, 2009. https://www.factcheck.org/2009/09/obamas-health-care-speech/.

p. 126 'really critical to getting the thing to pass'. Viebeck, Elise. "ObamaCare Architect: 'Stupidity' of Voters Helped Bill Pass." *TheHill*, February 4, 2016. https://thehill.com/policy/healthcare/223578-obamacare-archi-tect-lack-of-transparency-helped-law-pass.

p. 126 'too stupid to understand the difference'. Calamur, Krishnadev. "Obamacare Architect Apologizes For Remarks On The Law's Passage." NPR, November 12, 2014. https://www.npr.org/sections/thet-wo-way/2014/11/12/363537837/obamacare-architect-apologizes-for-remarks-on-the-laws-passage.

p. 126 'it ends up being the same thing'. "Al Ose: Pass FairTax to Get Rid of Hidden Taxes." madison.com, December 9, 2014. https://madison.com/ct/news/opinion/mailbag/al-ose-pass-fairtax-to-get-rid-of-hidden-taxes/article_d318b8f6-c7b3-53f7-b9d1-d6517aff4e6a.html.

p. 126 'worse still when an adolescent does'. "Will You Still Need Me, When I'm Sixty-Four?" *American Thinker*. Accessed May 14, 2020. https://www.americanthinker.com/articles/2009/08/will_you_still_need_me_when_im.html.

p. 126 'out of their health plans'. "PolitiFact - Valerie Jarrett Says 'Nothing in Obamacare Forces People out of Their Health Plans.'." Accessed May 2020. https://www.politifact.com/factchecks/2013/oct/30/valerie-jarrett/valerie-jarrett-says-nothing-obamacare-forces-peop/.

p. 127 'preventive care, birth control, pregnancy'. "Obama, under Fire for Health Law Stumbles, Tries to Hit Reset with Supporters." FOX News Network, February 2, 2015. https://www.foxnews.com/politics/obama-under-fire-for-health-law-stumbles-tries-to-hit-reset-with-supporters.

p. 127 'coverage cut in half'. Lim, Naomi. "Bill Clinton Calls Obamacare 'the Craziest Thing in the World,' Later Tries to Walk It Back." Cable News Network, October 5, 2016. https://www.cnn.com/2016/10/04/politics/bill-clinton-obamacare-craziest-thing/index.html.

p. 127 'televised on C-SPAN'. "The Obameter." PolitiFact. Accessed May 2020. https://www.politifact.com/truth-o-meter/promises/obameter/promise/517/health-care-reform-public-sessions-C-SPAN/.

p. 127 'TV on Amazon'. "Obama: Using Obamacare Website as Easy as Buying 'a TV on Amazon'." CNSNews.com. Accessed May 2020. https://www.cnsnews.com/mrctv-blog/craig-bannister/obama-using-obamacare-website-easy-buying-tv-amazon.

p. 127 'we will call you out'. *The Washington Post*. Accessed May 2020. http://voices.washingtonpost.com/thefix/white-house/the-obama-address-first-though.html.

p. 127 'cancelled on them had junk plans'. "Some Canceled Insurance Policies Were 'Junk' Targeted by Law." *Tampa Bay Times*, August 29, 2019. https://www.tampabay.com/news/health/some-canceled-insurance-policies-were-junk-insurance-targeted-by-law/2151587/.

p. 127 'The penalty is not a tax'. Harrington, Scott. "The Individual Mandate as a Tax: What the Court Said." *Forbes*, June 29, 2012. https://www. forbes.com/sites/scottharrington/2012/06/28/the-individual-mandate- as-a-tax-what-the-court-said/#1f9ca58d6aea.

p. 128 'Where were people enrolled in 2013?' "Health Insurance Coverage in the United States: 2013." The United States Census Bureau, July 25, 2018. https://www.census.gov/library/publications/2014/demo/ p60-250.html.

p. 128 'Where were people enrolled in 2017?' "Health Insurance Coverage in the United States: 2017." The United States Census Bureau, April 16, 2019. https://www.census.gov/library/publications/2018/demo/ p60-264.html.

p. 134 '1.6 pitches per inning'. Williams, Mark T. "MLB Umpires Missed 34,294 Ball-Strike Calls in 2018. Bring on Robo-umps." *BU Today*, April 8, 2018. https://www.bu.edu/articles/2019/mlb-umpires-strike- zone-accuracy/.

p. 135 'Supreme Court rulings have made the following decisions'. Marcum, Anthony. "Those 5-4 Decisions on the Supreme Court? 9-0 is Far More Common." *Washington Post*, June 28, 2018. https://www.washington- post.com/news/posteverything/wp/2018/06/28/those-5-4-decisions- on-the-supreme-court-9-0-is-far-more-common/.

p. 136 'seven million went without coverage'. Norris, Louise, and Louise Norris. "Will You Owe a Penalty under Obamacare?" healthinsurance. org, May 13, 2020. https://www.healthinsurance.org/obamacare/ obamacare-penalty-calculator/.

p. 136 'many tax filers didn't answer whether they had healthcare coverage'. "Results of the 2017 Filing Season," n.d. https://www.treasury.gov/tigta/auditreports/2018reports/201840012fr.pdf.

p. 136 'because of hardship or for other reasons'. "Most Uninsured Will Be Exempt from Penalties." PNHP. Accessed May 2020. https://pnhp.org/news/most-uninsured-will-be-exempt-from-penalties/.

p. 137 'dancing on the barstool'. Rhodan, Maya. "Michelle Obama Tells Jimmy Fallon Young People Are 'Knuckleheads' Who Need Obamacare." *Time*, February 21, 2014. https://time.com/9201/michelle-obama-jimmy-fallon-tonight-show-obamacare/.

p. 137 'Eighty-seven percent of people in the Obamacare'. Findlay, Steven. "Health Insurance Costs Crushing Many People Who Don't Get Federal Subsidies." Kaiser Health News, December 14, 2018. https://khn.org/news/health-insurance-costs-crushing-many-people-who-dont-get-federal-subsidies/.

p. 139 'Other more controversial provisions applied later'. Hoar. "Correction, Please! [New American, The]." InsuranceNewsNet, February 29, 2012. https://insurancenewsnet.com/oarticle/Correction-Please-[New-American-The]-a-332136#.Xr8mHmhKhPY.

p. 140 'just 7 percent of income'. Fontinelle, Amy. "A Brief History of Taxes in the U.S." Investopedia, April 2, 2020. https://www.investopedia.com/articles/tax/10/history-taxes.asp.

p. 141 'The infamous "Cornhusker Kickback'. Jordon, Steve, and World-Herald. "What Was the 'Cornhusker Kickback,' the Deal That Led to Nelson's Crucial ACA Vote?" Omaha.com, July 21, 2017. https://www.omaha.com/livewellnebraska/obamacare/what-was-the-cornhusker-kickback-the-deal-that-led-to/article_a2eb3a1d-df14-513b-a141-c8695f6c258e.html.

p. 142 'These deals were the most notable'. "Full List of Backroom Health Deals in Deem and Pass Healthcare Bill." Americans for Tax Reform. Accessed May 2020. https://www.atr.org/full-list-backroom-health-deals-inbr-a4672.

p. 142 'It's easy to remember the failed Obamacare website'. Muschick, Paul. "Obamacare Website Crash Stemmed from Extreme Government Incompetence." The Morning Call, March 27, 2019. https://www.mcall.com/news/watchdog/mc-obamacare-website-failure-watchdog-20160224-column.html.

p. 143 'Penalties apply to employers for not offering adequate coverage'. Kim-Brunetti, Joanna H. "Coming Soon: Employer Mandate Penalties From the IRS." AccountingWEB, April 18, 2017. https://www.accountingweb.com/tax/irs/coming-soon-employer-mandate-penalties-from-the-irs.

p. 143 'The Cadillac Tax (tax on high-cost plans) originally applied in 2017'. "Cadillac Tax." Cigna. Accessed May 2020. https://www.cigna.com/employers-brokers/insights/informed-on-reform/cadillac-tax.

p. 145 'Obamacare led to many unintended consequences'. Johnson, Andrew. "100 Unintended Consequences of Obamacare." National Review, October 1, 2013. https://www.nationalreview.com/2013/10/100-unintended-consequences-obamacare-andrew-johnson/.

p. 145 'Elimination of healthcare coverage for retirees and spouses'. "Is IBM, Time Warner Move to Eliminate Retiree Health Benefits the New Normal?" Challenger, Gray & Christmas, Inc., September 11, 2013. https://www.challengergray.com/press/blog/ibm-time-warner-move-eliminate-retiree-health-benefits-new-normal.

p. 145 'UPS'. "UPS Denies Insurance Coverage of Spouses and Cites ACA as Reason." McBrayer PLLC. September 24, 13. https://www.mcbrayerfirm.com/blogs-Healthcare-Law-Blog,ups-denies-insurance-coverage-of-spouses-and-cites-aca-as-reason.

p. 145 'Limiting employees to under thirty hours per week to avoid penalties'. "US Employers Slashing Worker Hours to Avoid Obamacare Insurance Mandate." Guardian News and Media, September 30, 2013. https://www.theguardian.com/world/2013/sep/30/us-employers-slash-hours-avoid-obamacare.

p. 145 'Limiting employees to under thirty-hours per week to avoid penalties'. Graham, Jed. "ObamaCare Employer Mandate: A List Of Cuts To Work Hours, Jobs." Investor's Business Daily, September 5, 2014. https://www.investors.com/politics/policy-analysis/obamacare-employer-mandate-a-list-of-cuts-to-work-hours-jobs/.

p. 146 'Cutting benefits for part-timers'. O'Connor, Clare. "Target Joins Home Depot, Walmart, Others In Cutting Health Care For Part-Timers, Citing Obamacare." *Forbes*, January 22, 2014. https://www.forbes.com/sites/clareoconnor/2014/01/22/target-joins-home-depot-walmart-others-in-dropping-health-care-for-part-timers-citing-obamacare/#51a62c4c16a8.

p. 146 'Downsizing in the healthcare industry'. Robeznieks, Andis. "Downsizing." Modern Healthcare, March 16, 2013. https://www.modern-healthcare.com/article/20130316/MAGAZINE/303169951/downsizing.

p. 146 'Bureau of Economic Research studied the impact of Obamacare'. Passy, Jacob. "Businesses Eliminated Hundreds of Thousands of Full-Time Jobs to Avoid Obamacare Mandate." MarketWatch, November 24, 2017. https://www.marketwatch.com/story/businesses-eliminated-hundreds-of-thousands-of-full-time-jobs-to-avoid-obamacare-mandate-2017-11-24.

p. 146 'the provisions of Hillarycare led to Obamacare provisions'. Facebook. com/obamacarefacts. "What Is HillaryCare?" Obamacare Facts, March 10, 2020. https://obamacarefacts.com/what-is-hillarycare/.

p. 148 'Obamacare has already been devastating to the market'. Fehr, Rachel, Rabah Kamal, and Cynthia Cox. "Insurer Participation on ACA Marketplaces, 2014-2020." The Henry J. Kaiser Family Foundation, November 21, 2019. https://www.kff.org/private-insurance/issue-brief/insurer-participation-on-aca-marketplaces-2014-2020/.

CHAPTER 5

p. 154 'Studies have shown that Medicare pays seventy cents on the dollar, and Medicaid pays fifty cents'. Shatto, John D., and M. Kent Clemens. "Projected Medicare Expenditures under an Illustrative Scenario with Alternative Payment Updates to Medicare Providers." CMS, n.d. https://www.cms.gov/files/document/illustrative-alternative-scenario-2020.pdf.

p. 154 'Studies have shown that Medicare pays seventy cents on the dollar, and Medicaid pays fifty cents'. Masterson, Les. "CBO Reports Show Private Insurers Pay Physicians, Hospitals Far More than Medicare." *Healthcare Dive*, June 27, 2017. https://www.healthcaredive.com/news/cbo-reports-show-private-insurers-pay-physicians-hospitals-far-more-than-m/445949/.

p. 154 'Studies have shown that Medicare pays seventy cents on the dollar, and Medicaid pays fifty cents'. Lopez, Eric, Tricia Neuman, Gretchen Jacobson, and Larry Levitt. "How Much More Than Medicare Do Private Insurers Pay? A Review of the Literature." The Henry J. Kaiser Family Foundation, May 1, 2020. https://www.kff.org/medicare/issue-brief/how-much-more-than-medicare-do-private-insurers-pay-a-review-of-the-literature/.

p. 154 'Studies have shown that Medicare pays seventy cents on the dollar, and Medicaid pays fifty cents'. "Medicaid Physician Fees after the ACA Primary Care Fee Bump." Urban Institute, n.d. https://www.urban.org/sites/default/files/publication/88836/2001180-medicaid-physician-fees-after-the-aca-primary-care-fee-bump_0.pdf.

p. 154 'Studies have shown that Medicare pays seventy cents on the dollar, and Medicaid pays fifty cents'. King, Robert. "Study: Rates Charged by Hospitals to Private Insurers Vastly Outpace Medicare, Medicaid Rates." FierceHealthcare, January 7, 2020. https://www.fiercehealthcare.com/hospitals-health-systems/study-private-hospital-payment-rates-vastly-outpace-medicare-medicaid.

p. 157 'As the author and economist Daniel Mitchell describes'. Mitchell, Daniel J. "Paul Krugman Is Learning the Wrong Lesson from Denmark: Daniel J. Mitchell." Foundation for Economic Education, August 22, 2018. https://fee.org/articles/paul-krugman-is-learning-the-wrong-lesson-from-denmark/.

p. 158 'they haven't read *This Time Is Different: Eight Centuries of Financial Folly*'. "Stay Connected for the Latest Books, Ideas, and Special Offers." The Trustees of Princeton University. Accessed May 2020. https://press.princeton.edu/books/paperback/9780691152646/this-time-is-different.

p. 160 'While Venezuelans are eating zoo animals instead of starving'. Reuters. "Thieves Stealing Venezuela Zoo Animals to Eat Them, Say Police." The Guardian. Guardian News and Media, August 17, 2017. https://www.theguardian.com/world/2017/aug/17/thieves-stealing-venezuela-zoo-animals-to-eat-them-say-police.

p. 160 'Every three hours a woman dies due to breast cancer'. Fox News. "Women Want to Escape Venezuela so Badly They Sell Hair, Breast Milk, Sex." *New York Post*, December 24, 2018. https://nypost.com/2018/12/24/

women-so-desperate-to-escape-venezuela-they-sell-hair-breast-milk-sex/?utm_source=facebook_sitebuttons&utm_medium=site+buttons&utm_campaign=site+buttons&fbclid=IwAR24kKEdX9nUUv-VSo5pHtro341E7KY8KeDXnnT06OSZOAg4zqGHBD9DzyBU.

p. 160 'thousands of dollars a year in healthcare'. Nierenberg, Danielle, "PolitiFact - How Much Would Bernie Sanders' Health Care Plan Cost the Middle Class?" Politifact. Accessed April 2020. https://www.politifact.com/article/2016/jan/13/how-much-would-bernie-sanders-health-care-plan-cos/.

p. 161 'greed are destroying the middle class of America'. Better World Quotes - "Bernie Sanders on The Middle Class." Accessed April 2020. https://www.betterworld.net/quotes/bernie/bernie23.htm.

p. 161 'Medicare isn't the problem. It's the solution' Reich, Robert. "Medicare Isn't the Problem, It's the Solution." *San Francisco Chronicle*, December 8, 2011. https://www.sfgate.com/opinion/reich/article/Medicare-isn-t-the-problem-it-s-the-solution-2374512.php.

p. 161 'a federal jobs guarantee, and criminal justice reform'. "Alexandria Ocasio-Cortez Quotes." BrainyQuote. Xplore. Accessed April 2020. https://www.brainyquote.com/quotes/alexandria_ocasiocortez_926325.

p. 161 'That is part of the cost of our system'. Rutz. "Dem Socialist Ocasio-Cortez Defends Single-Payer Health Care by Citing Reduced 'Funeral Expenses'." *Washington Free Beacon*, August 9, 2018. https://freebeacon.com/issues/ocasio-cortez-defends-single-payer-health-care-reduced-funeral-expenses/.

p. 161 'recent polling from the Kaiser Family Foundation'. Waldman, Deane. "Medicare for All Is a Socialist's Dream - and an American Nightmare." *TheHill*, July 30, 2018. https://thehill.com/opinion/healthcare/399283-medicare-for-all-is-a-socialists-dream-and-an-american-nightmare.

p. 161 'You take a billion dollars'. "No One Ever Makes a Billion Dollars. You Take a Billion Dollars: Alexandria Ocasio-Cortez Slams Billionaires for Exploiting Workers | Markets Insider." *Business Insider.* Accessed April 2020. https://markets.businessinsider.com/news/stocks/aoc-accuses-billionaires-exploiting-workers-paying-slave-wages-2020-1-1028842799.

p. 161 'Denmark, not Venezuela'. "Sanders & Socialism: Debate Between Nobel Laureate Paul Krugman & Socialist Economist Richard Wolff." Democracy Now! Accessed April 2020. https://www.democracynow.org/2020/2/24/paul_krugman_richard_wolff_socialism_debate.

p. 161 'Who's the banana republic now?'. "Close The Gaps: Disparities That Threaten America." Sen. Bernie Sanders, August 5, 2011. https://www.sanders.senate.gov/newsroom/must-read/close-the-gaps-disparities-that-threaten-america.

p. 163 'I was right'. "Chavista Celebrities Refuse to Say They Were Wrong about Socialism." *American Thinker.* Accessed April 2020. https://www.americanthinker.com/blog/2017/06/chavista_celebrities_refuse_to_say_they_were_wrong_about_socialism.html.

p. 164 'Venezuela, with four billion dollars in wealth'. D'Amato, Pete. "Being the ex-President's daughter pays off: Hugo Chavez's ambassador daughter is Venezuela's richest woman." *Daily Mail*, August 10, 2015. https://www.dailymail.co.uk/news/article-3192933/Hugo-Chavez-s-ambassador-daughter-Venezuela-s-richest-woman-according-new-report.html.

p. 165 'Everyone will be a millionaire!'. King, Don Roy. "SNL Transcripts: Steve Martin: 11/04/78: A Special Message From the President of the United States." *SNL* Transcripts Tonight, January 3, 2019. https://snl-transcripts.jt.org/78/78dcarter.phtml.

p. 165 'the path is socialism'. "Hugo Chavez Quotes." BrainyQuote. Xplore. Accessed April 2020. https://www.brainyquote.com/quotes/hugo_chavez_177589.

p. 166 'to whom they belong'. "Fidel Castro Quotes." BrainyQuote. Xplore. Accessed April 2020. https://www.brainyquote.com/quotes/fidel_castro_175161.

p. 166 'children in the world who don't even have a piece of bread?' "Fidel Castro Quote." AZQuotes. Accessed April 2020. https://www.azquotes.com/quote/1544315.

p. 166 'our prostitutes are college graduates'. "Fidel Castro Death: 'History Will Absolve Me' and Other Quotes." NBCUniversal News Group, November 26, 2016. https://www.nbcnews.com/storyline/fidel-castros-death/fidel-castro-death-history-will-absolve-me-other-quotes-n688521.

p. 167 'inflation over the past two decades'. "Inflation, Inflation Expectations, and the Phillips Curve: Working Paper 2019-07." CBO, August 2, 2019. https://www.cbo.gov/publication/55501.

p. 168 'those effects that must be foreseen'. Kanopiadmin. "That Which Is Seen, and That Which Is Not Seen: Claude Frédéric Bastiat." Mises Institute, August 18, 2014. https://mises.org/library/which-seen-and-which-not-seen.

p. 170 '*The Waste Report* that showed the government's expenditures'. "Dr. Rand Paul Releases 2018 'Festivus' Edition of 'The Waste Report'."

Senator Rand Paul. Accessed May 2020. https://www.paul.senate.gov/news/dr-rand-paul-releases-2018-%E2%80%98festivus%E2%80%99-edition-%E2%80%98-waste-report%E2%80%99.

p. 171 'support was just 37 percent'. Suderman, Peter. "New Poll: Medicare for All Is Popular Until You Explain How It Works." *Reason*, January 24, 2019. https://reason.com/2019/01/24/new-poll-shows-medicare-for-all-is-popul/.

p. 172 'premiums, deductibles, coinsurance, copays, and other costs'. "Medicare Costs at a Glance." Medicare. Accessed May 2020. https://www.medicare.gov/your-medicare-costs/medicare-costs-at-a-glance.

p. 175 'bottom of the OECD list rather than at the top'. "How to Cure Health Care." Hoover Institution. Accessed May 2020. https://www.hoover.org/research/how-cure-health-care-0.

p. 175 'no change was made because of free coverage'. "No, My Study Didn't Find Medicare for All Would Lower U.S. Health Costs by $2 Trillion." Economics21.org, June 4, 2019. https://economics21.org/blahous-study-didnt-find-medicare-for-all-lowers-costs-two-trillion.

p. 176 'current dysfunctional healthcare system'. Burke, Cathy. "Bernie Sanders: 'Medicare For All' Expensive, Current System Even More So." Newsmax Media, Inc., June 16, 2019. https://www.newsmax.com/politics/sanders-2020-medicare-healthcare/2019/06/16/id/920580/.

p. 176 'Vermont considered Single Payer until its state taxes'. Roy, Avik. "Six Reasons Why Vermont's Single-Payer Health Plan Was Doomed From The Start." *Forbes*, December 22, 2014. https://www.forbes.com/sites/theapothecary/2014/12/21/6-reasons-why-vermonts-single-payer-health-plan-was-doomed-from-the-start/.

p. 176 'California's price tag was $400 billion'. Novak, Jake. "Op-Ed: Demo-crats' Single-Payer Health-Care Dream Just Became a Nightmare." CNBC, May 24, 2017. https://www.cnbc.com/2017/05/24/california-proves-sin-gle-payer-health-care-is-too-expensive-commentary.html.

p. 177 'A 2016 Kaiser Family Foundation report'. Furchtgott-Roth, Diana. "7 Obamacare Failures That Have Hurt Americans." *MarketWatch*, March 25, 2016. https://www.marketwatch.com/story/7-obamacare-failures-that-have-hurt-americans-2016-03-24.

p. 178 'stock up with the finest meats you could buy'. "John Stossel: Insur-ance Makes Healthcare Far More Expensive." YouTube, August 29, 2009. https://www.youtube.com/watch?v=3WnS96NVlMI.

p. 179 '2017 study by Bankrate.com'. "Millennials Struggle with Financial Vices." Bankrate.com. Accessed May 2020. https://www.bankrate.com/pdfs/pr/20170626-Financial-Vices.pdf.

p. 180 'happiest country in the world—Bhutan'. "The Happiest Country in the World - Bhutan!" *Youthreporter*. Accessed May 2020. https://www.youthreporter.eu/de/beitrag/the-happiest-country-in-the-world-bhutan.15468/.

CHAPTER 6

p. 183 'thirty-seventh country in the world in healthcare out of 191 coun-tries'. "World Health Organization Assesses the World's Health Systems." World Health Organization, July 29, 2013. https://www.who.int/whr/2000/media_centre/press_release/en/.

p. 185 'US healthcare compares poorly with ten other nations'. "New 11-Country Study: U.S. Health Care System Has Widest Gap Between

People With Higher and Lower Incomes." Commonwealth Fund, July 13, 2017. https://www.commonwealthfund.org/press-release/2017/new-11-country-study-us-health-care-system-has-widest-gap-between-people-higher.

p. 186 'Source: American Enterprise Institute (AEI)'. Perry, Mark. "Putting America's Enormous $19.4T Economy into Perspective by Comparing US State GDPs to Entire Countries." AEI. Accessed May 2020. https://www.aei.org/carpe-diem/putting-americas-enormous-19-4t-economy-in-to-perspective-by-comparing-us-state-gdps-to-entire-countries/.

p. 187 'claims Cuba's healthcare system is better than that of the US'. Rodriguez, Rene. "Cuban Healthcare Is Painted Rosy in 'Sicko,' Critics Say." *Miami Herald*. Accessed May 2020. https://www.miamiherald.com/news/nation-world/article1928212.html.

p. 188 'claim it was an objective measure of quality'. Atlas, Scott W., Nathan Glazer, Yuval Levin, Hoover Institution, and Stanford University Medical Center. "The Worst Study Ever?" *Commentary Magazine*, October 30, 2015. https://www.commentarymagazine.com/articles/scott-atlas/the-worst-study-ever/.

p. 189 'wrote about the WHO study in 2009'. Bialik, Carl. "Ill-Conceived Ranking Makes for Unhealthy Debate." *The Wall Street Journal*. Dow Jones & Company, October 21, 2009. https://www.wsj.com/articles/SB125608054324397621.

p. 189 'later wrote for the *Journal of New England Medicine*'. Shafrin, Jason. "Are WHO Rankings Entirely Worthless?" Healthcare Economist, April 27, 2010. https://www.healthcare-economist.com/2010/04/27/are-who-rankings-entirely-worthless/.

p. 189 'Time claimed in 2014'. Hellmann, Melissa. "Survey Ranks the U.S. Health Care System Lowest in Performance." Time, June 17, 2014. https://time.com/2888403/u-s-health-care-ranked-worst-in-the-developed-world/.

p. 191 'United States than in other developed countries'. Atlas, Scott W. In Excellent Health: Setting the Record Straight on America's Health Care. Hoover Press, September 1, 2013. https://books.google.com/books?id=PyPVROq1jSgC.

p. 191 'study by Robert Ohsfeldt of Texas A&M and John Schneider of the University of Iowa'. Perry, Mark. "U.S. vs. Europe: Life Expectancy and Cancer Survival." AEI, August 16, 2009. https://www.aei.org/carpe-diem/us-vs-europe-life-expectancy-and-cancer-survival/.

p. 192 'ethnicity than any other developed nation'. Atlas, Scott. "Survival of the Smallest." Hoover Institution, January 23, 2012. https://www.hoover.org/research/survival-smallest.

CHAPTER 7

p. 195 'marked the upward surge of mankind'. Amadeo, Kimberly. "Greed Is Good...or Is It?" The Balance, May 30, 2019. https://www.thebalance.com/greed-is-good-or-is-it-quote-and-meaning-3306247.

p. 196 'more of something (such as money) than needed'. "Greed." Merriam-Webster. Accessed May 2020. https://www.merriam-webster.com/dictionary/greed.

p. 196 'Pension funds are owned by widows and orphans'. "Q&A With Ben Stein." C. Accessed May 2020. https://www.c-span.org/video/?280479-1%2Fqa-ben-stein.

p. 197 'jail for seven years for unrelated securities fraud'. Jr., Tom Howell. "'Pharma Bro' Martin Shkreli Gets 7 Years in Prison for Fraud." The *Washington Times*, March 9, 2018. https://www.washingtontimes.com/ news/2018/mar/9/martin-shkreli-pharma-bro-7-years-prison-fraud/.

p. 197 'Heather Bresch (daughter of Democratic Senator Joe Manchin)'. Kasperkevic, Jana, and Amanda Holpuch. "EpiPen CEO Hiked Prices on Two Dozen Products and Got a 671% Pay Raise." Guardian News and Media, August 24, 2016. https://www.theguardian.com/business/2016/ aug/24/epipen-ceo-hiked-prices-heather-bresch-mylan.

p. 197 'greed, which is constant like gravity'. Sowell, Thomas. "Random Thoughts, by Dr. Thomas Sowell." Creators Syndicate, August 11, 2009. https://www.creators.com/read/thomas-sowell/08/09/random-thoughts-7defa.

p. 198 'movie rental company he called Netflix'. Syndicate, Creators. "John Stossel: Netflix and Blockbuster - the Overlooked Economics Lesson These Two Giants Can Teach Us." Fox Business, January 23, 2020. https://www.foxbusiness.com/money/netflix-blockbuster-econom-ics-lesson-john-stossel.

p. 200 'not so much that they could do nothing'. "Should You Leave It All to the Children?" *Fortune*, September 29, 1986. Accessed May 2020. https://archive.fortune.com/magazines/fortune/fortune_ archive/1986/09/29/68098/index.htm.

p. 200 'imagined offenses or from a sense of inadequacy'. "Guilt." *Merri-am-Webster*. Accessed May 2020. https://www.merriam-webster.com/ dictionary/guilt.

p. 201 'we live like kings'. McBride, Lorraine. "Bill Bailey: 'Comedy's a Reck-less and Foolhardy Job'." Telegraph Media Group, October 18, 2015.

https://www.telegraph.co.uk/finance/personalfinance/fameandfor-tune/11933516/Bill-Bailey-Comedys-a-reckless-and-foolhardy-job.html.

p. 202 'Source: Author's Analysis'. "Henry VIII." History.com. A&E Television Networks, November 9, 2009. https://www.history.com/topics/british-history/henry-viii.

p. 204 'Okay, Boomer'. Romano, Aja. "'OK Boomer' Isn't Just about the Past. It's about Our Apocalyptic Future." *Vox*, November 19, 2019. https://www.vox.com/2019/11/19/20963757/what-is-ok-boomer-meme-about-meaning-gen-z-millennials.

p. 204 'through the little window'. Rosling, Hans. "Transcript of 'The Magic Washing Machine.'" TED. Accessed May 2020. https://www.ted.com/talks/hans_rosling_the_magic_washing_machine/tran-script?language=en.

p. 206 'fav'rite number is one, two, three'. "Calloway - I Wanna Be Rich Lyrics." MetroLyrics. Accessed May 2020. https://www.metrolyrics.com/i-wanna-be-rich-lyrics-calloway.html.

p. 206 'Til there are no rich no more'. "I'd Love to Change the World." *Wikipedia*. Wikimedia Foundation, April 20, 2020. https://en.wikipedia.org/wiki/I'd_Love_to_Change_the_World.

p. 207 'Small and medium-sized businesses account for 50% of total employment in the US economy'. Kiersz, Andy. "The Impact of Small Business on the US Economy in 2 Extreme Charts." *Business Insider*, June 16, 2015. https://www.businessinsider.com/us-employment-by-firm-size-has-a-fat-tailed-distribution-2015-6.

p. 209 'cumulatively made since inception'. Griswold, Alison. "It took Amazon 14 years to make as much in net profit as it did last quarter."

Quartz, February 1, 2018. https://qz.com/1196256/it-took-amazon-amzn-14-years-to-make-as-much-net-profit-as-it-did-in-the-fourth-quarter-of-2017/#:~:text=For%20a%20sense%20of%20scale,-years%20as%20a%20public%20company.

p. 210 'Charities Aid Foundation'. Eleftheriou-Smith, Loulla-Mae. "These Are the World's Most Generous Countries." Independent Digital News and Media, February 2, 2016. https://www.independent.co.uk/news/world/americas/america-new-zealand-and-canada-top-list-of-world-s-most-generous-nations-a6849221.html.

p. 211 '$250 billion 2012, per the CBO and Joint Commission on Taxation'. "Reduce Tax Preferences for Employment-Based Health Insurance." Congressional Budget Office, November 13, 2013. https://www.cbo.gov/budget-options/2013/44903.

p. 211 'Home interest deductions'. "Mortgage Interest Deduction Is Ripe for Reform." Center on Budget and Policy Priorities, October 11, 2017. https://www.cbpp.org/research/mortgage-interest-deduction-is-ripe-for-reform.

p. 211 'Earned Income Tax credits'. Flores, Qiana, and Jessica Hathaway. "Tax Credits for Working Families: Earned Income Tax Credit (EITC)." Accessed May 2020. https://www.ncsl.org/research/labor-and-employment/earned-income-tax-credits-for-working-families.aspx.

p. 211 'Charitable contributions'. Hoffman, Marc. "CRS Reports on Tax Issues Relating to Charitable Contributions and Organizations." Planned Giving Design Center. Accessed May 2020. https://www.pgdc.com/pgdc/crs-reports-tax-issues-relating-charitable-contributions-and-organizations.

p. 212 'highest class—households making $100,000 plus in constant dollars—increased by 21 percent'. Perry, Mark. "Yes, the US Middle Class Is Shrinking, but It's Because Americans Are Moving up. And No, Americans Are Not Struggling to Afford a Home." AEI, n.d. https://www. aei.org/carpe-diem/yes-the-us-middle-class-is-shrinking-but-its-be- cause-americans-are-moving-up-and-no-americans-are-not-strug- gling-to-afford-a-home/.

p. 214 'average person also had more wealth than 40 percent of the popula- tion'. Robertson, Lori. "Sanders' Wealth Inequality Stat." FactCheck.org, May 19, 2016. https://www.factcheck.org/2016/01/sanders-wealth-in- equality-stat/.

CHAPTER 8

p. 218 'entice providers to practice medicine'. Bartlett, Steve, and Stu Neatby. "Doctor Shortage - Connecting the Dots and Seeking Solutions for Atlantic Canada: The Telegram." Health-Care-Challenges | In-Depth | The Telegram, February 14, 2019. https://www.thetelegram.com/ in-depth/health-care-challenges/doctor-shortage-connecting-the- dots-and-seeking-solutions-for-atlantic-canada-284540/.

p. 218 'entice providers to practice medicine'. Pym, Hugh. "Can the NHS Get All the Doctors and Nurses It Needs?" BBC, June 3, 2019. https://www. bbc.com/news/health-48501330.

p. 219 'urgent care centers that compete with Emergency Rooms'. Finnegan, Joanne. "Now More than 9,000 Urgent Care Centers in the U.S., Indus- try Report Says." *FierceHealthcare*, February 26, 2020. https://www. fiercehealthcare.com/practices/now-more-than-9-000-urgent-care- centers-u-s-industry-report-says.

p. 219 'larger number of patients helps to defray fixed costs'. Gee, Emily, and Ethan Gurwitz. "Provider Consolidation Drives Up Health Care Costs." Center for American Progress. Accessed May 2020. https://www.amer-icanprogress.org/issues/healthcare/reports/2018/12/05/461780/provid-er-consolidation-drives-health-care-costs/.

p. 219 'One idea is to change the Certificate of Need (CON) requirements'. Brooklyn Roberts. "State 'Certificate of Need' Laws Need to Go." *The Hill*, October 26, 2019. https://thehill.com/opinion/healthcare/467572-state-certificate-of-need-laws-need-to-go.

p. 219 'Medical schools that are not graduating enough physicians'. "A Solu-tion for the U.S. Doctor Shortage and the Medical School Bottleneck." RealClearEducation. Accessed May 2020.

p. 220 'along with state legislators'. "Revisiting the Rationing of Medical Degrees in the United States." Contexts. Accessed May 2020. https://contexts.org/articles/revisiting-the-rationing-of-medical-degrees-in-the-united-states/.

p. 220 'the AMA, along with state legislators, has helped to limit the number of physicians practicing in the US'. Dale Steinreich. "100 Years of Medical Robbery." Mises Institute, June 10, 2004. https://mises.org/library/100-years-medical-robbery.

p. 220 'declining up to one-third of applicants (recently)'. "Nursing Schools Are Rejecting Thousands of Applicants—in the Middle of a Nursing Shortage." CNNMoney. Accessed May 2020. https://money.cnn.com/2018/04/30/news/economy/nursing-school-rejections/index.html.

p. 221 'recent study by Tufts University'. Herper, Matthew. "The Cost Of Developing Drugs Is Insane. That Paper That Says Otherwise Is Insanely Bad." *Forbes*, October 16, 2017. https://www.forbes.com/sites/matthe-

wherper/2017/10/16/the-cost-of-developing-drugs-is-insane-a-paper-
that-argued-otherwise-was-insanely-bad/.

p. 222 'quality-adjusted life year (QALY) gained exceeds 50,000 British
Pounds'. "Responses to TA Methods Addendum Public Consulta-
tion…Technology-Appraisals/VBA-Consultation-Comments.pdf."
Nice.org, n.d. https://www.nice.org.uk/media/Default/About/what-
we-do/NICE-guidance/NICE-technology-appraisals/VBA-Consulta-
tion-Comments.pdf.

p. 222 'The US market represents 45 percent of pharmaceutical sales'.
Laporte, John. "Topic: Pharmaceutical Industry in the U.S." www.
statista.com. Accessed May 2020. https://www.statista.com/topics/1719/
pharmaceutical-industry/.

p. 222 'or seven years for rare-disease drugs'. "Drug Patent Life: How Long
Do Drug Patents Last?" DrugPatentWatch, February 22, 2019. https://
www.drugpatentwatch.com/blog/how-long-do-drug-patents-last/.

p. 222 'concept that is being debated is drug reciprocity'. Miller, Henry I.,
John J. Cohrssen, Bush, Robert Wesson Fellow in Scientific Philosophy,
Stanford University's Hoover Institution, FDA's Office of Biotechnology,
Council, and House Energy and Commerce Committee. "Drug Reciproc-
ity Could Save Lives in the U.S." *City Journal*, July 31, 2018. https://www.
city-journal.org/html/drug-reciprocity-16082.html.

p. 223 'ability to prescribe medicine without a prescription'. Luthra, Shefali.
"Shopping At The Apotheke: Compare German Pharmacies With Your
Corner Drugstore." *Kaiser Health News*, August 30, 2019. https://khn.
org/news/german-pharmacy-apotheke-comparing-health-system/.

p. 223 'general CPI by 1.8 percent per year over the past seventy years'. "CPI Home."
U.S. Bureau of Labor Statistics. Accessed May 2020. https://www.bls.gov/cpi/.

p. 223 'Demand in healthcare will continue to increase demographically'. Sawyer, Bradley, and Gary Claxton. "How Do Health Expenditures Vary across the Population?" Peterson-Kaiser Health System Tracker. Accessed May 2020. https://www.healthsystemtracker.org/chart-collection/health-expenditures-vary-across-population/.

p. 226 'About the only thing we use more of is technology'. Goodman, John C. "Socialized Failure." *National Review*, May 7, 2009. https://www.nationalreview.com/magazine/2009/05/25/socialized-failure/.

p. 226 'it costs $94,000, with similar results'. Fox, Maggie. "Hepatitis C Cure Eludes Patients as States Struggle with Costs." NBCUniversal News Group, July 20, 2018. https://www.nbcnews.com/health/health-news/hepatitis-c-cure-eludes-patients-states-struggle-costs-n870846.

p. 227 'water supply when others thought air was the cause'. Frerichs, Ralph R. "John Snow and the Broad Street Pump: On the Trail of an Epidemic." Accessed May 2020. https://www.ph.ucla.edu/epi/snow/snowcricketarticle.html.

p. 228 'quantities and prices of certain drugs sold'. "Potential Effects of a Ban on Direct-to-Consumer Advertising of New Prescription Drugs." CBO, n.d. https://www.cbo.gov/sites/default/files/112th-congress-2011-2012/reports/5-25-prescriptiondrugadvertising.pdf.

p. 229 'estimated that thirteen new drugs would be developed each year'. Kennedy, Joe. "The Link Between Drug Prices and Research on the Next Generation of Cures." Information Technology and Innovation Foundation, September 9, 2019. https://itif.org/publications/2019/09/09/link-between-drug-prices-and-research-next-generation-cures.

CHAPTER 9

p. 238 'In 1935, Congress passed—and President Franklin D. Roosevelt signed into law—the Social Security Act'. "Social Security." Social Security History. Accessed May 2020. https://www.ssa.gov/history/reports/crsleghist2.html.

p. 238 'bill temporarily lowering the payroll tax'. Miller, Mark. "Would Obama's Payroll Tax Cut Hurt Social Security?" Thomson Reuters, September 9, 2011. https://www.reuters.com/article/idUS263140017120110909.

p. 238 'The latest report shows that Social Security'. *ABC News.* Accessed May 2020. https://abcnews.go.com/Politics/social-security-running-money-benefits-track-reduced-2035/story?id=62557507.

p. 238 'The Social Security eligibility age has gone up, not down'. Lorie Konish. "The Social Security Retirement Age Could Go up. Here's Why That Change Won't Be Easy." CNBC, November 15, 2019. https://www.cnbc.com/2019/11/13/why-raising-social-securitys-full-retirement-age-wont-be-easy.html.

p. 238-239 'suggesting the Medicare eligibility age to follow suit by raising it from age sixty-five to sixty-seven'. "Raising Medicare's Age of Eligibility to 67 Would Achieve Significant Savings, But Shift Costs To 65- and 66-Year-Olds, Other Individuals, Employers and Medicaid, New Analysis Shows." KFF, May 16, 2013. https://www.kff.org/medicare/press-release/news-release-raising-the-age-of-medicare-eligibility/.

CHAPTER 10

p. 246 'compelling Americans to lead sicker and shorter lives'. Bailey, Ron. ""President Trump: Competition Is the Solution to High Drug

Prices." *Reason*, May 11, 2018. https://reason.com/2018/05/11/president-trump-competition-is-the-solut/.

p. 246 'here is a synopsis of the US compared to other countries' healthcare'. "International Health Care System Profiles." Canada: International Health Care System Profiles. Accessed May 2020. https://international.commonwealthfund.org/countries/canada/.

p. 248 'waiting for the specialist to perform the procedure'. Fraser Institute. Accessed May 2020. https://www.fraserinstitute.org/studies/waiting-your-turn-wait-times-for-health-care-in-canada-2018.

p. 248 'Canada employs "loser pays" court costs'. Kagan, Robert. "Do Lawyers Cause Adversarial Legalism? A Preliminary Inquiry." American Bar Foundation, n.d. https://www.jstor.org/stable/828429?seq=1.

p. 249 'leading to the boy becoming permanently disabled'. Fayerman, Pamela. "A Public Health System That Failed a Canadian Boy: The Saga of Walid Khalfallah." *Vancouver Sun*, November 18, 2012. https://vancouversun.com/news/staff-blogs/a-public-health-system-that-failed-a-canadian-boy-the-sad-saga-of-walid-khalfalla/.

p. 249 'where a judge denied the parents appeal'. Perraudin, Frances. "Alfie Evans's Father Begs Pope Francis to 'Save Our Son'." Guardian News and Media, April 18, 2018. https://www.theguardian.com/uk-news/2018/apr/18/alfie-evans-father-pope-francis-save-son-life-support.

p. 249 'NHS denied the baby's transfer; British Courts agreed'. "Charlie Gard: The Story of His Parents' Legal Fight." BBC, July 27, 2017. https://www.bbc.com/news/health-40554462.

p. 249 'cured the cancer that the UK doctors said was incurable'. Adams, Joel. "Ashya King Cleared of Cancer Three Years after His Parents

Abducted Him from Hospital for Treatment Abroad." Telegraph Media Group, March 3, 2018. https://www.telegraph.co.uk/news/2018/03/03/ashya-king-cleared-cancer-three-years-parents-abducted-hospital/.

p. 250 'NHS ambulances waiting for hospital care'. Campbell, Denis. "16,900 People in a Week Kept in NHS Ambulances Waiting for Hospital Care." Guardian News and Media, January 4, 2018. https://www.theguardian.com/society/2018/jan/04/16900-people-in-a-week-kept-in-nhs-ambulances-waiting-for-hospital-care.

p. 250 'thirty hours in the hospital hallway'. Campbell, Denis, and Pamela Duncan. "NHS Memo Reveals Two Patients Died after Waiting for A&E Care." Guardian News and Media, January 29, 2019. https://www.theguardian.com/society/2019/jan/29/nhs-memo-reveals-two-patients-died-after-waiting-for-ae-care.

p. 250 'the NHS in 2019 proposed "group appointments"'. Butterworth, Benjamin. "How NHS Plans to See Your GP in Groups of up to 15 Will Work." inews, September 6, 2019. https://inews.co.uk/news/health/how-will-gp-group-appointments-work-506659.

p. 250 'Four million patients are waiting for care today'. Campbell, Denis. "NHS Patients Waiting for Hospital Care Top 4m for First Time in a Decade." *Guardian News and Media*, August 10, 2017. https://www.theguardian.com/society/2017/aug/10/patients-waiting-planned-nhs-england-hospital-care-top-4-million-for-first-time-in-a-decade.

p. 250 '50 percent higher than in the US'. NHS. Accessed May 2020. https://www.nhs.uk/news/medical-practice/death-rate-much-higher-in-english-than-us-hospitals/.

p. 250 'UK health system a humanitarian crisis'. "NHS Faces 'Humanitarian Crisis' as Demand Rises, British Red Cross Warns." *Guardian*

News and Media, January 6, 2017. https://www.theguardian.com/society/2017/jan/06/nhs-faces-humanitarian-crisis-rising-demand-british-red-cross.

p. 250 'UK doctor union'. Triggle, Nick. "More Five-Day Doctor Strikes Announced." BBC, September 1, 2016. https://www.bbc.com/news/health-37250258.

p. 250 'nurse union strikes'. "Health Strike: RCN Nurses in Second Day's Strike." BBC, January 8, 2020. https://www.bbc.com/news/uk-northern-ireland-51026043.

p. 251 'number of physicians were 50 percent worse than anticipated prior to Obamacare'. Pham, Kevin. "America's Looming Doctor Shortage: What Policymakers Should Do." The Heritage Foundation. Accessed May 2020. https://www.heritage.org/health-care-reform/report/americas-looming-doctor-shortage-what-policymakers-should-do.

p. 251 '900 million dollars in false billings to Medicare and Medicaid. Berlinger, Joshua. "Hundreds Arrested for $900 Million Worth of Health Care Fraud." CNN, June 23, 2016. https://www.cnn.com/2016/06/23/health/health-care-fraud-takedown/index.html.

CHAPTER 11

p. 256 '655.2 deaths per million people in the US'. RealClearPolitics. Accessed June 2020. https://www.realclearpolitics.com/coronavirus/country/united-states/.

p. 256 '1.8 to 3.4 percent death rates from the CDC'. "Severe Outcomes Among Patients with Coronavirus Disease 2019 (COVID-19) — United States, February 12–March 16, 2020." Centers for Disease Control, March 18, 2020. https://www.cdc.gov/mmwr/volumes/69/wr/pdfs/mm6912e2-H.pdf.

p. 256 '3.4 percent from the WHO'. "WHO Director-General's Opening Remarks at the Media Briefing on COVID-19 - 3 March 2020." World Health Organization. Accessed June 2020. https://www.who.int/dg/speeches/detail/who-director-general-s-opening-remarks-at-the-media-briefing-on-covid-19---3-march-2020.

p. 257 'The data provided by the COVID Tracking Project'. *The Atlantic*. Accessed August 2020. https://docs.google.com/spreadsheets/u/2/d/e/2PACX-1vR-wAqp96T9sYYq2-i7TjOpvTf6XVHjDSMIKBdZHXiCGGdNC0ypEU9NbngS8mx-ea55JuCFuua1MUeOj5/pubhtml#.

p. 258 'compare COVID-19 to other viruses in recent history'. "The Worst Outbreaks in U.S. History." *Healthline Media*, October 5, 2018. https://www.healthline.com/health/worst-disease-outbreaks-history.

p. 260 'The data is significantly skewed, as this chart shows'. "US Coronavirus Cases and Deaths: Track COVID-19 data daily by state and county." USA Facts. Accessed September 2020. https://usafacts.org/visualizations/coronavirus-covid-19-spread-map/.

p. 260 'The CDC does not produce COVID-19 deaths by individual age'. "Provisional COVID-19 Death Counts by Sex, Age, and State." CDC. Accessed September 2020. https://data.cdc.gov/NCHS/Provisional-COVID-19-Death-Counts-by-Sex-Age-and-S/9bhg-hcku.

p. 261 'the CDC only provided enough information to create this graph'. "Morbidity and Mortality Weekly Report (MMWR)." CDC. Accessed September 2020. https://www.cdc.gov/mmwr/index.html.

p. 262 'to set up a "strawman" argument that everyone was misinterpreting their figures'. "CDC Says Only 6% Of COVID Deaths Cited COVID Alone. Here's What That Means." *Daily Wire*, September 2, 2020. https://www.dailywire.com/news/cdc-says-only-6-of-covid-deaths-cited-covid-alone-heres-what-that-means.

p. 263 'The table shows data by US city for counties with the largest number of deaths from COVID-19'. ArcGIS Dashboards. Accessed May 2020. https://www.arcgis.com/apps/opsdashboard/index.html#/bda7594740fd40299423467b48e9ecf6.

p. 264 'There were only two cities in the US with direct flights from Wuhan, China: New York City and San Francisco'. *ABC News.* Accessed May 2020. https://abcnews.go.com/Health/disaster-motion-flights-coronavirus-ravaged-countries-landed-us/story?id=70025470.

p. 265 'The actual case rate is unknown'. Hein, Alexandria. "Coronavirus Antibody Testing Finds Bay Area Infections May Be 85 Times Higher than Reported: Researchers." FOX News Network, April 17, 2020. https://www.foxnews.com/health/coronavirus-antibody-testing-finds-bay-area-infections-85-times-higher-reported-researchers.

p. 266 'incentive may be misaligned with the goal of accurate measurement'. "Physicians Say Hospitals Are Pressuring ER Docs to List COVID-19 on Death Certificates. Here's Why." Foundation for Economic Education, April 29, 2020. https://fee.org/articles/physicians-say-hospitals-are-pressuring-er-docs-to-list-covid-19-on-death-certificates-here-s-why/.

p. 266 'April 14, 2020, the state of New York added 3,778 to its rolls as it changed counting methods'. Honan, Katie, and Leslie Brody. "New York City Adds 3,778 People to Its Coronavirus Death Toll." *The Wall Street Journal.* Dow Jones & Company, April 14, 2020. https://www.wsj.com/articles/nursing-homes-remain-a-concern-as-new-yorks-coronavirus-outbreak-appears-to-plateau-11586892250.

p. 271 'has had reasonably good results with under 10,000 deaths'. Worldometer, accessed November 26, 2020. https://www.worldometers.info/coronavirus/country/sweden/.

CHAPTER 12

p. 274 'especially the 87 percent receiving subsidies to purchase Obamacare'. Norris, Louise. "The ACA's cost-sharing subsidies." Healthinsurance. org, September 23, 2019. https://www.healthinsurance.org/obamacare/ the-acas-cost-sharing-subsidies/.

p. 276 'it is likely that the actual cost of M4A would be substantially greater'. Blahous, Charles. "The Costs of a National Single-Payer Healthcare System." Mercatus Center, 2018. https://www.mercatus.org/system/ files/blahous-costs-medicare-mercatus-working-paper-v1_1.pdf.

EPILOGUE

p. 286 'by paying performance-based pay'. "The Executive Pay Cap That Backfired." *ProPublica*. Accessed May 2020. https://www.propublica. org/article/the-executive-pay-cap-that-backfired.

ACKNOWLEDGMENTS

'd like to thank my reviewers: Dave Dettinger; Kurt Giesa; Derek Guyton; Joe Korabik; Carolyn MacIver; Pete Plamann; Dale Yamamoto; Jian Yu; Ann Yurkowitz; and my publisher, Amplify Publishing, especially Michelle Meredith, Julia Steffy, and Naren Aryal.

ABOUT THE AUTHOR

R ich Yurkowitz is a healthcare actuary who has spent forty years studying healthcare. Rich has analyzed proposed legislation and national and state programmatic changes along the way. He has published articles about COVID-19 and been quoted on healthcare topics throughout his career. He graduated from the University of Wisconsin –Madison with a degree in actuarial science. He lives in Milwaukee with his wife and three children.